Official Guide to Texas State Parks

Official Guide to

TEXAS STATE PARKS

TEXT AND PHOTOGRAPHS BY
LAURENCE PARENT

FOREWORDS BY

ANDREW SANSOM
Executive Director, Texas Parks and Wildlife

AND

DOLPH BRISCOE AND JAMES "RED" DUKE

UNIVERSITY OF TEXAS PRESS, AUSTIN

Another "Learn about Texas" publication from
TEXAS PARKS AND WILDLIFE PRESS

I would like to thank Patricia Parent, Patsie and James Caperton, Dale and Delilah Linenberger, Frank Moster, Patrick Fischer, Murty and Teniece Sullivan, Todd Skinner, Andy Skiba, Amy Whisler, and Shannon Justice for their hospitality and help with the photos. I am grateful to many employees of the Texas Parks and Wildlife Department for their assistance with my photos and information. Thanks also go to my editors, Georg Zappler, Shannon Davies, and Mandy Woods, and to my designer, Ellen McKie, for bringing it all together.

Printed in China
Third printing, 2002

∞ The paper used in this publication meets the minimum requirements of American National Standard for Information Sciences—Permanence of Paper for Printed Library Materials, ANSI Z39.48-1984.

Designed by Ellen McKie

LIBRARY OF CONGRESS
CATALOGING-IN-PUBLICATION DATA

Parent, Laurence.
Official guide to Texas state parks / text and photographs by Laurence Parent — 1st ed.
p. cm.
Includes index.
ISBN 0-292-76575-4 (pbk. : alk. paper)
1. Parks—Texas—Guidebooks.
2. Texas—Guidebooks. I. Title.
F384.3.P36 1997
976.404'63—dc20 96-22956

PAGES II–III
Caddo Lake State Park

PAGE VIII
Bluebonnets at Inks Lake State Park

PAGE X
Sauer-Beckmann Farm at Lyndon B. Johnson State Historical Park

PAGE XII
Gorman Falls at Colorado Bend State Park

Contents

Foreword

Andrew Sansom

The incomparable diversity of Texas will take your breath away. Our state has more species of vertebrate animals and vascular plants and more variation in its ecological landscape than any other state in the Union. And from the land has sprung a cultural heritage every bit as rich and variegated as our natural history. The state parks of Texas are a reflection of this abundant cultural and natural inheritance and provide a window to our unique and intense sense of place.

On these pages Laurence Parent has captured the magnificent collection of special places managed for your enjoyment and understanding and held in trust for our children. These are the state parks of Texas, the natural areas, and the historical sites, presented by a most eloquent interpreter.

Today our state parks are more than repositories of our heritage as Texans. They form the resource base for the fastest growing industry in Texas—that of tourism and outdoor recreation—and they represent an incredible bargain to hundreds of thousands of visitors seeking quality experiences at affordable prices.

And yet, even as their meaning grows in our lives and in the economic fabric of Texas, the state parks are under assault as never before. Many varied user groups, from hunters to mountain-bikers to rock climbers to bird-watchers, vie for access to every acre. The infrastructure in many of our grandest parks, including water systems and buildings, dates back to the New Deal of the 1930s, when members of the Civilian Conservation Corps (CCC) and the Work Projects Administration (WPA) put these structures together, brick by brick. Today these essential support systems are aging and in increasing need of major restoration and repair. In part to address this daunting challenge, there exists a growing entrepreneurial spirit among the men and women who maintain our state parks and present them to the public.

We at the Texas Parks and Wildlife Department are privileged to be stewards of these precious places, but find ourselves increasingly caught between the opposing aims of protecting them for future generations and at the same time providing you, the user, with enhanced opportunities to experience them.

The beauty you will discover in these pages should encourage you not only to visit the Texas state parks but also to support them. In the years ahead, your advocacy on behalf of these crown jewels of the Texas heritage will become increasingly critical. This is so because, beyond economics, beyond the pleasure these special places can bring to their hundreds of thousands of visitors, the state parks of Texas are islands of hope where we are inspired to protect the legacy of our great state for generations of Texans to come.

ANDREW SANSOM
Executive Director
Texas Parks and Wildlife

Foreword

Dolph Briscoe and James "Red" Duke

For too many people, today's world is defined by concrete, steel, and shining glass. It is vital, therefore, that we have the means to leave behind the rambling, honking, screeching hubbub of the cities and listen to nature's lessons carried in the song of birds, the rustling of leaves, and the cracking of twigs beneath our feet.

While many of nature's lessons provide simple, everlasting truths, others, unfortunately—especially those illuminating the role of humans in nature—are not so evident. Nature is in a constant state of flux; it cannot be locked in a single moment in time and preserved forever in its pristine form. Humans have always been part of nature's changing parade, sometimes following its lead, sometimes changing the speed, and sometimes getting out of step.

We contribute most, however, when we become informed stewards of nature's riches. Through understanding the complex processes of nature and applying common sense, we can make informed decisions and become active caretakers of our natural resources, managing these gifts so that they are renewed for future generations.

The land within Texas' state parks has been set aside so that visitors can hike through tangled woods, watch butterflies flitting in sunlit meadows, feel the Gulf Coast waves wash across their feet, sleep under the stars of a jet-black night, and experience nature in myriad other ways. In this book, Laurence Parent has captured the beauty of these areas, which form some of the most striking natural classrooms in Texas.

Governor Dolph Briscoe
Chairman, Natural Resources Foundation of Texas
Dr. James "Red" Duke
Board Member, Natural Resources Foundation of Texas

Using this Guide

Guidebook organization

This guide is divided into seven sections, each one representing a different geographic region within Texas. Each section begins with some general information about the region, and is followed by descriptions of every park within that region, listed alphabetically. The state map and table of contents at the front of the book will aid in finding specific parks. In addition, color-coded symbols appear at the top of each page, with a different color being used for each region.

Park descriptions

For each park, a short essay provides some historical, biological, and geological background, along with park highlights and recreational opportunities. The Depression-inspired Civilian Conservation Corps (CCC) is frequently mentioned as having been responsible for the skillful construction of many of the buildings and other facilities that are still in use today at numerous parks; the TPWD's booklet *The Civilian Conservation Corps in Texas State Parks* provides a more detailed history of the CCC and its work in Texas. Following each park description is a summary of visitor information, including park size and operating schedule, camping availability, and facilities. This Visitor Information section also lists the nearest town (or towns) with such services as gas stations, restaurants, and lodging. The park's address and phone number are also provided, allowing you to call or write for more information.

Camping

At campgrounds described in the Visitor Information section as having partial hookups, water and electricity are available. Those described as having full hookups also have sewage connections. Most parks with camping facilities have a dump station even if no sewage connections are available.

Camping reservations are not generally necessary at the state parks. However, on spring, summer, and fall weekends, campgrounds at many parks often fill up, so reservations are advisable at those times. In addition, campgrounds can sometimes fill up on summer weekdays, particularly at some popular water-oriented parks with lakes or rivers, or on the coast. *All camping reservations are handled through a central reservation number in Austin: (512) 389-8900. Be sure to call that number, not the individual state parks, to reserve a site.*

Park hours

Most parks, especially those with campgrounds, are open every day, all year round. Some parks, particularly state historical parks, may be more limited in terms of the days and hours during which they are open. An effort has been made to give some idea of operating times in the Visitor Information sections of these parks. However, schedules sometimes change, both seasonally and for operational reasons. Before driving long distances, you may want to call ahead for a current schedule. In winter, a few of the larger parks with campgrounds may close for a short time to allow public hunts to take place.

Rules and regulations

Regulations are aimed at both protecting the park and providing a pleasant experience for visitors. To preserve the parks, please refrain from removing plants—including wildflowers—as well as minerals and artifacts. Firewood gathering is not allowed, but often bundles are sold at park headquarters. Otherwise, bring your own.

Please don't litter, damage park facilities, or leave fires unattended. Firearms and hunting are not allowed, except during special hunts. Public display and consumption of alcohol are prohibited. Be courteous to your campground neighbors and keep music and voices low at night.

Official Guide to
Texas State Parks

Amarillo
Panhandle Plains
Wichita Falls
Lubbock
Gainesville
Denison
Texarkana
Fort Worth
Dallas
El Paso
Midland
Prairies & Lakes
Big Bend Country
Piney-woods
Hill Country
Austin
Houston
Orange
San Antonio
Del Rio
Gulf Coast
South Texas Plains
Laredo
Corpus Christi
Brownsville

Big Bend Country

Most state parks in the Big Bend Country lie west of the Pecos River, in what is often called the Trans-Pecos region. The area is a land of superlatives. It contains the largest county, the largest state park, the deepest canyons, and the only mountains in the state. Lying right next to those mountains, which have some of the state's coldest, snowiest, and windiest weather, is the hottest and driest region in Texas. One of the longest rivers in North America, the Rio Grande, bounds West Texas along its southern and western flanks. The Trans-Pecos contains the most spectacular scenery in Texas and harbors two national parks.

Most of the area lies within the Chihuahuan Desert, a vast province of North America that stretches from deep inside Mexico, through West Texas, and into southern New Mexico. Low-elevation areas of the desert usually receive less than 10 inches of rain annually, allowing only sparse, hardy vegetation to grow.

Many desert plants have defenses that allow them to survive in the harsh, dry environment. Leaves tend to be small and waxy to limit transpiration; cacti do away with them altogether. Plants such as the ocotillo, which usually looks like a bundle of dead, upright, spiny sticks, only grow leaves after receiving sufficient rain. Annuals grow, bloom, and die quickly during short wet spells. Many plants grow spines or thorns and secrete chemicals that make their foliage toxic or bad-tasting to deter grazing animals.

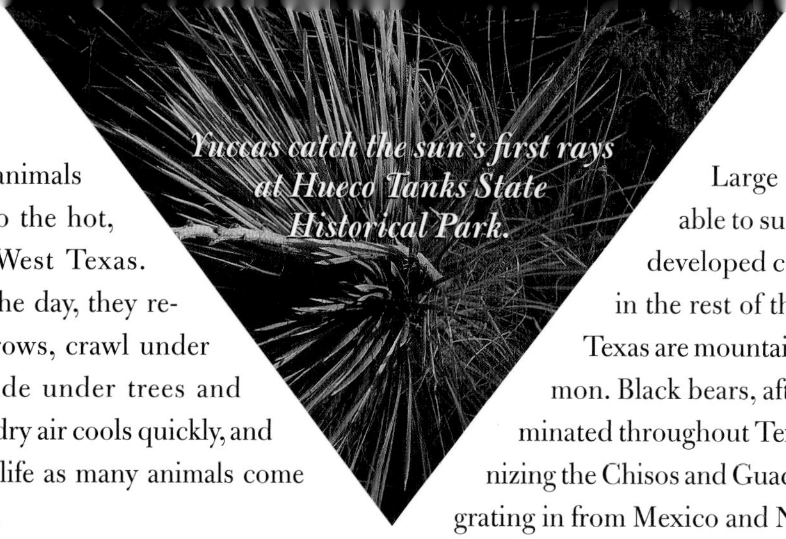

Yuccas catch the sun's first rays at Hueco Tanks State Historical Park.

Like the plants, animals have also adapted to the hot, dry conditions of West Texas. During the heat of the day, they retreat into their burrows, crawl under ledges, or seek shade under trees and shrubs. At dusk, the dry air cools quickly, and the desert comes to life as many animals come out to feed and hunt.

Mountain ranges are sprinkled across this dry desert country, seeming to float like islands on a vast desert sea. On an absolute scale, the mountains are not especially large; the highest peak, found in the Guadalupe Mountains, rises to only 8,749 feet above sea level. However, some of the mountains rise as much as 5,000 or 6,000 feet above the low-lying desert, and thus appear quite impressive.

These large changes in elevation cause moving air masses to rise and cool over these mountain ranges, condensing out additional precipitation. The highest ranges, such as the Guadalupe and Davis mountains, can receive as much as 10 or 15 inches more rain than surrounding desert lowlands. In stark contrast to the barren landscape of the desert below, forests grow on the moist, cool slopes of the ranges and grasslands cloak the foothills. Oaks, junipers, and pinyon pines cloak the middle slopes of the mountains. Tall ponderosa pines and even a few aspens can be found in the Guadalupe, Davis, and Chisos mountains, the three highest ranges.

Except for the area around El Paso, West Texas is very lightly populated. The Spaniards largely avoided the Trans-Pecos, calling it *el despoblado*, or the unpopulated land. Only a few small, widely spaced towns dot the empty region. Apart from these and the oil and gas fields lying on the eastern edge of the area, only sprawling ranches and parks cover the land.

Large predators have been able to survive better in this undeveloped country than they have in the rest of the state. Only in West Texas are mountain lions relatively common. Black bears, after having been exterminated throughout Texas, have been recolonizing the Chisos and Guadalupe mountains, migrating in from Mexico and New Mexico.

Humans have lived in West Texas for at least 10,000 years. Unlike the Anasazi in the Southwest, the early Texas peoples did not leave large masonry villages and cliff dwellings to mark their passing. However, they did create panels of painted and carved artwork on the walls of remote canyons and caves throughout the region. Notable examples of their work can be found at Hueco Tanks and Seminole Canyon state historical parks. Examples of homes and military outposts dating from the region's frontier days may be found in three state parks—Fort Lancaster, Fort Leaton, and Magoffin Home.

Fittingly, four of the largest state parks and several large wildlife management areas lie in the wide open spaces of West Texas. Big Bend Ranch State Natural Area contains 275,000 acres and borders on Colorado Canyon, one of the most spectacular segments of the Rio Grande. Chinati Mountains State Park offers everything from dry desert hills to lush, spring-filled canyons. Devils River State Natural Area lies on the far eastern fringe of the Big Bend country and has a mixed ecosystem of West Texas and Hill Country species. Franklin Mountains State Park encompasses the Franklin Mountains almost in their entirety, creating an island of wilderness in the heart of urban El Paso. From the cool mountain heights of Davis Mountains State Park to the deep canyons of Big Bend Ranch, West Texas contains some of the state's most notable parks.

Big Bend Country

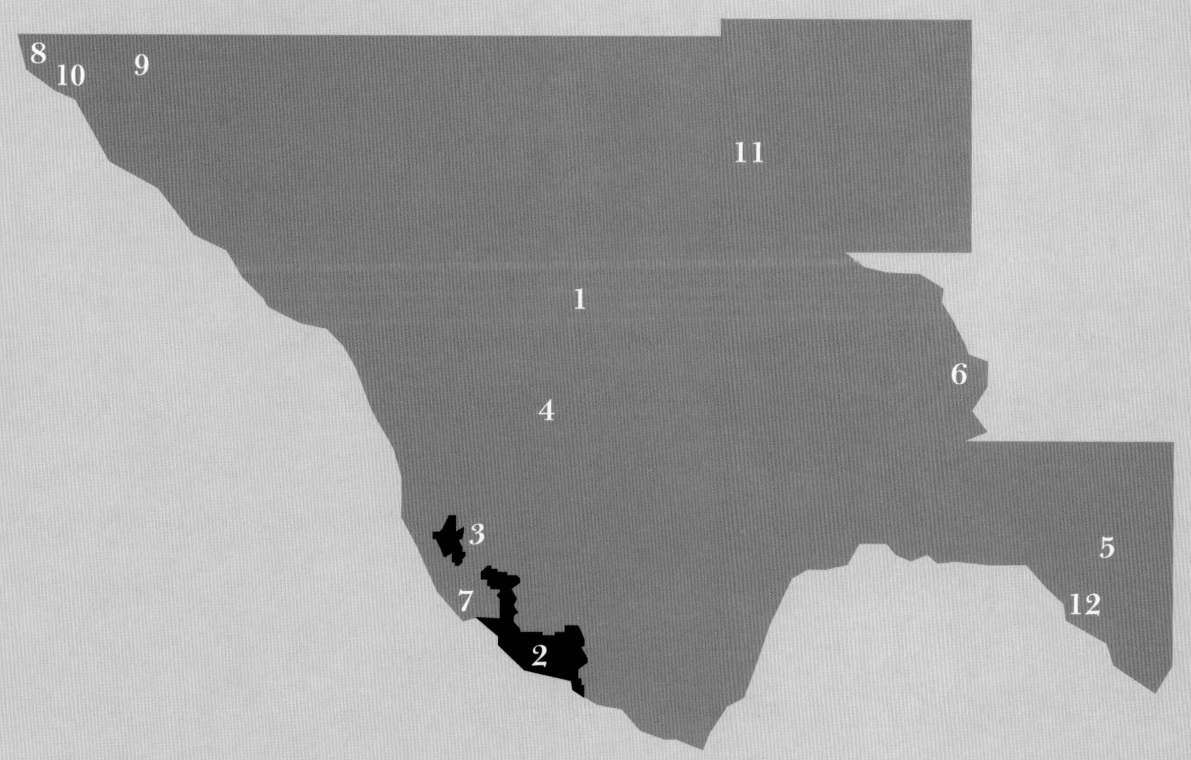

1 Balmorhea State Park
2 Big Bend Ranch State Park
3 Chinati Mountains State Park
4 Davis Mountains • Indian Lodge State Parks
5 Devils River State Natural Area
6 Fort Lancaster State Historical Park
7 Fort Leaton State Historical Park
8 Franklin Mountains State Park
9 Hueco Tanks State Historical Park
10 Magoffin Home State Historical Park
11 Monahans Sandhills State Park
12 Seminole Canyon State Historical Park

Balmorhea State Park

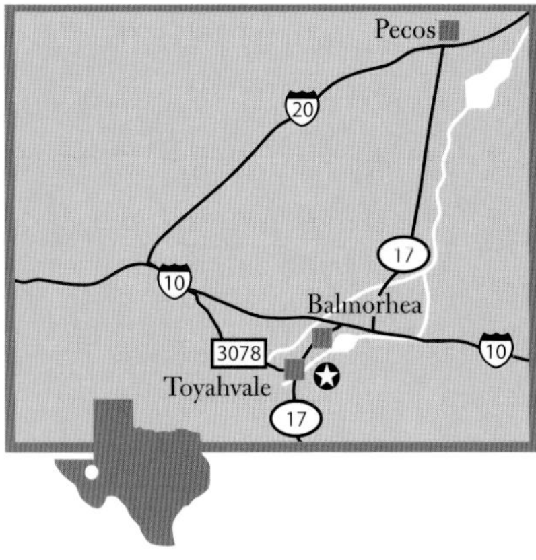

In the dry desert flatlands on the north side of the Davis Mountains, the clear, cold waters of San Solomon Spring gush forth, creating a startlingly green oasis of fields and tree-lined canals for many miles downstream. The spring produces between 15 and 26 million gallons per day from a deep pool in Balmorhea State Park. Its waters irrigate 10,000 acres in the farming towns of Balmorhea, Saragosa, and Toyahvale, and even form a small lake.

Most of the spring's water comes from precipitation falling on the Davis Mountains. The water seeps underground, then flows slowly through subsurface faults and porous rock layers, known as aquifers, to several springs in the Balmorhea area. San Solomon Spring, an artesian spring, is the largest. Artesian springs are under pressure and flow out above the water table, in contrast to gravity springs, that flow from below the water table.

Unfortunately, heavy groundwater pumping has lowered area water tables and dried up many West Texas springs. Comanche Springs in Fort Stockton had flow rates comparable to those of San Solomon and irrigated more than 6,000 acres before it stopped flowing in 1961. Two artesian springs near San Solomon Spring, Phantom Lake and Giffin, still flow, although at much reduced rates. Additional groundwater pumping could cause these two springs, and possibly even San Solomon, to fail.

These desert springs are effectively islands, separated from each other by miles of desert. Unique species of plants and animals evolved in the highly localized spring environments. Two endangered species, the Comanche Springs pupfish and the Pecos mosquito fish, live only in the park and a few other West Texas springs.

For thousands of years, San Solomon Spring provided water to early peoples. Later, the spring was a watering hole for Spanish explorers, gold-seekers, and other West Texas travelers. Some Mexican farmers built the first irrigation canals in the mid-nineteenth century. Other more elaborate systems were added over the following years. During the Depression, the Civilian Conservation Corps built the pool around the

LEFT:
Divers descend into the spring
TOP:
Dusk at Balmorhea
ABOVE:
Swimmers enjoy pool

spring, as well as the bathhouse, residences, and the San Solomon Springs Court motel units. The huge pool is 1.75 acres in area and 30 feet deep, and has a capacity of 3.5 million gallons. The water is a constant 72°F–76°F. With a continuous fresh inflow, chlorination is unnecessary.

San Solomon Spring has drawn people for thousands of years and continues to do so today. Local residents flock to the pool during the hot summers for swimming and relaxation. The spring itself boils up through the sandy bottom in the deepest part of the pool, attracting many scuba divers, who come from all over the area to dive in the clear, deep pool. There, they can swim by perch and schools of minnows and hunt for reclusive catfish hiding under rock ledges.

Texas Parks and Wildlife, in partnership with local groups and federal agencies, is restoring the San Solomon Springs Ciénega, a desert wetland at the park. Visitors can enjoy some of the ciénega's unique aquatic inhabitants through an underwater viewing window.

VISITOR INFORMATION

46 acres. Open all year. Hot in summer. Pool is open all year from 8 A.M. until a half hour before sunset. Swim at your own risk; open to certified divers and classes. Small campground with partial hookups and showers. Motel units, some with kitchenettes, are popular; reserve ahead. Limited visitor services available in Balmorhea; full services in Fort Davis, Pecos, and Fort Stockton. For information: Balmorhea State Park, Box 15, Toyahvale, TX 79786, (915) 375-2370.

Big Bend Ranch State Park

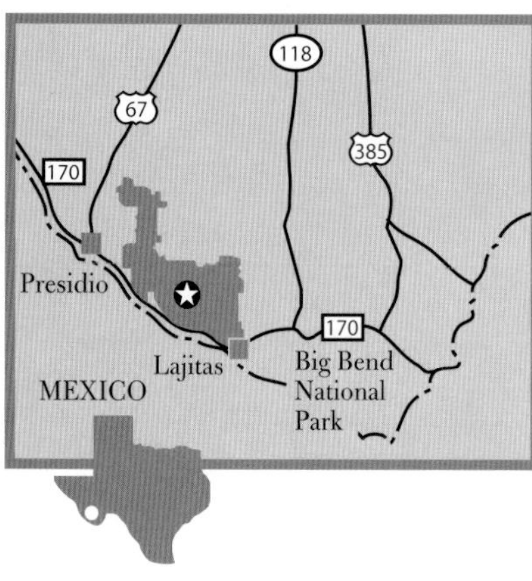

Deep in a remote corner of West Texas lie over a quarter million acres of Chihuahuan Desert that invite exploration. The Parks and Wildlife Department purchased the enormous tract in 1988, roughly doubling the size of the state-park system. Big Bend Ranch State Park fronts the Rio Grande between Lajitas and Presidio, and contains a rugged mix of desert mountains, canyons, and grasslands.

The Rio Grande flows through sheer-walled Colorado Canyon and forms the southern boundary of the park. The reddish-brown, iron-stained walls of the canyon were carved by the Rio Grande through the Bofecillos Mountains of Texas and the Sierra Rica of Mexico. Between 25 and 40 million years ago, before the river cut the canyon, massive volcanoes exploded on both sides of the river, spewing forth dark lava and layers of white ash to form the mountain ranges. Texas Highway FM 170, the River Road, follows the canyon, squeezed between mountains and the river. To the north of the highway is the Solitario, a huge dome of rock, called a laccolith, pushed upward from below by intruding igneous rocks.

The highway traverses one of the most scenic sections of Big Bend Ranch; it may be the most spectacular drive in Texas. The entire park lies within the Chihuahuan Desert. Except for small riparian areas along the Rio Grande and around springs and small permanent watercourses, desert vegetation dominates. Dryland grasses, such as blue, side-oats, and black grama, and chino, are common where they have not been heavily

Moonrise over volcanic tuff formations

grazed. Lechuguilla is prolific; it is an indicator plant of the Chihuahuan Desert, meaning that it lives nowhere else. It grows in a compact rosette of stiff, green blades tipped with sharp spines. Many an unwary hiker has speared an ankle on the omnipresent lechuguilla.

Other common desert plants include sotol, ocotillo, creosote, and mesquite, as well as many cactus species. Much of the wildlife is centered around water sources, where reeds, willows, salt cedar, cottonwood, and ash create a lush habitat. Commonly seen animals in the park include mule deer, javelina, and many species of lizards. Lucky visitors might spot rare or reclusive animals such as the mountain lion, golden eagle, bobcat, peregrine falcon, or zone-tailed hawk. The western mastiff bat, with an average wingspan of about twenty-two inches, is one of the most interesting residents of Big Bend Ranch.

Humans arrived in the area at least 10,000 years ago, living in nomadic groups that hunted game and gathered edible fruits, nuts, berries, leaves, and roots. The earliest groups left few traces other than projectile points and other stone tools. Evidence of later groups, in the form of campsites, rock art, burials, and stone artifacts, dots Big Bend Ranch. By A.D. 1200, some groups were practicing primitive agriculture along the Rio Grande upstream from the area that is now Big Bend Ranch. They lived in organized villages and were influenced by the Pueblo cultures of New Mexico. The Spaniards arrived about 400 years ago, but made only sporadic efforts to control and settle the Big Bend area north of the Rio Grande. They called it *el despoblado*—the unpopulated land. The presence of Comanches and Apaches limited settlement of the area until the late nineteenth century.

TOP:
Bluebonnets and desert marigolds
BOTTOM:
Colorado Canyon

Ranchers moved into the area after the Indian threat ended, and also at this time silver mining began at Shafter, just north of the park. Extensive mercury mining developed on the east side of the park around Terlingua. Profitable ore eventually ran out in both mining districts; most operations ceased by the 1940s. Until tourism developed, ranching and farming along the Rio Grande floodplain remained the chief economic activities.

The scenic route of Texas Highway FM 170, the River Road, provides an excellent introduction to Big Bend Ranch. Before starting, stop in at the Barton Warnock Environmental Education Center in Lajitas. It has an extensive museum describing the human and natural history of the region, an elaborate desert garden, and a bookstore, plus information and permits. Fort Leaton State Historical Park near Presidio also has information and permits, along with historical exhibits and a bookstore. Big Bend Ranch's administrative headquarters, 300 yards west of Fort Leaton, handles reservations for programs, camping, and lodging at Sauceda (in the center of the park), in addition to providing permits and information.

Popular activities include hiking and backpacking along trails ranging in length from 1.5 miles to more than 20 miles. The park also has a private-guide program into the interior. Boating the Rio Grande through Colorado Canyon is one of the most popular pursuits in the park. The deep, spectacular canyon has long calm stretches punctuated by occasional moderate rapids, floatable by both rafts and canoes. First-time floaters may want to consider taking a trip with outfitters based in Lajitas, Terlingua, or Study Butte. Anglers will enjoy pursuing catfish in the

TOP:
Closed Canyon
BOTTOM:
Rio Grande

muddy waters of the Rio Grande. Private guides lead interpretive bus tours of the interior areas once a month.

Big Bend Ranch State Park is one of the crown jewels of the state-park system. Its spectacular scenery and large size offer worthy competition to its better-known neighbor, Big Bend National Park.

VISITOR INFORMATION

269,714 acres. Open all year. Very hot from late spring through early fall. Most popular during Thanksgiving, Christmas, and spring-break holidays. Primitive car campsites with composting toilets along the river; no water or hookups. Ten additional car campsites in the interior; more are planned. Primitive backcountry camping for backpackers. Primitive equestrian area. Group accommodations with meals at the former ranch headquarters by reservation. Picnicking, fishing. Barton Warnock Education Center in Lajitas features a museum and bookstore. During extended hikes or river trips, it is advisable to use shuttle services in Lajitas and Terlingua rather than leaving car unattended for long periods. Scenic drive along paved Tx Hwy FM 170 is very steep, winding, and narrow in places and may not be suitable for large RVs or trailers. Dry water crossings can flood rapidly during heavy rains. This is lightly traveled, desert wilderness country; be prepared with adequate water, food, sunscreen, clothing, and other items before attempting hikes or river trips. Full visitor services available in Lajitas, Presidio, and Terlingua. For information: Big Bend Ranch State Park, P.O. Box 2319, Presidio, TX 79845, (915) 229-3416.

Chinati Mountains State Park

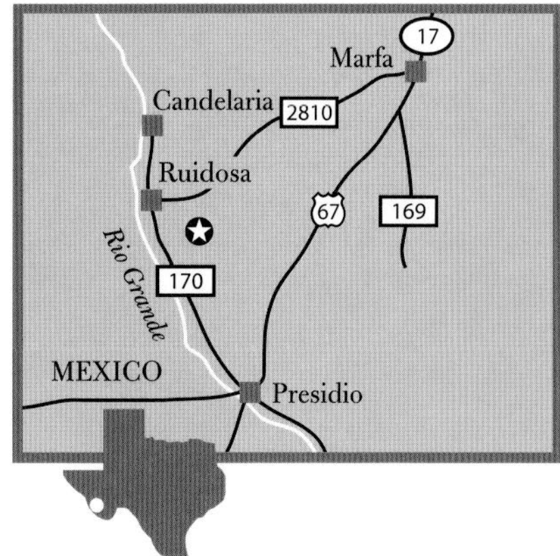

One of the state's newest and largest parks lies deep in West Texas in the Chinati Mountains northwest of Presidio. The igneous mountain range is the fourth highest in Texas, exceeded in height only by the Guadalupe, Davis, and Chisos mountains. The rugged mountains offer everything from dry desert hills to lush, spring-filled canyons. Craggy peaks and sheer granite bluffs tower over the sprawling park.

The land was donated to the state by the Mellon Foundation as part of its effort to secure nationally significant sites as gifts to the people of the United States. The Chinati donation was the largest ever for the Texas Parks and Wildlife Department. As well as giving the land to the state, the Mellon Foundation also set up an endowment for the county to offset the loss in property taxes.

Like the rest of the Trans-Pecos area, the Chinati Mountains are in the Chihuahuan Desert, a vast area that stretches from southern New Mexico through West Texas and deep into Mexico. Like all deserts, it is characterized by an average annual rainfall of less than 10 inches at lower elevations. However, mountain areas, such as the Chinati range, trap additional moisture when air masses rise and cool as they push over high-elevation areas. Thus, in contrast to the lowland desert areas, the upper levels of the park have grasslands and even some areas of scrub woodland.

The former owners built an unpaved, but maintained, road system and several simple stone cabins to enhance their enjoyment of the property. Initial access to this new park will be in the form of guided tours on a reservation basis and will be managed by Big Bend Ranch State Park. Early development will probably include campsites and hiking trails, as well as renovation of some of the existing buildings.

VISITOR INFORMATION

Approximately 40,000 acres. No access at present. Hiking, wildlife observation. Full visitor services available in Presidio. For information: Chinati Mountains State Park, c/o Big Bend Ranch State Park, P.O. Box 1180, Presidio, TX 79845, (915) 229-3416.

Claret-cup cactus

Davis Mountains • Indian Lodge State Parks

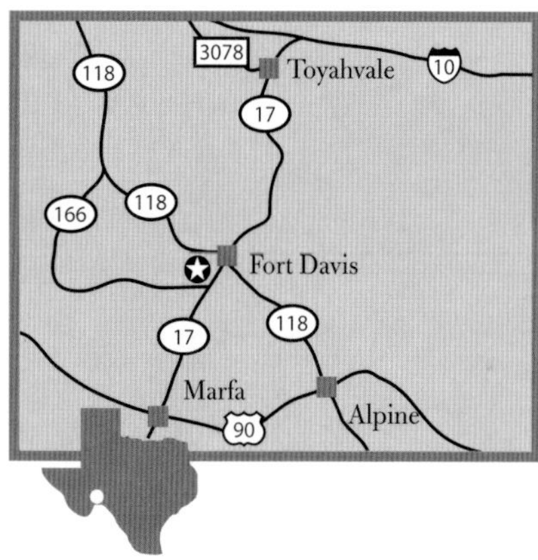

To find mountains in Texas, you have to go to the far western part of the state, often called the Trans-Pecos region. Only six counties in Texas—big counties, admittedly—have mountain ranges. The Trans-Pecos is dotted with mountains, most of them small in extent, not exceptionally high, and vegetated with desert plants. The three highest ranges, the Guadalupe, Davis, and Chisos mountains, are exceptions. They are large enough and high enough to create their own weather. As winds blow over the mountains, the air rises and cools and condenses out additional precipitation, sometimes as much as ten inches more than the surrounding desert receives. The extra moisture and coolness of the higher elevations foster the growth of forests on the mountain slopes. Davis Mountains and Indian Lodge State Parks lie in the largest and most lush range of the three.

The Davis Mountains form the second highest range in Texas, reaching the high point on 8,382-foot Mount Livermore, but they encompass the largest area. The mountains were named for Jefferson Davis, the U.S. secretary of war who ordered construction of the frontier military installation, Fort Davis.

Between 35 and 39 million years ago, volcanoes erupted violently, spewing ash and lava across the land that would become the Davis Mountains. During this time, volcanic activity was occurring all along a wide belt between Montana and Mexico. The Davis Mountains were in one of the largest centers of this activity, and there the eruptions were centered around two large areas, the Paisano volcano west of Alpine and the Buckhorn Caldera northwest of Fort Davis. Today erosion has rounded off the rough edges of the mountains and vegetation has covered the slopes, but dark cliffs of ancient lava flows still mark the mountains' violent past.

the CCC are still used in the lobby and some of the rooms. A swimming pool, cool summer evenings, and mountain views are among the lodge's attractions.

Davis Mountains State Park's scenic drive leads to a high ridge above Limpia Creek, where views stretch for miles. To the east lies the town of Fort Davis, the old fort, and sprawling grasslands dotted with mountains. To the west rise the high, wooded peaks of the Davis Mountains, one of which, Mount Locke, is crowned with the white domes of McDonald Observatory. In late summer, afternoon thunderstorms march across the mountains, trailing curtains of rain. The temperature falls and the fresh scent of moist earth permeates the air. Rainbows dance across the broad sweep of grasslands at the base of the mountains as the sun sets in the western sky. Davis Mountains and Indian Lodge State Parks provide a cool, scenic retreat during the long, hot Texas summers.

The extra precipitation that falls on the Davis Mountains spurs the growth of lush vegetation that is in contrast to the surrounding sea of dry desert. The lower slopes are blanketed with rich grasslands that foster large numbers of pronghorn antelope. In the middle elevations, Emory and gray oak and one-seed junipers cloak the hills. Slightly higher up, pinyon pines appear, and finally, on the highest slopes, tall ponderosa pines grow, mixed with a few aspens.

Davis Mountains and Indian Lodge State Parks lie in the mountain foothills, with a mix of grassland and juniper-oak woodland. The parks' mix of habitats draws a large number of bird species, of which one of the most interesting is the Montezuma quail. The bird has a very limited range in North America; the two parks are the only places in Texas with public access where it can be seen.

Fort Davis National Historic Site, the best preserved frontier fort in the Southwest, adjoins the state park's eastern boundary. The fort was established in 1854 to protect travelers and settlers in West Texas from attacks by Apaches and Comanches. It was garrisoned in part with black troops, known as buffalo soldiers by the Indians. Except for interruptions during the Civil War, the military post was occupied by troops until 1891. A scenic hiking trail connects the state park to the old fort.

Historic Indian Lodge, tucked in a bucolic setting in Keesey Canyon in Davis Mountains State Park, draws many people. It was built in 1933, during the Depression, by the Civilian Conservation Corps (CCC). The architecture was modeled after southwestern Indian pueblos and has adobe walls more than 18 inches thick and exposed roof beams. Some of the original furnishings made by

LEFT:
Indian Lodge
ABOVE:
View from the scenic drive

VISITOR INFORMATION

2,770 acres. Open all year. Warm days, cool nights in summer make Davis Mountains State Park very popular at that time of year. Can be cold in winter, with occasional snows. Moderate-sized campground with partial and full hookups. Primitive backpacking campsites in remote park area north of Tx Hwy 118. Indian Lodge State Park has 39 rooms, swimming pool, restaurant. Lodge is very popular; reserve well in advance. Scenic drive, hiking and nature trails, picnicking. Interpretive center. Full visitor services available in Fort Davis. For information: Davis Mountains State Park, P.O. Box 1458, Fort Davis, TX 79734, (915) 426-3337; Indian Lodge, P.O. Box 1458, Fort Davis, TX 79734, (915) 426-3254.

Devils River State Natural Area

The dirt road winds endlessly through the dry, dusty hills north of Del Rio, giving little hint of the oasis ahead. After 18 miles, the county road enters Devils River State Natural Area, a remote 20,000-acre preserve. The hilly terrain is dry and treeless near the headquarters, but a surprise awaits visitors. Downstream from there, in the bottom of the dry canyon of Dolan Creek, springs gush out of the bedrock. The first spring encountered is José Maria Spring, with its oases of pecans, live oaks, and sycamores. A short distance farther downstream, just above Dolan Creek's confluence with the Devils River, more springs pour into the creek on private land as well as on the Nature Conservancy's Dolan Falls Preserve. Along the Devils River, just above the confluence with the creek, massive springs pour a flood of clear, cool water into the river within the natural area. The clear, rushing waters of Dolan Creek and the Devils River exist in sharp contrast to the steep, dry, treeless hills above.

Over the course of millions of years, Dolan Creek, the Devils River, and their tributaries have carved deep canyons into the thick limestone beds of the western part of the Edwards Plateau. This area marks the convergence of the vegetation of three ecological areas—the Chihuahuan Desert to the west, the Edwards Plateau/Hill Country to the east, and the Tamaulipan brushlands of northern Mexico to the south. Most of the natural area is dry, with grasses, shrubs, and cacti dominating. At permanent sources of water, lush groves of trees and other plants thrive.

Humans have lived in the area for at least 11,000 years, leaving pictographs painted in rock shelters, as well as artifacts and campsites. In historic times, Apaches controlled the region, followed by Comanches, Kiowas, and Kickapoos. Because of conflict between settlers and various Indian groups, the area was little explored until the middle of the nineteenth century. In 1881, the railroad was

LEFT, TOP:
Canoeists on Devils River
LEFT, MIDDLE:
Mountain-biker
LEFT, BOTTOM:
Springs along river
ABOVE:
Devils River

built through the country to the south, opening the Devils River area to settlement. In 1883, Erasmus Fawcett settled the area now occupied by the natural area and the Nature Conservancy preserve, and established a sprawling sheep and goat ranch.

The area is still very lightly settled today, with large, widely scattered ranches. The Texas Parks and Wildlife Department and the Nature Conservancy purchased their land from some of these ranchers, including some of the descendants of Erasmus Fawcett. Unfortunately, much of the land has been greatly altered by human activities. Dolan Creek and the Devils River were once lined by continuous stands of pecans, oaks, and sycamores, but overgrazing of much of the watershed speeded erosion and water runoff, contributing to massive floods in the 1930s and 1950s. The muddy torrents washed away large parts of the woodland areas, along with vast quantities of topsoil. With proper management and years of healing, however, the two preserves may one day recover more of their original character.

Because of its limited staff and minimal facilities, Devils River State Natural Area may only be visited by those making advance reservations. Bring all necessary food, water, gas, and other supplies; this is one of the remotest areas of Texas. The Nature Conservancy's adjoining preserve, with the impressive Dolan Falls, is generally only open to members on guided field trips.

VISITOR INFORMATION

19,989 acres. Open by reservation only. Hot in summer. Limited primitive camping and bunkhouse space. Hiking, mountain-biking. Full visitor services available in Del Rio. For information: Devils River State Natural Area, HCR 1, Box 513, Del Rio, TX 78840, (830) 395-2133. The Nature Conservancy of Texas is based in San Antonio and can be reached at (210) 224-8774.

Fort Lancaster State Historical Park

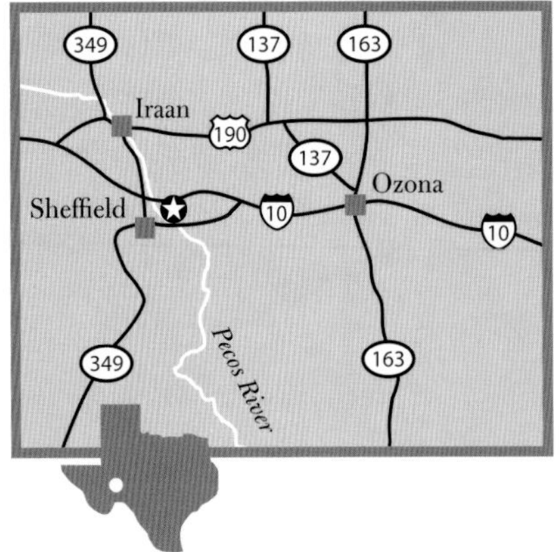

between San Antonio and El Paso. The fort was one of four built to protect the route from attacks by Apaches and other Indian tribes. Initially it consisted of tents and other temporary structures, but as time allowed, the troops constructed more durable stone and adobe quarters out of native materials gathered nearby—wood from oak trees, adobe mud, and limestone—and finished lumber from Fort Davis. By 1860, the fort had some twenty-five permanent buildings and an average complement of seventy-two men and four officers.

Ruins of Fort Lancaster

Fort Lancaster is almost lost in the vast emptiness of West Texas, tucked as it is into the valley of the Pecos River and its tributaries. Even with today's paved highways and air-conditioned automobiles, the landscape still seems harsh and desolate. To the soldiers who occupied the fort, it must have seemed like the remotest corner of the world.

The post was established as Camp Lancaster in August 1855 on the east bank of Live Oak Creek, about a half mile above the creek's confluence with the Pecos River. A year later, it became Fort Lancaster. The site was located near an important ford of the Pecos River on the military road

The isolated garrison faced difficult odds in its battles with the Apaches. In the empty country, the Apaches, who knew the terrain intimately, could roam at will and raid parties of travelers. The Apaches were some of the best guerrilla fighters the world has ever seen, attacking swiftly and withdrawing before the opposition could organize. Scouting and punitive expeditions by the troops, as few in number as they were and with so much country to cover, were rarely productive. The soldiers' principal duty became that of providing an escort for mail carriers, gold miners, wagon trains, and settlers. One high point for the troops, in the midst of this dangerous, difficult duty, came when the experimental camel train of Secretary of War Jefferson Davis stopped at the fort for the night in July 1857.

Although the Apache threat remained serious, the Civil War brought the fort's short history to an end. When Texas joined the Confederacy, the fort was abandoned and the troops marched to San Antonio to surrender on March 19, 1861. The Confederacy attempted to garrison the fort for a few months in 1861–1862, but it was soon abandoned to the elements. Travelers still used it as a stopping place, and after the war, in 1867 and 1871, U.S. troops used it briefly as a bivouac, but the fort's glory days were over.

The park visitor center contains interpretive displays and artifacts from the old fort and provides a good introduction to its history. After viewing the exhibits, walk out onto the quiet site. Stone chimneys reach skyward and mesquite grows over tumbled-down walls, but the American flag still flies over the parade ground. Listen closely; maybe you'll hear the sound of distant gunfire, the clatter of horses' hooves, or the sound of a lonesome bugle. More than one hundred years later, the ruins of Fort Lancaster still stand guard over the valley of the Pecos River.

VISITOR INFORMATION

82 acres. Open all year, 8 A.M.–5 P.M. Hot in summer. Historic buildings and interpretive center. Limited food and gas available in Sheffield; full visitor services in Iraan and Ozona. For information: Fort Lancaster State Historical Park, P.O. Box 306, Sheffield, TX 79781, (915) 836-4391.

Fort Leaton State Historical Park

With the end of the Mexican-American War in 1848, Mexico ceded disputed parts of Texas and most of the Southwest to the United States. On August 8 of that year, Benjamin Leaton and three American partners crossed the Rio Grande into Texas at Presidio del Norte. He and his party had been employed by the governments of Sonora and Chihuahua as bounty hunters and paid to hunt down Indians. He was notorious for terrorizing the people of Chihuahua; one contemporary referred to him in his journal as a "noble desperado."

Leaton acquired a tract of land on a low bluff on the north side of the Rio Grande, just downstream from the town of Presidio, and built a massive adobe fortress to house his family, employees, and business and to protect them against Indian raids. Leaton farmed the floodplain and began trading with bands of Apaches and Comanches. Both Mexican and American authorities accused him of encouraging the Indians to raid Mexican settlements for livestock that they could then trade for guns and ammunition. Even today, some local residents recall him as *un mal hombre*—a bad man.

After Leaton died in 1851, the violence associated with him seemed to linger. His widow married Edward Hall, a local customs agent. Hall moved into Leaton's home, from which he operated a freight business. He later borrowed a large sum of money from John Burgess, one of Leaton's bounty-hunting partners. Hall put up the adobe fortress as collateral and was foreclosed upon in 1864 when he failed to repay Burgess. Hall refused to leave the fort and was murdered shortly thereafter.

Burgess and his family then moved into Fort Leaton and established a successful freighting business on the busy San Antonio–Chihuahua Trail. In 1875, Burgess was murdered

Fort Leaton

by Bill Leaton, Ben Leaton's youngest son, in revenge for the murder of his stepfather, Edward Hall, but the Burgess family continued to live in the fort until 1926.

After the fort was abandoned, it deteriorated rapidly under the assault of the elements and vandals. In the 1930s, local residents partly restored the historic structure, but it again fell into disrepair. Finally, it was donated to the state and restored by the Parks and Wildlife Department.

The walls of Fort Leaton still loom over the fertile farmlands downstream from La Junta de los Rios, the Spaniards' name for the confluence of the Rio Grande and the Rio Conchos. Exhibits document the cultural history of the area, from the Indians who first farmed the floodplain, to the Spanish explorers, to the arrival of Ben Leaton and other Americans.

VISITOR INFORMATION

18 acres. Open all year, 8 A.M.–4:30 P.M. Day use only. Historic building, interpretive exhibits, picnicking. Full visitor services available in Presidio. For information: Fort Leaton State Historical Park, P.O. Box 2439, Presidio, TX 79845, (915) 229-3613.

RIGHT:
Franklin Mountains hiker
FAR RIGHT:
View from North Franklin Peak

Franklin Mountains State Park

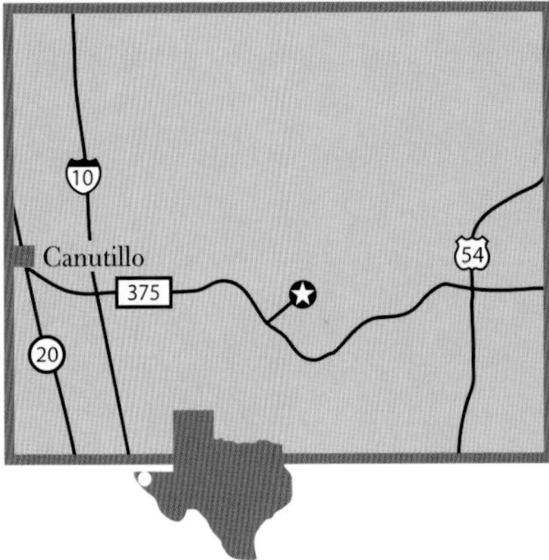

The massive fault-block of the Franklin Mountains rises abruptly from the broad, cultivated valley of the Rio Grande to the west and the flat desert basin of the Hueco Bolson to the east. The river cuts through the mountains on the south side, separating the Franklin range from mountains lying across the river in Mexico. In that cut, or river pass, sprawls the heart of El Paso. Two horns of the city curve up to the north, flanking the mountains on both east and west and forming a large, horseshoe-shaped urban area. Within that urban horseshoe is the wild, rugged terrain of Franklin Mountains State Park.

To Anglo-Americans who visited them early in the nineteenth century, the Franklin Mountains were full of menace and hidden dangers. They were a "chain of frowning mountains" to George Kendall, who, along with three hundred others, was taken prisoner by Mexicans, having been sent by the Republic of Texas on an expedition to Santa Fe in 1841.

In 1951, noted artist and author Tom Lea wrote of the range,

Mount Franklin is a gaunt, hardrock mountain, standing against the sky like a piece of the world's uncovered carcass. The plants that grow along Mount Franklin's slopes are tough plants, with thirsty roots and meager leaves and sharp thorns that neither hide nor cover the mountain's rough rock face. Mount Franklin is a lasting piece of our planet, unadorned.

Although a small range, the Franklin Mountains rise an impressive 3,400 feet above El Paso, reaching the highest point on the summit of North Franklin Peak, 7,192 feet above sea level. The desert mountains follow a long ridge running north from El Paso to the New Mexico state line. Due to the low precipitation and steep slopes, sparse Chihuahuan Desert vegetation cloaks the mountain slopes.

All desert plants adapt to survive in harsh, dry environments. Many plants have small, waxy leaves to reduce water loss through transpiration and thorns to discourage browsing animals. The barrel cactus, common in the Sonoran Desert of Arizona, finds its easternmost outpost in the United States in Franklin Mountains State Park. The distinctive cactus grows into ponderous individual stems up to four feet tall and two feet in diameter. Many of the very old plants have been damaged or destroyed by people cutting into them in the vain hope of finding a reservoir of water. Many others have been stolen from the park for use in gardens. Consequently, they are becoming quite rare in the Franklin Mountains.

Desert vegetation does not completely dominate the mountains. Here and there, tucked into hidden canyons, lie cool oases of trickling water and deep shade. The Franklins are too dry to have any large springs, but even the tiny trickles of water support lush stands of cottonwood, velvet ash, and hackberry.

These permanent waterholes are invaluable to desert wildlife. Mule deer, rabbits, and ground squirrels frequent the springs for water, browse, nuts, and berries. Hummingbirds come for flower nectar, while other birds search for wild grapes growing at the springs. Predators, such as bobcats, foxes, and coyotes, come too, drawn by the water and higher concentrations of prey animals. Even an occasional mountain lion appears in the park.

Early people also visited the mountains. At Mundy's Spring, ancient mortar holes in the rock remain from the grinding of mesquite beans and acacia pods. Members of the Jornada branch of the Mogollon Indians inscribed petroglyphs on canyon walls in the Franklin Mountains between A.D. 900 and 1400.

Alvar Núñez Cabeza de Vaca may have been the first European to pass

through the area, in 1536. In 1541, the Espejo/Chamuscado expedition is known to have come through. Juan de Oñate, in 1598, was the first Spaniard to attempt to colonize the Rio Grande Valley and northern New Mexico. Since then, the El Paso area has been governed by Spain, Mexico, the Republic of Texas, the Confederacy, and ultimately, the United States.

Today, the state park encompasses most of the mountains and is one of the largest state parks in Texas. The Castner Range, an old artillery range that is part of Fort Bliss, takes a large bite out of the east side of the mountain range. No longer used by the Army, it includes some of the most scenic parts of the mountains. The federal government may eventually turn it over to the state for the park, but because unexploded ammunition is probably still scattered across the area, a thorough cleanup would be necessary before it could be opened to public use.

Wilderness dominates the park at present, with little in the way of areas developed for use. The Tom Mays picnic area, with tables and shelters but no water, lies off the Trans-Mountain Highway on the west side and is open for day use. El Paso operates a similar recreation area in McKelligon Canyon on the southeast side within the park boundaries. Eventually more facilities will probably be added.

Many good hiking trails already exist. From the Tom Mays picnic area, trails lead to both East and West Cottonwood Spring, as well as to Mundy's Spring, Indian Peak, and the old tin mines on the east side. The springs are very small and delicate and easily trampled by heavy human feet.

At the turn of the century, tin ore was found and mined on the east side of the range. The mines are small and have been fenced off to prevent entry because of the risk of collapse and also because human visitors would disturb the bats that have set up house in the dark tunnels.

One trail climbs all the way to North Franklin Peak, the top of the range. The spectacular view stretches from mountains far south in Mexico one hundred miles north to 12,000-foot-high Sierra Blanca Peak in New Mexico. From there, El Paso and Ciudad Juárez seem silent and far away. Amid the craggy peaks and cactus-covered canyons, solitude awaits the hiker.

VISITOR INFORMATION

23,867 acres. Open all year. Day use only. Hot in summer, rare snows in winter. Extensive hiking trails, picnicking, no water. Full visitor services available in El Paso. For information: Franklin Mountains State Park, 1331 McKelligon Canyon Road, El Paso, TX 79930, (915) 566-6441.

Hueco Tanks State Historical Park

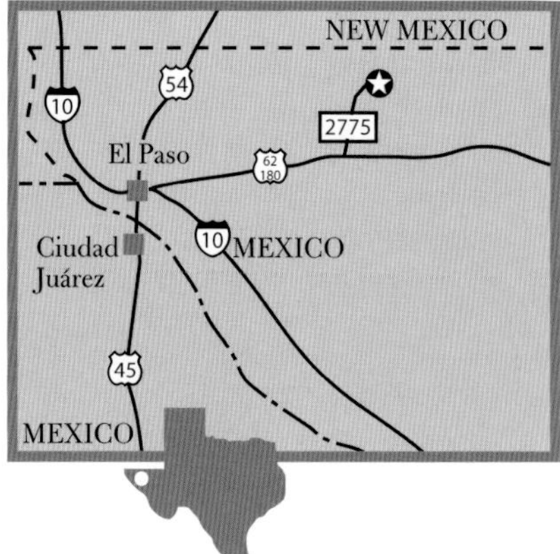

Although Hueco Tanks is nationally famous today as a winter rock-climbing center, humans have been visiting the site for at least 10,000 years. Always, either directly or indirectly, the attraction has been the rocks of Hueco Tanks. The park centers around three small, rocky mountains that tower several hundred feet above the flat alluvial slope of the Hueco Mountains. These "mountains" are, in fact, tumbled-down piles of boulders, interlaced with cliffs and caves.

Geologists believe the three mountains originated as magma, or molten rock, that intruded into layers of sedimentary rocks that had been laid down by an ancient sea. The magma cooled and hardened into a

RIGHT:
Mask pictograph
OPPOSITE PAGE, TOP:
Rock climber on "Klingon Warship"
OPPOSITE PAGE, BOTTOM:
Natural stone arch

prominent trees are one-seed junipers, Arizona oaks, and hackberries.

The first humans known to have been present at Hueco Tanks belonged to the Folsom culture. Evidence indicates that these people of 10,000 years ago relied heavily on now-extinct animals such as giant bison, camels, and mammoths. They left few traces other than their distinctive projectile points.

As the climate became drier, later nomadic groups relied on hunting smaller game and on harvesting edible plants. The water available in the natural rock tanks became more important. Additionally, the many

low-grade granite called syenite porphyry. Over time, the softer sedimentary rocks were eroded away, leaving the syenite mounds standing alone, like islands floating on the flat desert.

Although the syenite was harder than the sedimentary rocks, the forces of erosion slowly shaped it, too. Rain and wind wore down the rocks; freezing and thawing of water split off pieces; and even plants took their toll—lichen slowly ate away at the rock surface, while roots widened cracks. The weathering process created holes and depressions in the rock—*huecos* in Spanish—leading to the park's name. These huecos trapped rainwater that attracted wildlife and humans to the rocky outcrops.

The bare rocks not only collect pools of rainwater, they also funnel extra water into canyons and cracks filled with soil. The extra water, combined with the coarse igneous soil, enables a relict oak-juniper woodland to survive in the midst of the dry Chihuahuan Desert. During the cooler, wetter period of the last ice age, woodlands dominated the Hueco Tanks area. As the climate warmed and dried, the trees disappeared except in special habitats like Hueco Tanks. Analysis of ancient pack-rat nests shows that there were still pinyon pines at Hueco Tanks 13,000 years ago, but today the most

caves and overhangs eroded from the syenite provided shelter from the elements. During this time, called the Early Archaic period (between 8,000 and 5,000 years ago), the first rock art, consisting of abstract designs, was created in this area that now forms the park. Later, during the Middle and Late Archaic periods (from 5,000 to 1,500 years ago), the rock art consisted of hunting scenes with stylized humans and animals. Around A.D. 1000, a culture based on farming appeared in the area, allowing a less nomadic lifestyle. The people of this culture, known as the Jornada branch of the Mogollon, left a stunning array of rock art in many parts of the park. As with the earlier art, most of their work was in the form of pictographs, being painted onto the rock rather than carved. Their art is characterized by distinctive geometric shapes, stylized animals, hundreds of "masks," and figures reminiscent of classic Pueblo Indian motifs.

The Mogollon had vanished by the time the Spaniards arrived in the sixteenth century. The latter found instead hunter-gatherer groups, whom they called Sumas and Mansos, along the Rio Grande, and the Apaches. The last Indian rock art at Hueco Tanks was done by the Apaches. Their paintings included men on horses, a sign of their encounters with horse-mounted Europeans.

Because the Apaches dominated Hueco Tanks, the Spaniards and Mexicans avoided the area. The United States acquired the Southwest in 1848 after the Mexican-American War, and the California Gold Rush of 1849 spurred a large westward migration. One of the early emigrant routes passed by Hueco Tanks, because of its water. Later, the Butterfield Overland Mail used the same route from 1858 to 1859. The ruins of the stage stop can still be seen in the park.

In the late nineteenth century, the tanks became part of a ranch. In the 1960s, massive land development was started at Hueco Tanks but failed. For a brief time it was operated as a county park, before becoming a state historical park in 1969. Since that time, the Parks and Wildlife Department has worked to restore natural drainage systems within the park, reseed overgrazed areas, and protect the rock art from vandalism.

People no longer come to Hueco Tanks for the water; the rocks themselves attract visitors. The syenite of Hueco Tanks is very durable, rough-surfaced, and noncrumbly. Because of this, as well as the fact that it forms towering cliffs and challenging overhangs, the park attracts many rock climbers. In winter, when popular climbing sites such as Yosemite are cold and snowed in, climbers from all over the country descend on Hueco Tanks. Indeed, most people cannot resist scrambling up the rock slopes and boulders of the three mountains. Observant hikers will find many ancient pictographs, along with stone-grinding holes. The rock art is very old and fragile and should not be touched or disturbed in any way.

VISITOR INFORMATION

860 acres. Open all year. Hot and dry in summer, except for occasional late-summer thunderstorms. Busiest on spring and fall weekends. To prevent vandalism of the rock art, the park has stricter entrance requirements and regulations than most state parks. These include visitor registration and orientation, locked gates at night, and limits on the number of people allowed in the park at any one time. No pets. Campfires and charcoal fires prohibited throughout park. Small campground with partial hookups and showers. Hiking, picnicking. Rock climbers must register. Climbing is prohibited in rock-art areas. Bolts, pitons, and other rock-destroying aids are not allowed. Full visitor services available in nearby El Paso. For information: Hueco Tanks State Historical Park, 6900 Hueco Tanks Road #1, El Paso, TX 79938, (915) 857-1135.

Magoffin Home State Historical Park

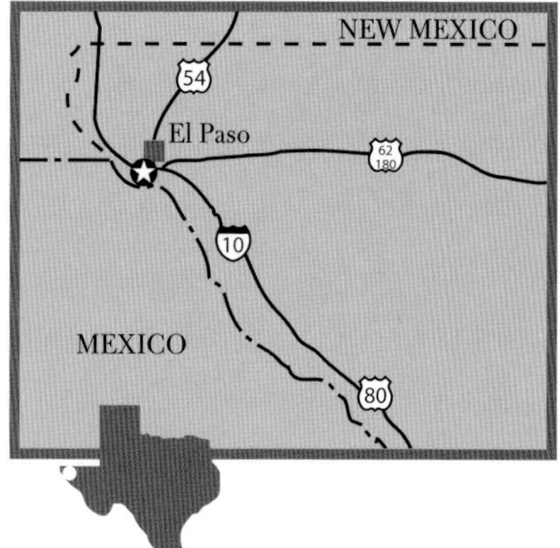

The Magoffin Home was built in 1875 by Joseph Magoffin, a son of one of the first Anglo settlers in the El Paso area. His father, James Wiley Magoffin, was born in Kentucky in 1799, but went to Mexico in search of adventure and business opportunities. He became a merchant and U.S. consul in Saltillo and then moved to Ciudad Chihuahua. He married María Gertrudes de los Santos Valdéz de Veremende, the daughter of a former governor of the state of Coahuila.

After the Mexican-American War ended, James Magoffin settled in 1849 on the banks of the Rio Grande across from the Mexican settlement of El Paso del Norte, today known as Ciudad Juárez. To conduct his trading business, he built a store, warehouses, and an adobe home which slowly grew into a small settlement known as Magoffinsville. Important visitors to the area were usually entertained by the Magoffins and the first Fort Bliss was built at Magoffinsville in 1854. The Rio Grande, in a devastating flood, destroyed much of the settlement in 1868, the same year that James Magoffin died.

OPPOSITE PAGE:
Cave at Hueco Tanks
BELOW:
Magoffin Home

James Magoffin's son Joseph had come to Magoffinsville to help with his father's business in 1856. During the Civil War he left the area and joined the Confederate cause. Afterwards he returned and worked as a bookkeeper until he managed to reclaim the family property that had been confiscated at the end of the war. He became a business and civic leader and in 1873 helped incorporate the city of El Paso. He was elected mayor of El Paso several times in the succeeding years and continued to work at various businesses before dying in 1923. During his life, El Paso changed from a rough frontier town into a busy, sprawling city.

Joseph Magoffin built his home in 1875 using adobe brick and the Territorial style of architecture, which mixed the Pueblo Indian style with Greek Revival details on doors and windows. Originally the home had seven rooms flanking a central hall, but additions were gradually built, creating a central patio and, ultimately, twenty rooms. Members of the Magoffin family lived in the house until 1986, when Octavia Magoffin Glasgow died. Because of its historical value, the home had been purchased in 1976 by the City of El Paso and State of Texas. Many of the Magoffin family furnishings still fill the house and give a view of early life on the western frontier.

VISITOR INFORMATION

1.5 acres. Open all year for guided tours daily, 9 A.M.–4 P.M. Historic home on landscaped grounds. Full visitor services available in El Paso. For information: Magoffin Home State Historical Park, 1120 Magoffin Avenue, El Paso, TX 79901, (915) 533-5147.

Monahans Sandhills State Park

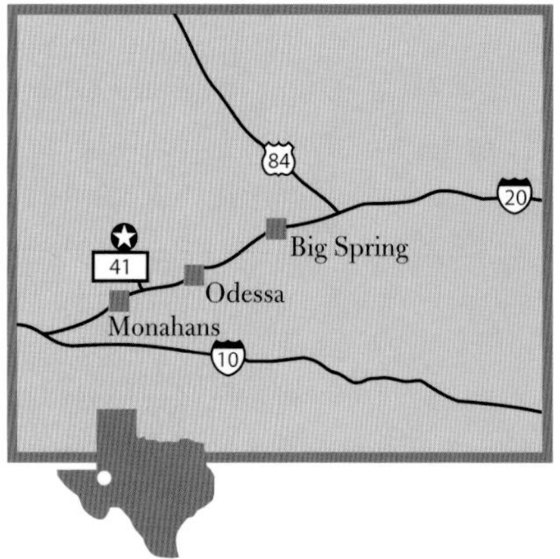

Originally derived from Triassic sandstone to the west, the sand has been deposited by winds in a narrow belt on the west side of the caprock that bounds the High Plains. The first major dune-building period began about 25,000 years ago as the climate became drier.

Miniature oak trees, usually less than three feet tall even when mature, cover much of the stabilized dunes. The shin oaks, *Quercus havardii*, are well adapted to the arid, windy climate, with roots as long as seventy feet reaching down to the shallow groundwater. In contrast to the oak's small stature, the acorns on the trees are quite large.

Dune sunset

Like bits of the vast Sahara Desert, fields of sand dunes lie tucked away in parts of windswept West Texas. The best-known is a huge field of dunes in the Permian Basin, a small part of which lies in Monahans Sandhills State Park. Much of the huge dune field has been stabilized by vegetation, but the state park contains an area with many active dunes. These dunes, some as much as seventy feet high, constantly move and change in shape in response to the wind. The dune field is about 200 miles long and stretches from southern Crane County far into southeastern New Mexico.

The shallow groundwater tapped by the oaks attracted humans to the dunes as much as 12,000 years ago. Indians found abundant fresh water beneath the sands, as well as plentiful game, acorns, and mesquite beans. More than 400 years ago, Spanish explorers became the first Europeans to visit the dunes, but despite the attraction of the shallow groundwater, most travelers avoided the area because of the difficulty of crossing the dunes.

The dunes' relative isolation ended in the 1880s when the builders of the Texas and Pacific Railroad chose Monahans as a water stop between Big Spring and the Pecos River. In the 1920s, discovery of oil beneath the sand hastened the area's development.

Present-day visitors find easy access to the park from Interstate 20. The park road winds through the dunes, some of them vegetated and others active. Children love the steep slopes of the dunes and sandsurf, roll, and tumble down them. Campgrounds and picnic areas are hidden away in valleys between the dunes, along with mesquites and desert willows.

Climb a dune and look out on the vastness of the Permian Basin. Dunes stretch to the horizon under the endless blue sky. The wind will soon erase your tracks, leaving the dunes untouched for the next visitor.

Wind-sculpted dunes

VISITOR INFORMATION

3,840 acres. Open all year. Hot in summer. Moderate number of campsites with partial hookups. Interpretive center, picnicking, nature and equestrian trails. Use care not to get lost when hiking in the dunes. Park store, sandsurfing-disk rental. Full visitor services available in Monahans. For information: Monahans Sandhills State Park, P.O. Box 1738, Monahans, TX 79756, (915) 943-2092.

Seminole Canyon State Historical Park

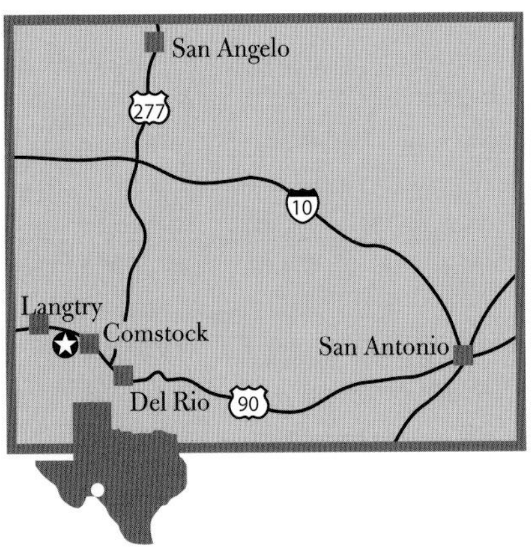

For thousands of years, early peoples lived in the large rock shelters tucked into deep canyons near the confluence of the Pecos River and the Rio Grande. Smoke from their cooking fires blackened the ceilings of these shelters and large, flat rocks were polished smooth from years of use as work tables. Striking panels of rock art were painted, and today form the most prominent remnants of these peoples' existence. Bold geometric shapes, humanlike figures interpreted as shamans, and stylized animals dance across rock faces, protected from the elements by shelter roofs and walls. Seminole Canyon State Historical Park contains some of the best of these ancient pictographs.

The area around the state park is stark, rocky, and dry. The sparsely vegetated terrain contains a mix of plants and animals from the Chihuahuan Desert, the Hill Country, and the South Texas brushlands. Most of the land is relatively flat, but the Pecos River, the Rio Grande, and their tributaries have carved surprisingly deep canyons through the underlying limestone. The cream-

Fate Bell Shelter

Pictograph

colored rock was created during the Cretaceous period, when ancient seas covered the area.

Humans are believed to have first lived here at least 12,000 years ago, at the end of the last ice age. The climate was cooler and wetter, with dense woodlands in the canyons and lush grasslands cloaking the uplands. These early people hunted now-extinct animals such as the mammoth and giant bison, but left no rock paintings.

By about 7,000 years ago, a new culture appeared whose members depended on gathering foodstuffs and hunting much smaller game than their predecessors had obtained. The dry, rocky terrain seems inhospitable, but they learned how to survive. Fruits gathered from prickly pear and strawberry cacti were eaten raw or used in other foods. Other fruits included those of the Texas persimmon and the yucca. The hearts of agaves and sotol plants were roasted for eating. Acorns and beans from the mesquite and catclaw acacia were ground into flour. Hunting added fat and protein to their diet.

They made projectile points, awls, scrapers, and knives by chipping them out of chert and flint. The tough fibers of the lechuguilla plant, the yucca, and the sotol were used to make twine, sandals, baskets, and many other items. When time permitted or religious ceremony required, these people painted rock-shelter walls using paints made from crushed iron ores and other substances mixed with animal fat. Starting 3,000 or 4,000 years ago, they created their artwork, some of the oldest pictographs in North America.

The dry air and deep shelters protected the rock art, leaving much of it still colorful and fresh after thousands of years. Many pictograph sites are known in the Lower Pecos area, some with a single painting, others with panels hundreds of feet long. Unfortunately, some sites have been damaged by vandals and other sites were flooded by the creation of Lake Amistad. Members of the state park staff conduct tours to one of the best locations, Fate Bell Shelter, in Seminole Canyon. The canyon was probably named for Seminole-Negro scouts stationed at Fort Clark in Brackettville during the 1870s. The moderately strenuous hike descends into the canyon, and leads to an enormous rock shelter containing hundreds of pictographs.

Another site, Panther Cave, can be reached by boat at the confluence of Seminole Canyon and the Rio Grande, now part of Lake Amistad. One of the paintings is an impressive panther that is fifteen feet long. The cave can be viewed from a distance by hiking or mountain-biking a 3-mile trail to a bluff overlooking the confluence. The trail crosses the abandoned grade of the Southern Pacific Railroad along the way. The railroad line was built to link El Paso with San Antonio. Crews worked from both ends of the line and reached the park area in 1882. Crossing the Pecos River Canyon presented a serious problem. Tons of black powder were used to blast tunnels and grades down to river level, where a low bridge was built over the Pecos. The track was subject to numerous rockfalls and collapses, so it was abandoned in 1892, when a bridge spanning the entire Pecos River Canyon was completed. At the time, the span, at 321 feet high, was the tallest in the world. The modern highway bridge on US 90, located just downstream from the railroad bridge, is the highest vehicle bridge in Texas.

The hiking trail ends at an impressive bluff 200 feet above the Rio Grande, a stark contrast to the flat, dry country that the rest of the trail crosses. Panther Cave lies across the lake waters of the mouth of Seminole Canyon, the large painted panther easily visible even to the naked eye. Take a good flashlight (for your return journey) and watch the sunset from the overlook. As the last golden rays of sunlight move up the canyon walls, try to imagine a prehistoric artist hard at work, painting the stone walls of Panther Cave.

VISITOR INFORMATION

2,173 acres. Open all year. Hot in summer. Guided tours of Fate Bell Shelter are conducted Wednesday through Sunday, 10 A.M. and 3 P.M. Private outfitters from Comstock and Lake Amistad, near Del Rio, lead boat tours to Panther Cave. Small campground with partial hookups and showers. Hiking, mountain-biking, picnicking, excellent interpretive museum at visitor center. Very limited visitor services available in Langtry and Comstock (no lodging); full services in Del Rio. For information: Seminole Canyon State Historical Park, P.O. Box 820, Comstock, TX 78837, (915) 292-4464.

Gulf Coast

The Texas Gulf Coast stretches for several hundred miles, from the Rio Grande delta on the Mexican border to the mouth of the Sabine River on the Louisiana border. State parks along the coast offer miles of beaches, important salt marshes, and historic lighthouses, battlefields, and plantations.

The Texas coast and inland coastal plain is a very flat, low-lying strip of land, 50–100 miles wide and more than 300 miles long, that adjoins the Gulf of Mexico. Few rocks are found along the coast; the region is blanketed by thick layers of sediment, deposited over millions of years by Texas rivers after being eroded from higher terrain to the north and west. The organic matter buried with these sediments later formed plentiful deposits of oil and gas.

Rises and falls of sea level greatly affect the coast. As ice ages have come and gone, so the sea level has changed considerably. When glaciers and ice caps lock up large quantities of water during an ice age, the sea level falls and the coast moves many miles offshore from where it is now. Conversely, when the ice melts, the sea level rises and floods many miles inland. About 18,000 years ago, during the peak of the last ice age, the shoreline moved many miles out into the Gulf and rivers cut deeper valleys as their gradient changed. When the ice age ended and the sea level rose, water flooded the valleys, creating large bays, such as Galveston and Corpus Christi.

Long, narrow barrier islands protect most of the coast and bays from storms. They were formed by the action

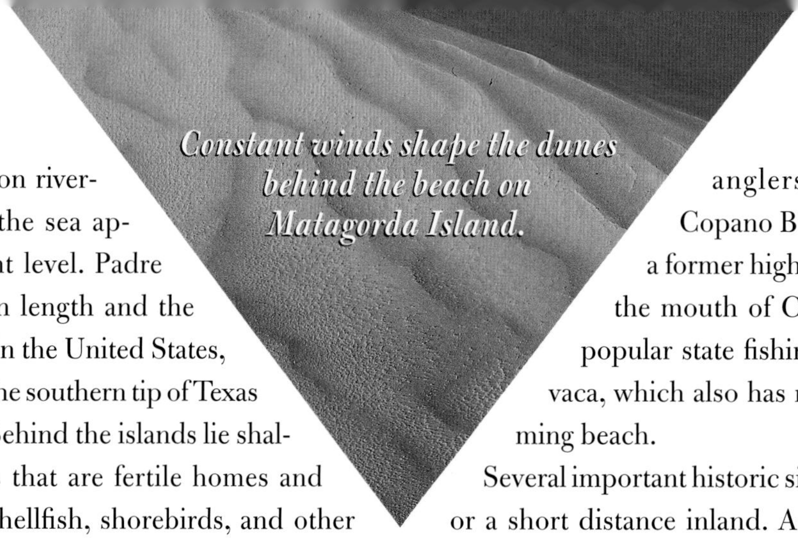

Constant winds shape the dunes behind the beach on Matagorda Island.

of wind and waves on river-deposited sand as the sea approached its current level. Padre Island, 113 miles in length and the longest such island in the United States, stretches from near the southern tip of Texas to Corpus Christi. Behind the islands lie shallow, protected bays that are fertile homes and nurseries for fish, shellfish, shorebirds, and other creatures.

A number of Texas's most popular parks lie on the barrier islands and similarly formed peninsulas. Mustang Island, Galveston Island, and Sea Rim state parks all offer miles of broad, sandy beaches and developed facilities. Matagorda Island is one of just two major islands on the Texas coast that is accessible only by boat. In addition to offering 38 miles of undeveloped beach, it harbors an historic lighthouse and endangered whooping cranes.

Several parks lie on the protected bays behind the barrier islands. Goose Island offers salt marshes, live-oak woodland, and a lengthy fishing pier. Many anglers also visit nearby Copano Bay State Fishing Pier, a former highway causeway across the mouth of Copano Bay. Another popular state fishing pier is at Port Lavaca, which also has marshes and a swimming beach.

Several important historic sites lie along the coast or a short distance inland. At San Jacinto Battleground, today marked by the 570-foot-tall limestone tower called the San Jacinto Monument, Texas rebels routed General Santa Anna's superior forces during the war for Texas's independence. The restored Battleship *Texas* rides gently in a slip at the park, adding another attraction. Other parks preserve historic mansions, plantations, and battlefields.

Parks such as those at Lake Corpus Christi and Lake Texana offer traditional water recreational activities, including sailing, waterskiing, fishing, and swimming. Miles of bicycle trails, an astronomical observatory, and plentiful alligators make Brazos Bend particularly unique. Most Gulf Coast parks offer campgrounds and picnic areas alongside their many other attractions.

Gulf Coast

1 Brazos Bend State Park
2 Christmas Bay State Park
3 Copano Bay State Fishing Pier
4 Fulton Mansion State Historical Park
5 Galveston Island State Park

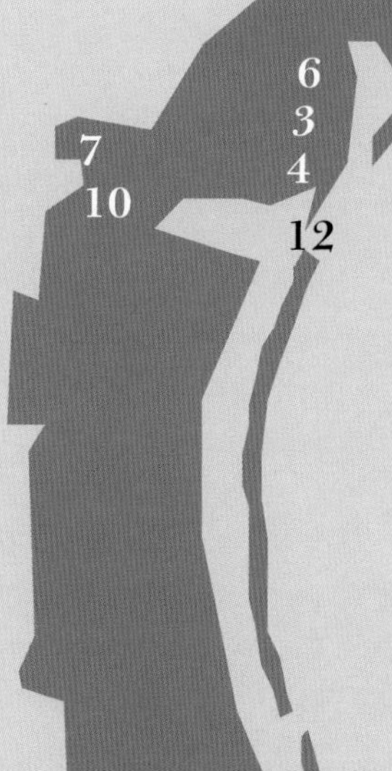

6 Goose Island State Park
7 Lake Corpus Christi State Park
8 Lake Houston State Park
9 Lake Texana State Park
10 Lipantitlan State Historical Park
11 Matagorda Island State Park
12 Mustang Island State Park
13 Port Isabel Lighthouse State Historical Park
14 Port Lavaca State Fishing Pier
15 Sabine Pass Battleground State Historical Park
16 San Jacinto Battleground and Monument • Battleship *Texas* State Historical Parks
17 Sea Rim State Park
18 Sheldon Lake State Park
19 Varner-Hogg Plantation State Historical Park

Brazos Bend State Park

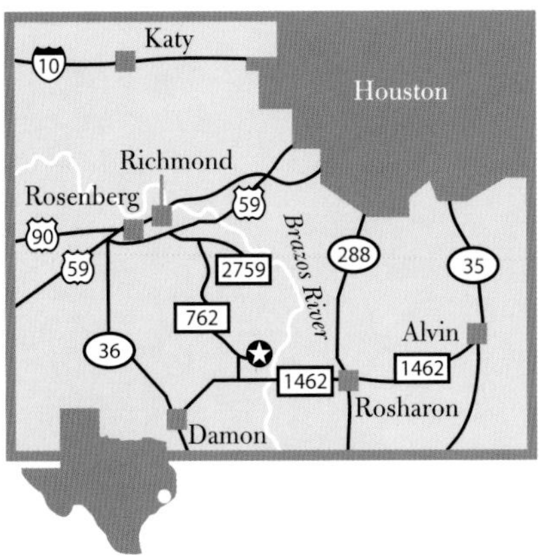

Massive live oaks arch over grassy Gulf Coast prairies. Primeval-looking alligators float motionless in sloughs and bayous, only their eyes and nostrils visible in the dark waters. White-tailed deer browse shrubs at dusk and dawn. At night, raccoons and bobcats slip through woods, stalking their prey. The edge of the bustling city of Houston lies only 20 miles away, but is little noticed in the Brazos River bottomland of Brazos Bend State Park.

The park occupies a small portion of the flat, vast coastal plain lining the Gulf of Mexico. The mighty Brazos River, one of the largest rivers in Texas, sweeps by the park, forming its eastern boundary. Most of the park lies in its floodplain, but there are areas of drier uplands. Big Creek meanders through the park, joining the river in the park's southeast corner. Over time the creek has created several oxbow lakes, formed when a curving meander is cut off from the main creek flow by erosion. Marshes and several small, shallow, man-made lakes add more watery areas to the park. The shallow, slow-

Water plants on lake

moving waters and warm climate favor the park's most famous resident, the American alligator. Large numbers of the reptiles live in the park, feeding on plentiful birds, fish, and other small animals.

More than 200 species of birds have been sighted at Brazos Bend. In addition to songbirds, the wetlands attract large numbers of migratory waterfowl, shorebirds, and wading birds.

Although the park is home to many species of wildlife, it is very recreation oriented. Fifteen miles of hiking and mountain-bike trails wind through the lush bottomlands. The scenic Red Buckeye Loop Trail in the southeast corner of the park circles around a peninsula of land between Big Creek and the Brazos River. Dense woods of sycamore, water oak, cottonwood, and many other trees arch over this narrow hiking trail. In March, the shrubby buckeyes bloom, forming a beautiful scarlet understory.

Other trails, broader and more open, follow the edges of the many lakes, bayous, and marshes. An observation tower and several platforms provide viewpoints for wildlife viewing, and fishing opportunities abound.

Within Brazos Bend lies one of the most unique features to be found in the Texas state-park system: the three domes of the George Observatory, nestling deep in the park woods. The largest telescope, with its substantial mirror measuring 36 inches in diameter, is used frequently for public viewing, unlike most similar telescopes at other observatories. Although the low elevation and the proximity to Houston do not provide ideal conditions for an observatory, it is much more accessible than remote mountaintop sites. The rounded white dome peers deep into the heavens while alligators swim through bayous below, forming an interesting contrast at one of Texas's most popular state parks.

VISITOR INFORMATION

4,897 acres. Open all year. Summers are hot and humid. Mosquito repellent is recommended in spring and summer. Campgrounds have partial hookups. Screened shelters, showers. Picnicking, hiking, cycling, fishing, wildlife viewing. Special handicapped-accessible trail with unique signage that can be interpreted by the blind. Because of the alligators, swimming is not allowed. Do not feed, annoy, or approach these large reptiles. Watch pets and children closely. Weather permitting, the observatory is open to visitors most Saturday evenings. Excellent gift and book store. Full visitor services available in Richmond, Rosenberg, and other nearby towns and cities. For information: Brazos Bend State Park, 21901 FM 762, Needville, TX 77461, (979) 553-5102.

Mountain-biker

Christmas Bay State Park

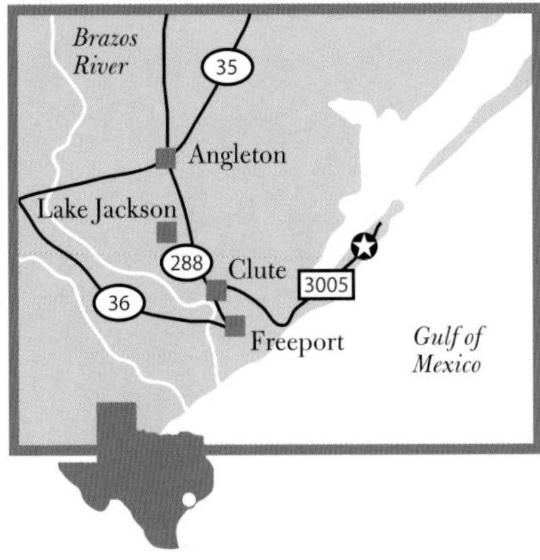

Christmas Bay State Park is an undeveloped coastal park located on Texas FM 3005 between Galveston and Surfside Beach. The park lies on Follets Island, a long, narrow peninsula extending northeast from Surfside Beach toward Galveston. Follets Island may have once been a true island, with a channel, or pass, separating it from the mainland. Between Follets Island and the mainland lie Christmas and Drum bays, two small bodies of water that are connected to the Gulf through larger West Bay and San Luis Pass, the channel between Follets and Galveston islands.

The park contains about 1.5 miles of beach frontage, as well as about 3 miles of water frontage on Christmas and Drum bays. The numerous shallow bays along the Texas coast, such as Christmas and Drum, provide important habitat for many species of fish and shellfish found in the Gulf of Mexico. Most sea creatures spend at least a portion of their lives in the shallow, fertile waters of these bays.

The state park has no developed facilities and is now managed by the General Land Office. Although anglers visit the marshes on the bay side of the park, the beach is probably the most popular destination. On this part of the coast the sand is generally firm enough to allow driving on the beach. Activities include swimming, surf fishing, beachcombing, and primitive beach camping.

VISITOR INFORMATION

485 acres. Open all year. Hot and humid in summer. Primitive camping on beach. Swimming, fishing, beachcombing, picnicking (no facilities). Full visitor services available in Surfside Beach and Freeport. For information: Christmas Bay State Park, c/o General Land Office, La Porte, TX 77571, (281) 470-1191.

Marshes lining bay

Copano Bay State Fishing Pier

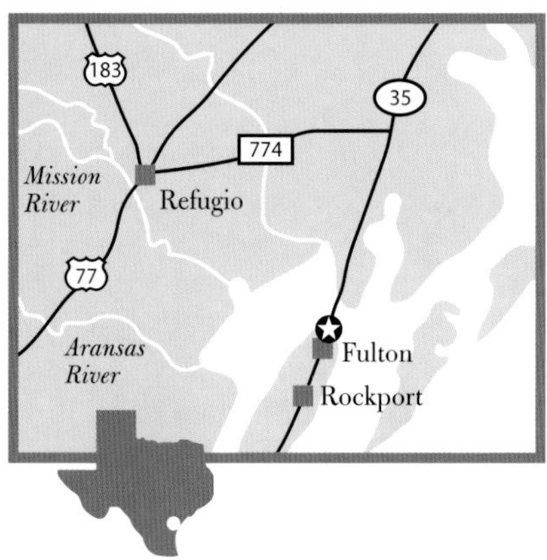

Copano Bay State Fishing Pier

Anglers wanting some elbow room can find it at the Copano Bay State Fishing Pier. Originally, the fishing pier was a long bridge, or causeway, that spanned the mouth of Copano Bay and saved highway traffic traveling up or down the coast from having to make a long detour around the bay. When a new highway causeway was constructed that was wider and stronger and thus able to handle heavier vehicles, the old one was closed to vehicles and converted into a fishing pier. Because taller boats are able to pass through the new causeway, which has a high section in the middle, the middle part of the old, lower causeway had to be removed. This leaves two separate sections of causeway, one of which stretches 6,190 feet from the north side, while the other extends 2,500 feet from the south side—plenty of room for a lot of anglers.

Copano Bay is a bay off a bay, rather than being directly connected to the Gulf of Mexico. It opens off the back side of Aransas Bay, which is separated from the Gulf by San Jose Island, a barrier island. Like most Texas bays, Copano Bay was a river valley when sea levels were lower during the last ice age. As the ice melted, the sea level rose and flooded the old river mouths and valleys. Texas Highway 35 and the fishing-pier segments span the mouth of the bay, connecting the Lamar and Live Oak peninsulas.

The shallow bays and their associated marshes are vital for the production of fish and shellfish in the Gulf of Mexico. Most of these creatures spend at least a portion of their life in the bays and marshes of the Texas coast. Anglers using Copano Bay State Fishing Pier take advantage of the fertile bay waters, where they can catch redfish, flounder, speckled trout, drum, sheepshead, and many other species.

VISITOR INFORMATION

6 acres. Open all year. Partially lighted fishing piers, boat ramp, fish cleaning tables, concession building, restrooms. Full visitor services available in Rockport and Fulton. For information: Copano Bay State Fishing Pier, P.O. Box 39, Fulton, TX 78358, (361) 729-7762.

Fulton Mansion State Historical Park

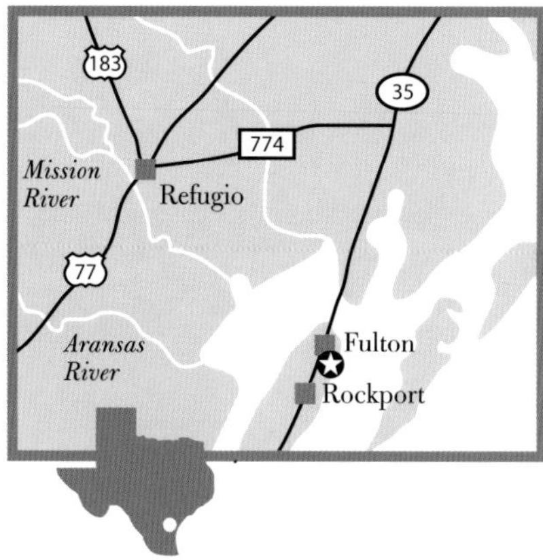

Prominent Fulton Mansion presides over sparkling Aransas Bay in complete contrast to the smaller beach homes and businesses that line the shore in Rockport and Fulton. When it was built in the 1870s, the ornate building must have dominated the area. The builder, George Fulton, first came to Texas in 1837 to fight in the war for Texas's independence, but he arrived too late to participate. During the following years, he worked as a land developer, machinist, engineer, newspaper reporter, teacher, draftsman, railroad superintendent, and bridge builder in Texas and other states. In 1868 he and his family moved back to Texas permanently to oversee his wife's inheritance when her father died.

With his wife's inherited South Texas land, Fulton, together with several partners, established an extensive cattle-ranching business. In 1874, the Fultons began construction of their home on the shores of Aransas Bay. They chose the French Second Empire style of architecture, with its characteristic mansard roof, for their 6,200-square-foot home. Most materials and construction equipment were shipped in from New Orleans and the East Coast at considerable expense. Fulton's previous engineering experience is evident in the mansion's construction. He built it to withstand hurricanes by using concrete and concrete blocks for the basement walls and 1-inch x 5-inch pine planks spiked together on top of each other to create solid upper walls. The floors were constructed in a similar manner and were a solid 5 inches thick.

Fulton installed all available modern conveniences inside the house, including running water, flush toilets, central heat, and a gas lighting system. He even built a water cooling system to preserve perishable food, and a simple clothes dryer. Finishing touches included walnut and cypress woodwork, chandeliers, fine rugs, and ornate furniture.

George Fulton died in 1893 and eventually his wife Harriet was unable to maintain the home on her own. She sold it in 1907, the first of several ownership changes that the house would undergo. Over time, the historic mansion was neglected and deteriorated physically. Finally, it was purchased by the Texas Parks and Wildlife Department in 1976 and restored to its former grandeur, to stand as an architectural monument on the Texas coast.

VISITOR INFORMATION

2.3 acres. Open all year for guided tours Wednesday through Sunday. Wear flat, soft-soled shoes to protect the floors and rugs. Historic building, picnicking. Full visitor services available in adjacent Rockport and Fulton. For information: Fulton Mansion State Historical Park, P.O. Box 1859, Fulton, TX 78358, (361) 729-0386.

Fulton Mansion

Galveston Island State Park

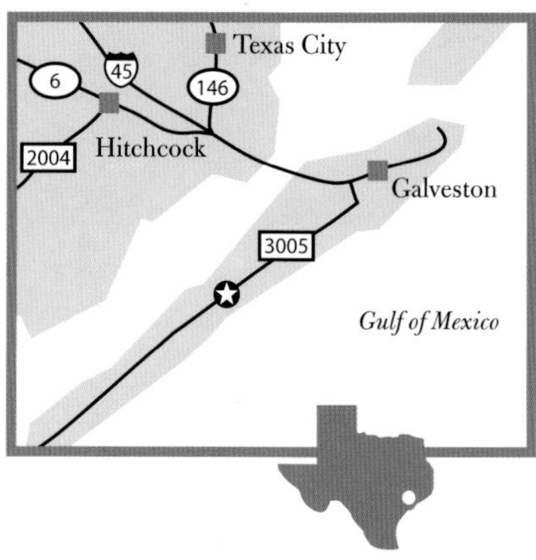

Galveston Island beach

Thousands of people visit Galveston Island State Park every year, drawn primarily by the 1.6 miles of beach fronting on the Gulf of Mexico. Galveston Island is a barrier island, formed by wave action and longshore currents in the shallow waters lining the Gulf. The island is not very old geologically; the rising and falling sea level that accompanies passing ice ages destroys and recreates barrier islands relatively quickly.

Behind the broad beach of the state park, winds have built dunes that are mostly anchored by vegetation. Behind the dunes lies a strip of coastal prairie covered with grasses and other plants. Salt marshes border the bay on the back side of the island and provide an excellent habitat for fish, crustaceans, and wading birds. The park spans the entire width of the island, from the beach to the salt marsh.

When Europeans first arrived on the Gulf Coast, nomadic Karankawa Indians lived on the island and in other coastal areas. Alvar Núñez Cabeza de Vaca was shipwrecked here in 1528 and held prisoner by the Karankawas for six years before making his way back to Mexico City. The Spaniards returned for a short time in the middle of the eighteenth century and set up a presidio named for the Spanish governor of Louisiana, Bernardo de Galvez. They soon left and the French gained control for a time. In 1817, Jean Lafitte and his band of pirates established a base called Campeche on the island. For several years, Lafitte preyed on Spanish ships, but he was finally run off after attacking an American ship.

The community that Lafitte left behind grew into a thriving port named Galveston, an anglicized version of the earlier presidio's Spanish name. During the Civil War, Galveston changed hands more than once during battles between the Union and the Confederacy. After the war, the port prospered, becoming the largest in Texas and the third largest in the nation. The fact that the city was on a low-lying barrier island, and as such was built on sand, proved to be unfortunate. In 1900, disaster struck when a hurricane blasted the island with 20-foot-high storm tides driven by winds blowing at 100 miles per hour. More than 6,000 people died and most of the island's buildings were leveled in the greatest natural disaster in American history. Since that time, however, the rebuilt city has thrived as a port and major tourist destination.

Many visitors to the island come to enjoy the sand and surf offered by Galveston Island State Park. Not only are swimming, sunbathing, and fishing possible, the quiet bayside marshes provide opportunities for hiking and birding. On summer evenings, outdoor musicals such as "Oklahoma!" and Paul Green's "The Lone Star" play at the Mary Moody Northen Amphitheater in the park. Although hurricanes strike the island occasionally, most of the time the park offers a quiet outdoor escape from the busy port of Galveston and inland cities such as Houston.

VISITOR INFORMATION

1,950 acres. Open all year. Hot and humid in summer. Mosquitoes can be thick behind the dunes in warm weather. Very popular, especially in summer. Large number of campsites with partial hookups and showers. Screened shelters. Swimming, fishing, picnicking, hiking and nature trails. Outdoor musicals on summer evenings, except Sunday. Full visitor services available in Galveston. For information: Galveston Island State Park, 14901 FM 3005, Galveston, TX 77554, (409) 737-1222.

Driftwood on beach

Goose Island State Park

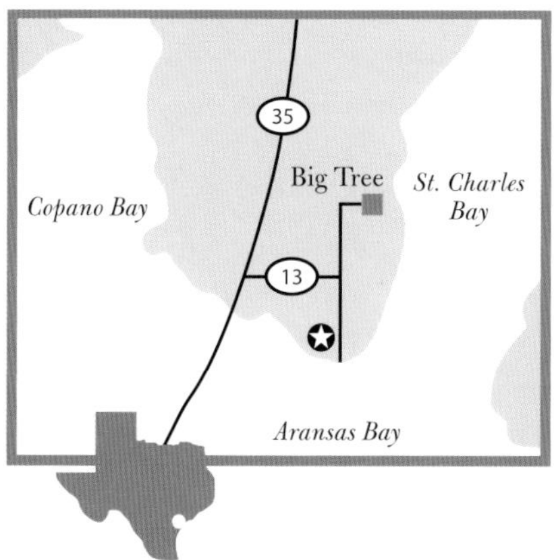

Goose Island State Park lies at the southern tip of the Lamar Peninsula, at the conjunction of Aransas, St. Charles, and Copano bays. Unlike most coastal areas in Texas, much of the coast around the state park is heavily wooded with live oaks and redbays. The outlying barrier islands, Matagorda and San Jose, probably offer some protection to this coastal area, making it easier for trees to survive on this stretch of the salty, storm-prone coast. The sandy strip of land upon which much of the state park lies was once a barrier island itself, during the Pleistocene era, when sea levels were higher.

Goose Island State Park provides an interesting mix of habitats, considering its small size. Goose Island itself, a small island barely separated by water from the mainland part of the park, only measures about 140 acres, but it contains a mix of salt marshes and tidal flats, as well as a small grassland area on the highest ground. In contrast, most of the mainland park area is a dense forest of wind-sculptured live oaks and redbays. Small patches of coastal prairie cover openings in the woods.

Two diverse types of creature draw many people to Goose Island—namely, birds and fish. A boat ramp and a 1,620-foot-long fishing pier make water access easy for anglers. The pier, lighted at night, stretches far into the bay to several islets and oyster banks. Popular fish include redfish, flounder, speckled trout, drum, and sheepshead.

The coastal area around Rockport is nationally famous for its birds; more than 400 species have been recorded here. With a mix of marshes, tidal flats, beaches, and open water, the coast attracts multitudes of wading and shore birds. Thickets of live-oak woodland and open coastal prairies provide different habitats for other species. Spring and fall migrations bring many songbirds and other migrants through every year. Probably the most famous bird in the area is the whooping crane. When standing, this large white bird is the tallest bird found in the United States. It is endangered and possibly the rarest bird in the country; only about 140 remain. The cranes summer in western Canada, but return every winter to Aransas National Wildlife Refuge and surrounding bay areas. The wildlife refuge is just across the narrow mouth of St. Charles Bay from Goose Island.

In addition to birds and fish, the state park offers swimming, picnicking, and boating opportunities. A

Tidal flats in Aransas Bay

short nature trail winds through the thick live-oak woods surrounding the mainland campground. The Goose Island Oak, generally known as "The Big Tree," is one of the most impressive sights on the coast. The enormous tree, estimated to be 1,000 years old, grows in a separate unit of the park about 2 miles northeast of the park headquarters. The state champion coastal live oak, it is 44 feet tall, has a trunk 35 feet in circumference, and has a crown spread of 89 feet. It has survived prairie fires, Civil War battles, and hurricanes too numerous to count. The tree is a fine symbol of the lasting appeal of the Texas coast at Goose Island State Park.

VISITOR INFORMATION

314 acres. Open all year. Hot and humid in summer. Mosquitoes can be fierce away from the shore in warm weather. Large number of campsites, split between woods and shore locations; partial hookups and showers. Swimming, boating, boat ramp, fishing, lighted fishing pier, short hiking/nature trail, birding, picnicking. Full visitor services available in Rockport and Fulton. For information: Goose Island State Park, 202 S. Palmetto St., Rockport, TX 78382, (361) 729-2858.

ABOVE:
Goose Island fishing pier
RIGHT:
CCC pavilion at Lake Corpus Christi
OPPOSITE PAGE, TOP:
CCC pavilion
OPPOSITE PAGE, BOTTOM:
Lake Corpus Christi

Lake Corpus Christi State Park

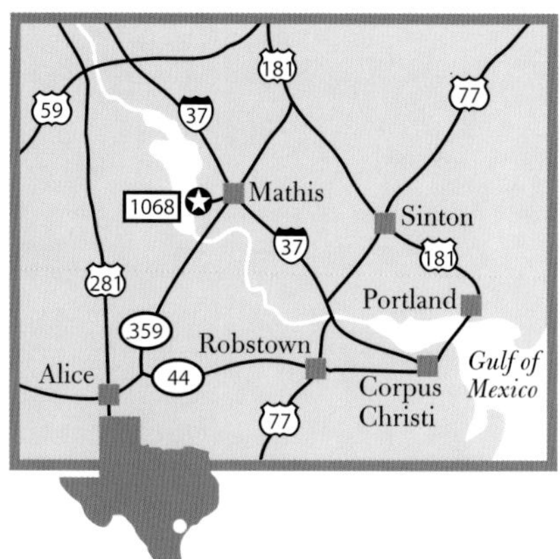

Lake Corpus Christi State Park has long been a cornerstone of the Texas state-park system. The park had its beginnings when the size of the local population grew in the early part of this century. Increased demand for water led to an earth-fill dam being built across the Nueces River in 1929. Unfortunately, the dam failed only ten months later. It was rebuilt in 1935 and the large but shallow new reservoir was named Lake Corpus Christi. Parkland was leased from the City of Corpus Christi and opened with little development.

The Civilian Conservation Corps

worked to improve the park during the Depression of the 1930s. The corps' most notable accomplishment was the construction of the pavilion and interpretive center on a high bluff overlooking the lake. The skillfully built limestone building is still attractive today, with stone arches framing views of the lake.

During the park's early days, a herd of longhorn cattle was established in the park to help maintain the breed's bloodlines in Texas. The cattle flourished and came into frequent conflict with park visitors. As a result, the animals were finally rounded up and sent to Fort Griffin State Historical Park.

Over the years, the Nueces River not only fed a constant supply of water to the lake, it also added copious amounts of silt and clay. The sediment gradually filled the reservoir, reducing its water-storage capability while the population of Corpus Christi continued to swell. In 1958, a new dam was completed that raised the water level and greatly increased the reservoir's capacity.

Long before European settlers arrived in the Corpus Christi area, various Indian groups lived along the lush Nueces River bottomland. At that time, most of the South Texas area was flat grassland interspersed with wooded riparian areas along streams and rivers. After Spanish and Anglo settlers arrived, natural fires were suppressed, so brush began to invade the grasslands. Imported cattle accelerated the process by favoring grasses for grazing and ignoring brush, and by bringing in seeds of plant species from other areas. Today a thick brushland of mesquite, acacia, huisache, yucca, and other plants dominates most of the park and, indeed, much of South Texas.

Many types of mammal are found in the park, including javelina, armadillos, jackrabbits, skunks, and raccoons. Some of the most popular animal species are birds, of which more than 300 species have been recorded at Lake Corpus Christi. The park gets an interesting mix of South Texas and Mexican species, songbirds, waterfowl, and wading birds. Its location on a major migration route increases the variety of species found.

The park not only provides a water supply and haven for wildlife, it offers visitors excellent recreational opportunities. Swimmers and boaters who tire of the rougher salt water of the nearby coast come to the state park. Waterskiers and sailboarders zip across the smooth lake waters, while anglers troll the depths, trying for black bass, striped bass, crappie, and catfish. Lake Corpus Christi State Park has been established for many years, and is still one of the top draws among Texas state parks.

VISITOR INFORMATION

288 acres. Open all year. Hot and humid in summer. Large number of campsites with partial and full hookups and showers. Screened shelters. Fishing piers, boat ramps, swimming, waterskiing, picnicking, and boat rental. Full visitor services available in Mathis and Corpus Christi. For information: Lake Corpus Christi State Park, P.O. Box 1167, Mathis, TX 78368, (361) 547-2635.

Lake Houston State Park

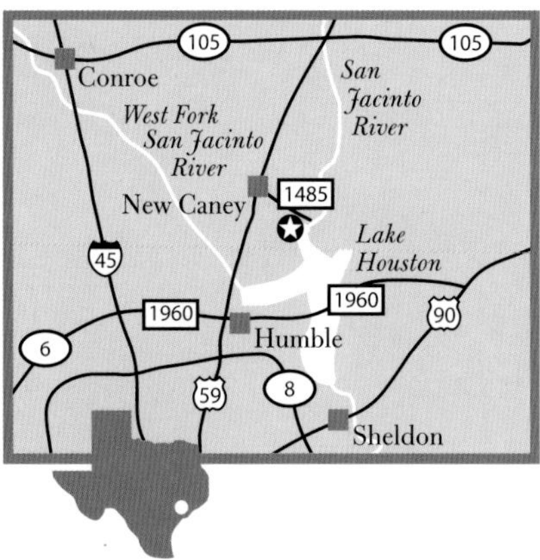

One of Texas's newest parks, Lake Houston State Park lies only a half hour north of Houston. Its name is somewhat misleading, because only the park's extreme southern end touches the far upper end of Lake Houston, and currently there is no easy access to that part of the park. However, the park offers plenty of other recreational opportunities for visitors.

A network of former logging roads provides miles of trails for hiking and biking, and it is also being developed for future equestrian use. The old roads wind through dense woods of magnolia, oak, loblolly pine, and other species typical of the East Texas Pineywoods. In wet bottomland areas, swampy cypress sloughs create a primeval atmosphere. Many types of animal, from songbirds to white-tailed deer, make their home under the dense forest canopy. As development spreads north from Houston, the 4,900-acre park will become increasingly important as a wildlife refuge.

The park occupies a wedge of land between the East San Jacinto River on the east and Caney Creek and Peach Creek on the west.

Fishing pier on oxbow lake

Although there is no lake access for boats, canoeing, fishing, and wading are possible in the creeks and rivers. Prior to its purchase in the early 1980s, most of the property was utilized as a hunting camp by the timber company Champion International. In 1990, an additional area—200 acres of a former girl scout camp—was purchased, and most park development is concentrated in the latter area. Two lodges are available for overnight rentals, and walk-in tent sites have been developed for camping.

Even without these more elaborate developments, park visitors can still walk or cycle through miles of park trails, enjoying the thick forest; birders can scan the trees for the many different species of birds that are drawn to the undeveloped woodland; anglers can try their skill at catching bass and catfish in the park waterways; and canoeists can paddle down the calm, slow-flowing creeks. Houston may be close by, but there is little sign of it deep in the woods of Lake Houston State Park.

VISITOR INFORMATION

4,913 acres. Open all year. Hot and humid in summer. Small number of walk-in tent campsites with showers. Fishing, canoeing, hiking, biking, and equestrian trails. Full visitor services available in Cleveland, Conroe, and Houston. For information: Lake Houston State Park, 22031 Baptist Encampment Road, New Caney, TX 77357, (281) 354-6881.

Lake Texana State Park

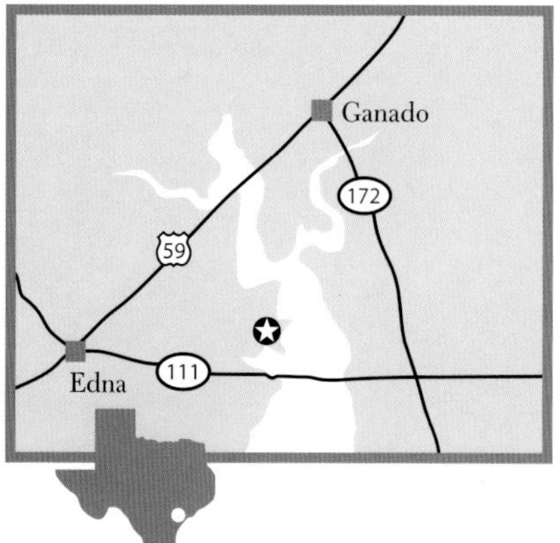

Lake Texana State Park lies on the shores of Lake Texana, an 11,000-acre reservoir filled by the waters of the Navidad River and smaller creeks. For its size, the lake is relatively shallow. It lies on the flat coastal plain, so there was not enough topographic relief to create a deep body of water on the Navidad River itself. Palmetto Bend Dam, a rolled earth-filled structure, was completed in 1979. To create a large lake on the flat terrain, the dam had to be almost 8 miles long with a maximum crest elevation of 55 feet. The dam backs

Lake Texana fishing pier

up water for 18 miles, resulting in a 125-mile shoreline that winds around many tributaries, both large and small.

The lake was named for the town of Texana, founded in 1832 along the Navidad River, a few miles downstream from the present dam. For years Texana was a prosperous inland port, but in 1883 it was bypassed by the New York, Texas, and Mexican Railroad. Today little remains of it but an historical marker.

Most of the land surrounding the park is prairie; some is used for grazing, while some has been plowed under for crops such as rice. Most of the park, however, lies within the old river valley on the edge of the lake and is wooded with live oaks, post oaks, pecans, water oaks, cedar elms, and other trees. Yaupon, American beautyberry, palmettos, and mustang grapes form the woodland understory.

The lake is relatively new, so dead, flooded timber still stands in some parts of it, providing excellent fish habitat. Anglers pursue largemouth bass, crappie, and catfish in all corners of the lake, and the park offers excellent fishing facilities, including three fishing piers, two of which are lighted, and a boat ramp.

Birding and wildlife watching are two other quiet activities enjoyed at Lake Texana. More than 225 bird species have been recorded here. Flooded rice fields and mudflats along the lakeshore attract shorebirds from the nearby coast, and spring and fall migrations can bring everything from waterfowl and songbirds to huge groups (known as kettles) of migrating hawks. The most prominent mammals are the white-tailed deer that, almost oblivious to people, wander through campsites and picnic areas. Though they are seen less often, other common animals include armadillos, raccoons, opossums, squirrels, alligators, and bobcats.

For more active recreation, the lake offers plenty of room for waterskiers and jet-skiers, as well as for sailboats. Swimmers can take advantage of multiple water-access points throughout the park. Lake Texana is a popular but quiet escape from urban life, drawing many people back year after year.

VISITOR INFORMATION

575 acres. Open all year. Hot and humid in summer. Large number of campsites with partial hookups and showers, split into two areas. Boating, waterskiing, boat ramp, fishing piers, picnicking, birding. Full visitor services available in Edna and Victoria. For information: Lake Texana State Park, P.O. Box 760, Edna, TX 77957, (361) 782-5718.

Sunset over lake

Lipantitlan State Historical Park

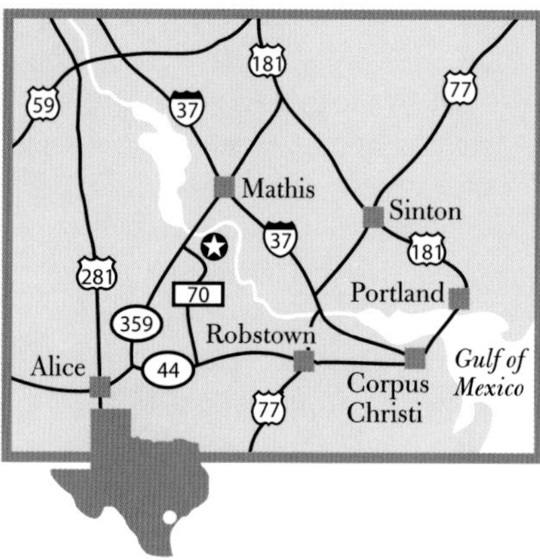

Lipantitlan State Historical Park is a small, little-developed park located near the Nueces River southeast of Lake Corpus Christi. The park is close to the site of Fort Lipantitlan, a post first built by the Spaniards in 1728 near a Lipan Apache village of the same name. The fort was abandoned after many Indians died in the Battle of Medina on August 18, 1813.

Reactivated by Mexican troops in 1831 to deter further Anglo-American colonization, the fort was little more than an earthen embankment surrounding unfinished barracks. In October 1835, Captain Philip Dimitt, commander of Texas forces at Goliad, sent a company led by Ira Westover to take the fort. The troops seized the fort on November 3 and stopped a Mexican counterattack the next day.

On June 7, 1842, volunteers under General James Davis successfully defended Fort Lipantitlan against an assault by General Antonio Canales and his "Republic of the Rio Grande" forces. The fort was abandoned after that battle and crumbled into ruin.

Today the small park bearing the old fort's name offers little more than the shade of old, gnarled mesquite trees. Other than an historical marker, little remains of the once hotly contested military post.

VISITOR INFORMATION

5 acres. Open all year. Hot and humid in summer. Historical marker, picnicking. No water or other facilities. Difficult to find; obtain directions at nearby Lake Corpus Christi State Park. Full visitor services available in Mathis and Corpus Christi. For information: Lipantitlan State Historical Park, c/o Lake Corpus Christi State Park, Box 1167, Mathis, TX 78368, (361) 547-2635.

Mesquite at Lipantitlan

Matagorda Island State Park

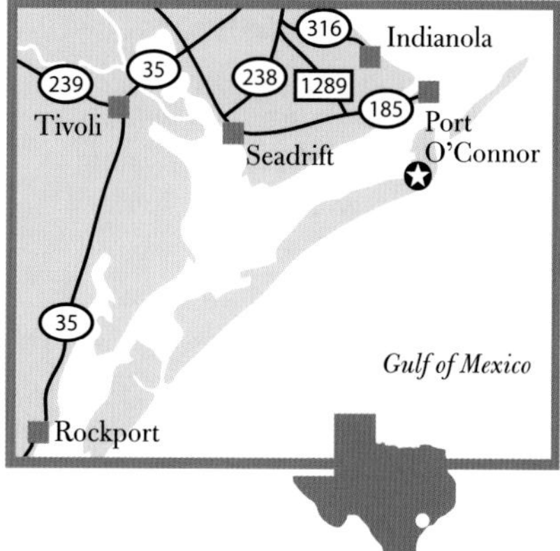

People who make the effort to visit Matagorda Island are rewarded with one of the emptiest, most isolated sections of the Texas coast. Matagorda is one of only two major coastal islands in Texas not connected to the mainland by bridges or ferries. To reach the island, it is necessary to take a boat—either your own or a chartered one—or the passenger ferry that runs on weekends and holidays.

Like the more famous Padre and Galveston islands, Matagorda is long and narrow: it measures 0.75–4.5 miles in width and 38 miles from end to end. The low-lying island is a barrier island, created from sand by longshore currents and wave action in the shallow waters at the edge of the Gulf of Mexico. Barrier islands are fragile and short-lived; changes in sea level and hurricanes can destroy them and rebuild them elsewhere. Even though the islands are not especially durable, they provide an important buffer for the mainland from hurricanes and tropical storms.

Unlike most coastal areas of Texas, the island is virtually undeveloped. A crumbling World War II air base and an historic lighthouse built in 1852 lie on the northeastern end of the island; the rest of Matagorda's 56,668 acres have only a scattered ranch building or two and some dirt roads. Except for park vehicles, no motorized transportation is allowed on the island, which is jointly managed by the state and federal governments as a state park, state wildlife management area, and national wildlife refuge.

Wildlife thrives on the empty, undeveloped island. Nineteen state or federally endangered or threatened species are found there, including the famous whooping crane. More than 300 species of birds use Matagorda as either a permanent home, a winter refuge, or a migratory stopover point. Habitat exists for wading birds, shorebirds, waterfowl, raptors, and songbirds. Whooping cranes spill over onto the island from Aransas National Wildlife Refuge, just across San Antonio Bay.

Mammals found on the island include white-tailed deer, coyotes, raccoons, and jackrabbits. Alligators lurk in freshwater marshes, preying on unwary animals that come too close. Western diamondback rattlesnakes and other reptiles are common in the grasslands behind the beach dunes. Rare sea turtles such as the Kemp's ridley use the island on occasion.

Fertile salt marshes behind the central grasslands provide nursery areas for shrimp, crabs, and many species of fish. Anglers commonly catch redfish, spotted trout, flounder, mackerel, and many other species in the waters surrounding the island.

Most visitors, including those using the ferry, come to the island by crossing Espiritu Santo Bay from Port O'Connor. The park office and docks are on the bay side of the island across from the town. The park operates a shuttle vehicle daily from the docks to the beaches on the gulf side of the island about 1.5 miles away. Mountain bikes are an excellent alternative means of getting around the island. Matagorda Island may take some effort to reach, but miles of empty gulf beaches are the reward.

VISITOR INFORMATION

7,325 acres. Open all year. Access only by boat or ferry. Passenger ferry operates on weekends and holidays; call park for schedules and fees. Primitive camping is permitted in the bay-side dock area and along two miles of gulf beach. Facilities include a limited number of picnic tables with shade shelters, pit toilets, and an outdoor cold-water rinse-off shower near the docks. No electricity, drinking water, concessions, or telephones on the island; bring plenty of food, water, and sunscreen. Fishing, swimming, surfing, sunbathing, picnicking, and birding; 80 miles of beach, as well as dirt roads and mowed paths, provide extensive hiking and mountain-biking opportunities. Limited visitor services available in Port O'Connor and Seadrift; full services in Port Lavaca. For information: Matagorda Island State Park, P.O. Box 117, Port O'Connor, TX 77982, (361) 983-2215.

Gulf Coast beach

Mustang Island State Park

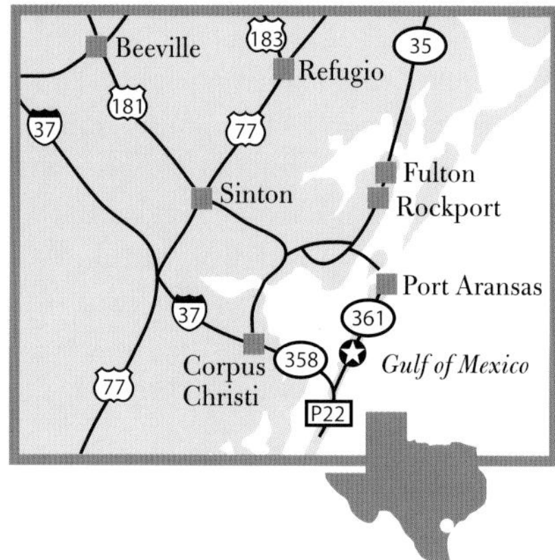

The surf washes ashore ceaselessly on the beaches of Mustang Island that face the Gulf of Mexico, sometimes with small, quiet rollers, other times with towering waves driven by hurricanes. The endless movement of the ocean seems to draw people to the island year after year. Mustang Island State Park, one of Texas's most popular state parks, occupies several miles of beach and marsh on the long, narrow island.

Mustang Island is a barrier island, one of many along the Texas coast; others include Padre, Matagorda, and Galveston islands. Barrier islands are formed when sand is deposited along the shore by wave action and long-shore currents and then built up into dunes by steady coastal winds. The islands form important buffers for the bays and mainland behind them, dulling the impact of violent gulf storms and tidal surges.

The low, sandy islands change constantly as dunes move and beaches erode. Sand eroded from one part of an island can be deposited elsewhere. Hurricanes and storms striking the barrier islands can radically alter them, opening new channels, or passes, between the Gulf and the bays or closing old ones. Fish Pass, within the state park, was formerly a small channel connecting Corpus Christi Bay and the Gulf, but has now sanded in and closed; large granite jetties that mark the mouth of the old channel now provide a favorite fishing site and surf break for surfers. Likewise, the channel that once separated Mustang and Padre islands, to the south of the state park, has closed also.

Behind the dunes of Mustang Island lie grasslands carpeted with salt-tolerant plants. Low areas in the grasslands fill with rainwater and become freshwater marshes vegetated with bulrushes and cattails. Close to the bay, fingers of salt water reach up into the island, creating salt marshes and mudflats, depending on the level of the tides. The marsh areas are a prime habitat for wading birds and small fish.

The varied habitats of the island provide homes for many creatures, large and small. Mammals range from small herbivores such as gophers and cottontails to predators like the coyote. Birdlife is abundant and attracts many park visitors. Water and shore birds, such as herons, gulls, pelicans, and terns, are commonly seen all year. In spring and fall, large numbers of migrants pass through the park.

Mustang Island jetty

Before Europeans arrived, the Karankawa Indians lived on Mustang Island and in other coastal areas. The Spanish explorer Alonso Alvarez de Piñeda first sailed this part of the Texas coast in 1519. Later, part of a Spanish treasure fleet was washed ashore on Padre Island in 1553, but the area was little visited until the eighteenth century, when the Spanish missionary effort was in full swing. Until several cattle ranches were established on the island in the 1850s, no settlements were built. Except for the small shipping town of Port Aransas at the north end, Mustang Island remained quiet and relatively undeveloped until a causeway was built to Padre Island in 1954. In 1972 the parkland was purchased and damage done by vehicles driving on the dunes was repaired. Today, many thousands of people visit Mustang Island State Park every year, to swim, surf, fish from the jetties, sunbathe, or just relax to the soothing sound of waves rolling onto the wide, sandy beach.

VISITOR INFORMATION

3,704 acres. Open all year. Hot and humid in summer. Very busy in summer, especially on weekends. Moderate-sized campground behind dunes, with partial hookups and showers; large primitive beach camping area with no hookups. Swimming area with bathhouse, rinsing showers. Swimming, fishing, picnicking. No glass containers allowed on beach. Breeze usually keeps mosquitoes off beach, but they can be fierce behind the dunes, especially on warm evenings. Avoid jellyfish and stingrays on beach and in water. Some visitor services available on north end of Padre Island at junction of Park Road 22 and Tx Hwy 361; full services in nearby Corpus Christi and Port Aransas. For information: Mustang Island State Park, P.O. Box 326, Port Aransas, TX 78373, (361) 749-5246.

Port Isabel Lighthouse State Historical Park

The Port Isabel Lighthouse was built in 1852 to guide shipping through Brazos Santiago Pass to Point Isabel. Prior to construction of the lighthouse, General Zachary Taylor used the site as a supply depot during the Mexican-American War. Fighting returned to the area during the Civil War, and the light was darkened for its duration.

Confederate troops held the site until 1863, when federal forces sent to strengthen the blockade on

Southern shipping gained control. Both sides used the lighthouse as a lookout during the war. Confederate troops captured 113 Union soldiers at a battle at nearby Palmito Ranch on May 13, 1865—ironically, more than a month after General Robert E. Lee had surrendered at Appomattox. The clash is believed to have been the last of the Civil War.

After the war the light was repaired, and it guided ships until 1905, when traffic declined. During this period, its use was interrupted from 1888 to 1894 owing to a squabble over ownership of the land under the lighthouse. In 1950, the lighthouse was acquired by the State Parks Board from private owners; it was dedicated as a state park in 1952, the centennial of its construction. The tower has been repaired and renovated and today looks out on a resort community. Of the 16 lighthouses that have been constructed along the Texas coast, only the Port Isabel Lighthouse is open to visitors.

VISITOR INFORMATION

0.88 acres. Open Wednesday through Sunday all year, 10–11:30 A.M. and 1–5 P.M., except Christmas Day. Historic building. Limited visitor services available in Port Isabel; full services on South Padre Island. For information: Port Isabel Chamber of Commerce, 421 East Queen Isabella Blvd., Port Isabel, TX 78578, (956) 943-2262.

LEFT:
Port Isabel Lighthouse
ABOVE:
Port Lavaca State Fishing Pier

Port Lavaca State Fishing Pier

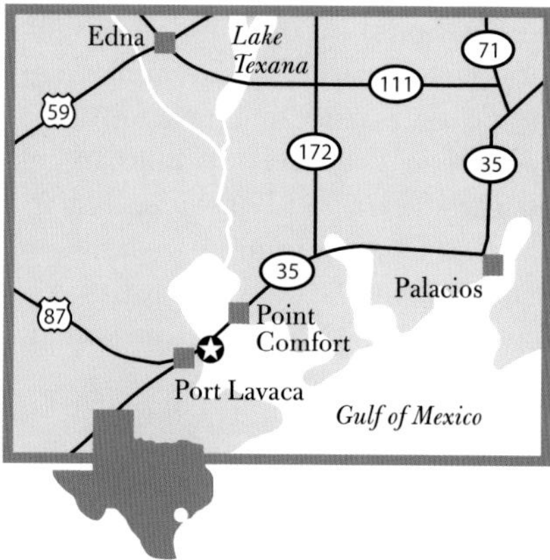

The Port Lavaca State Fishing Pier lies on the west side of Lavaca Bay, by the city of Port Lavaca. The pier itself is part of an old causeway that once spanned the bay. It is managed by the City of Port Lavaca, as part of Lighthouse Beach Park.

The pier extends out into Lavaca Bay, a prime nursery ground for many species of fish and shellfish. Most creatures found in the Gulf of Mexico spend at least part of their lives in the bays and marshes of the Texas coast. Anglers fishing off the pier can catch many different varieties of fish, including redfish, sheepshead, speckled trout, drum, and flounder.

Lavaca Bay is a small bay extending off bigger Matagorda Bay. Benefiting from the protection Matagorda Peninsula offers to Matagorda Bay, Lavaca Bay is somewhat protected from storms and other disturbances in the Gulf. Like most bays on the Texas coast, it formed when the sea level rose and drowned part of an old river valley—in this case, that of the Lavaca River and smaller tributaries.

Lighthouse Beach Park adjoins, and offers visitors a number of activities other than fishing. A small sandy beach allows swimming in the shallow bay waters, while tables serve picnickers. Campsites for RVs have full hookups. The park also has a long recycled-plastic boardwalk and interpretive exhibits in a small area of coastal marsh.

VISITOR INFORMATION

1.8 acres. Open all year. Hot in summer. Fishing pier with restrooms, boat ramp. Adjoining Lighthouse Beach Park has camping with full hookups, picnicking, swimming, and nature study. Full visitor services available in Port Lavaca. For information: Port Lavaca State Fishing Pier, 202 N. Virginia, Port Lavaca, TX 77979, (361) 552-5311.

Sabine Pass Battleground State Historical Park

Sabine Pass is a channel of water that connects the Gulf of Mexico with Sabine Lake and separates Texas and Louisiana. Today the waterway is calm, the quiet interrupted only by occasional oceangoing ships, shrimp boats, and pleasure craft, but during the Civil War the pass was the site of an important battle.

A bronze statue of Lieutenant Richard W. "Dick" Dowling overlooks the site of the conflict. During the Civil War, Texas was a major source of supplies for Confederate forces, although few battles took place on Texas soil. In an attempt to limit Texas's ability to supply the South, Union forces established a naval blockade of the Gulf coast. To circumvent the blockade, an industry of "blockade runners" developed in many Confederate ports, including Sabine City (now called Sabine Pass), a small town on the Texas shore. In 1862, the Union limited the blockade running at Sabine City by stationing ships outside the mouth of the pass and by entering the pass and destroying the fort located there, Fort Sabine. They soon left because the town was under quarantine with a yellow fever epidemic.

On July 3, 1863, Confederate forces surrendered at Vicksburg and lost control of the Mississippi River, freeing thousands of Union troops for service elsewhere. Plans were made to invade Texas, and to first take Beaumont in order to sever the railroad link between Texas and Louisiana. The plan was for an amphibious assault on Sabine Pass to be followed by the landing of 15,000 troops, who would take the Beaumont region.

Meanwhile, Texas defenses at Sabine Pass were in a pitiful condition. General John Magruder, Texas District commander, ordered a new shore battery named Fort Griffin to be built at the pass to replace Fort Sabine. Defense of the pass was left to two small gunboats and several small companies of the Texas Infantry. In July, second in command Dick Dowling, a native of Ireland, occupied Fort Griffin along with his company of rough Irish dockhands.

By the first week in September, the Union fleet, with 4,000 troops and supplies, was approaching the pass, but no more than 300 Confederate troops were within 50 miles of the area. The bulk of Magruder's troops had been sent to northwestern Louisiana. Magruder, hearing of the imminent invasion of Sabine Pass, ordered the few remaining troops to retreat. Dowling and his band of 48 mutinous Irishmen ignored the order and adopted the motto "Victory or death!"

Before dawn on September 8, following delays and mistakes on the part of the Union forces, the invasion began. Sandbars in the channel made travel difficult for the Union ships. The gunboat *Clifton* made the first entry, but remained out of range of Fort Griffin's guns. A second entry into the pass was led by the *Sachem*, one of the four Union gunboats. The *Arizona* then got stuck on a sandbar.

The *Sachem* moved into range of Fort Griffin's guns. Dowling's men finally opened fire, striking the gunboat at will while a strong current drove it aground on the Louisiana shore. The *Clifton* forged ahead, but was struck by a shot that cut its wheel rope. Currents pushed it aground on the Texas shore in close range of the fort's guns. In less than an hour, Dowling's men had captured two gunboats and 350 men. The remainder of the Union fleet retreated to New Orleans, not to return to Sabine Pass until after the end of the war. Not a single one of Dowling's men was injured in the battle.

Dick Dowling memorial

After recent losses at Vicksburg and Gettysburg, the Confederacy was heartened by the victory at Sabine Pass. Fort Griffin was not abandoned until a month after the war ended. Its flag was the next to last one to be lowered in the entire Confederacy. Although the Battle of Sabine Pass did not stop the ultimate defeat of the South, it did prevent a Union invasion of Texas and the resulting devastation suffered by many other Southern states. After the war Dick Dowling became a successful businessman, but sadly died of yellow fever a few years later, on September 28, 1867.

VISITOR INFORMATION

56 acres. Open all year. Hot and humid in summer. Small number of campsites with partial hookups. No showers. Replica of Fort Sabine, historical markers, interpretive pavilion, picnicking, fishing, boat ramp. Full visitor services available in Port Arthur. For information: Sabine Pass Battleground State Historical Park, P.O. Box 1066, Sabine Pass, TX 77655, (409) 971-2559.

San Jacinto Battleground and Monument • Battleship *Texas* State Historical Parks

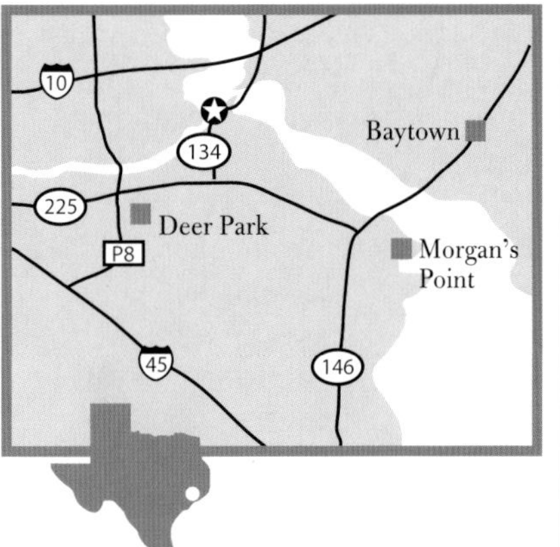

In March of 1836, the war for Texas's independence from Mexico was not going well for General Sam Houston and his Texan troops. On March 11, Houston abandoned Gonzales and retreated eastward in advance of the numerically superior forces of General Antonio Lopez de Santa Anna, the President of Mexico. Houston's poorly trained troops were restless, eager for revenge after the

View of San Jacinto Monument from Battleship Texas

Goliad massacre and the fall of the Alamo. Houston realized, however, that the Texans had little chance of winning over Santa Anna's much larger army without some sort of advantage.

On April 18, Houston arrived at Buffalo Bayou and found that Santa Anna had already sacked the small town of Harrisburg. Through a captured Mexican courier, he learned that Santa Anna had isolated himself from the bulk of his troops and had a force of about 750 men, slightly smaller than Houston's force of 820 men. Houston realized that his chance had come. On April 19, Houston and his men crossed to the south bank of Buffalo Bayou and marched east, setting up camp near Lynch's Ferry on April 20. An advance guard of the Texans captured a boatload of the Mexican Army's provisions at the ferry, providing food for the famished Texan soldiers.

A small party of Texans was dispatched to New Washington on Galveston Bay to learn Santa Anna's position. After a brief skirmish with the Mexican Army, the Texans retreated back to Houston's position near Lynch's Ferry, with the Mexican forces not far behind. Upon his arrival at nearby San Jacinto, Santa Anna tried to draw the Texans into battle. Skirmishes continued into the late afternoon, when Santa Anna established a camp about three-quarters of a mile east of Houston's position.

In a brief skirmish at sunset, a detail of Texan cavalry almost met with disaster, stoking Houston's fears about his poorly trained, individualistic troops. As darkness fell, both armies settled into camp for the night. Houston ordered his men to eat and rest, while he stayed up all night worrying. Santa Anna, realizing that Houston's force was slightly larger, built fortifications using saddles, baggage, and anything else available and hoped that reinforcements would soon arrive. Even though his men were exhausted, he kept them up all night on alert, believing that the Texans would attack at first light.

On April 21, dawn came with no attack and Santa Anna relaxed. At about 9 A.M. about 500 more Mexican troops arrived, to the chagrin of Houston and his men. Houston sent a small detail to destroy Vince's Bridge to delay additional Mexican reinforcements. At noon he held a council of war, at which no decision was reached.

That afternoon, Houston assembled his troops and laid out a plan of battle. The main force advanced quietly in a frontal assault, hoping for the advantage of surprise. Two other groups circled around to the left and right flanks of the Mexican camp. The Mexican troops had relaxed in the knowledge of their numerical superiority and many were eating and sleeping.

The Texans had advanced to within 200–300 yards of the Mexican position before they were discovered and the alarm sounded. The main group of Texans charged the camp, screaming, "Remember Goliad! Remember the Alamo!" A pitched battle quickly ensued, much of it hand to hand at the Mexican fortifications. The two other groups of Texans attacked the flanks, quickly overwhelming the Mexican camp. Houston was wounded, but fought on with his men. In less than twenty minutes, organized resistance ended and many Mexicans fled toward the San Jacinto River, hoping to swim to safety. Even though Houston and his officers tried to stop the slaughter, many Mexicans were killed by revenge-driven Texans even as they tried to surrender. As the sun set to the west, the battle ended, the marshes stained scarlet with blood. Nine Texans and 630 Mexicans lay dead or mortally wounded, a tremendous defeat for the Mexican Army.

Those with medical training did their best with minimal supplies to treat the Texan and Mexican wounded. The 700 uninjured Mexican troops were disarmed and placed under guard. A small number, including Santa Anna, escaped from the battle and headed westward to the several thousand troops waiting west of the Brazos River. Houston knew that if Santa Anna was able to reunite with the main body of his army, the

LEFT:
Battleship Texas
RIGHT:
San Jacinto Monument

war would continue, so he sent out scouts to search for the escapees the next day. By noon, Houston's men had captured Santa Anna, who was disguised as a private. Santa Anna ordered his troops to withdraw from Texas, securing independence for the Republic of Texas.

To commemorate the pivotal battle, the 570-foot-tall San Jacinto Monument was built, along with the San Jacinto Museum of History at the base. An elevator in the massive concrete and limestone tower takes visitors to an observation level near the top, under the crowning limestone star. On a clear day, the view encompasses the historic battleground and many square miles of Gulf Coast country east of Houston.

In a berth on Buffalo Bayou, on the opposite side of the park from the monument, lies the second major attraction of the state park: the mighty Battleship *Texas*. Today it rests quietly at its mooring, in stark contrast to the bitter battles in which it was involved during World Wars I and II.

The *Texas* was commissioned in 1914, at which time it was the most powerful ship in the world. It first saw service that year in Mexico, and then in Europe in 1918 during World War I. Between the two world wars, the *Texas* was continually modernized, the improvements including being converted from coal to oil fuel. When the Japanese attacked Pearl Harbor in 1941, the *Texas* was docked in Portland, Maine and escaped the destruction inflicted on many of its sister battleships. During the war in Europe, it saw action in several battles, including D-Day, the invasion of Europe on the Normandy coast, at which it was the flagship. Its massive 14-inch guns pounded salvo after salvo into German artillery positions at Omaha Beach to help landing troops gain a beachhead. After the war ended in Europe, the *Texas* steamed into the Pacific and fought in the battles at Iwo Jima and Okinawa.

In 1948, the *Texas* was decommissioned and presented to the State of Texas. It was berthed at the San Jacinto Monument until 1988, when it was removed to Galveston for a major overhaul and renovation; after 40 years, rust and corrosion had taken their toll on the massive ship. In 1990, the 573-foot *Texas*, on the way to being restored to its 1945 condition, was reopened to the public. Tours wind through the main deck and the maze-like compartments of the lower decks of the *Texas*, once one of the most fearsome weapons on Earth, and today the only surviving Navy ship to have served in both world wars.

VISITOR INFORMATION

1,005 acres. The park, battleship, monument, and San Jacinto Museum of History are open daily all year except Christmas Eve and Christmas Day. Call to verify times. Hot and humid in summer. Day use only. Historic structures, museums, theater presentation, interpretive markers, picnicking, fishing. Full visitor services available in Houston and suburbs. For information: San Jacinto State Historical Park, 3523 Highway 134, La Porte, TX 77571, (281) 479-2431; San Jacinto Museum of History, 3800 Park Road 1836, La Porte, TX 77571, (281) 479-2421.

Sea Rim State Park

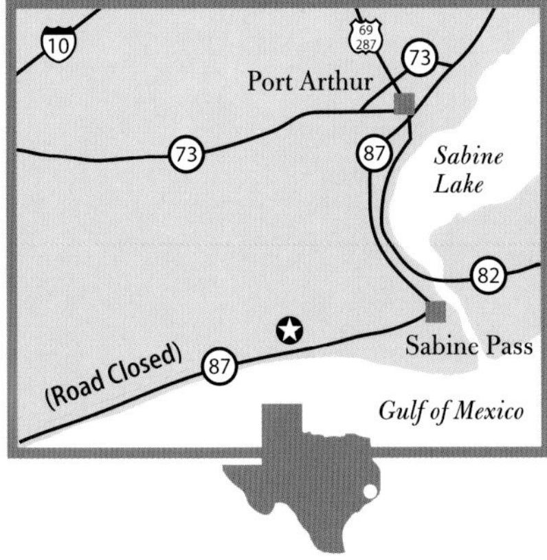

Sandy beaches line the vast majority of the Texas Gulf Coast, but at Sea Rim State Park, marshes extend into the surf along part of the shore. These "sea rim" salt marshes give the park its name. They grow in the layers of mud and silt swept westward along the coast from the Sabine River by longshore currents and deposited along the shore at Sea Rim. Farther west in the park, the typical sandy beaches and dunes reappear along the shore.

Most park visitors favor the beach, where they can swim, surf, fish, and sunbathe. A low ridge of dunes, mostly anchored by vegetation, backs the broad beach. Behind the dunes lies a vast area of lightly visited marshlands. A short boardwalk nature trail behind the dunes introduces visitors to the marsh area. Ponds form in the low-lying terrain through a combination of storms depositing large quantities of water and alligators digging holes during dry spells. Water in the ponds and wet areas has varying degrees of salinity, from almost fresh to as salty as sea water. Salinity is raised by storm tides carrying in salt water and by evaporation, while rains add fresh water. Plants in the marshes adapt to the salt water through having a high tolerance to salt.

Salt-tolerant grasses are the principal plant component of the marshlands. Reptiles and amphibians thrive in the shallow waters of ponds and sloughs in the marsh. Alligators, snakes, and turtles bask on the banks, but slide into the water at the approach of humans. Frogs leap into the water with a splash and disappear from sight.

Alligators were once endangered, but have made a remarkable comeback. Only a few are usually seen along the boardwalk trail, but many live in the marshlands unit behind Highway 87. The large sprawl of the marshlands unit takes up the largest part of the park, but is relatively unvisited, even though a boat ramp leads into a system of channels, ponds, lakes, and sloughs that are ideal for a canoe or shallow-draft boat with a small motor. In addition, a number of wooden platforms have been built in the marsh for camping and for observing wildlife.

Birds love the marshes at Sea Rim. Wading birds, such as herons, egrets,

and rails, stalk the shallow waters, hunting for crustaceans, fish, frogs, and other prey. Songbirds perch in the tall grasses, feeding on plentiful insects.

At dusk, the mammals come out to eat. Small rodents scurry through the tall grasses, foraging for seeds and tender shoots. Nutria and muskrats feed upon the marsh grasses and build their dens. Raccoons roam the marsh, feeding on anything they can catch. Even a few rarely seen river otters and minks make their home in the marsh.

People have learned that the fertile waters of the marsh wetlands are very important to fisheries in the Gulf of Mexico. The shallow, nutrient-rich waters act as a nursery for many fish and crustacean species, including redfish and shrimp. In addition, the marshes provide a habitat for large numbers of wintering waterfowl. The importance of the marsh habitat is emphasized by the nearby location of McFaddin, Texas Point, and Anahuac national wildlife refuges. The beach at Sea Rim State Park is very attractive, but the marshes make an interesting alternative destination.

LEFT:
Gulf Coast beach
ABOVE:
Beach at sunset

VISITOR INFORMATION

15,094 acres. Open all year. Hot and humid in summer. Insect repellent a necessity in the marshes. Do not approach, feed, or touch alligators. Modest number of developed campsites with partial hookups and showers. Primitive camping on designated beach area and marsh platforms. Interpretive exhibits, nature trail, swimming, picnicking, fishing, sunbathing, surfing, boat ramp, canoeing, boating, and birding. Full visitor services available in Port Arthur. For information: Sea Rim State Park, P.O. Box 1066, Sabine Pass, TX 77655, (409) 971-2559.

Sheldon Lake State Park

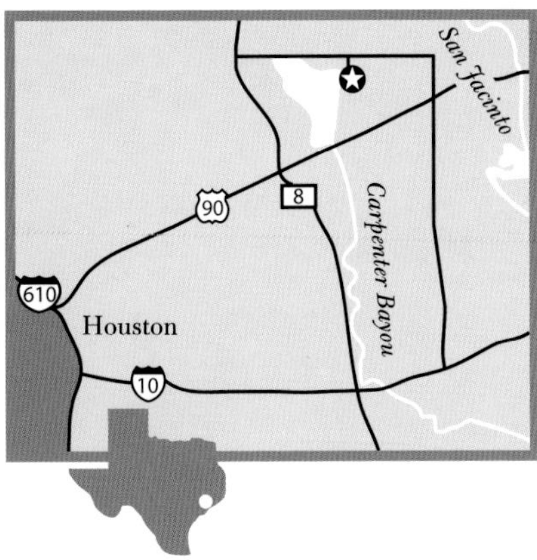

Sheldon Lake State Park is a combined state park/wildlife management area lying only about 13 miles northeast of downtown Houston. It consists of a 1,200-acre lake and surrounding land. Sheldon Reservoir was built in 1941 by damming the waters of Carpenters Bayou, a tributary of Buffalo Bayou. It was used during World War II as a water supply by wartime industries located on Buffalo Bayou. After the war, the federal government designated it as surplus and transferred it to the City of Houston. The city, in turn, conveyed the lake to an agency that was the predecessor of the Texas Parks and Wildlife Department.

The lake was converted into a waterfowl refuge and fishing lake. Florida bass, crappie, sunfish, and catfish were stocked, and surrounding land was farmed to provide grain for wintering geese and ducks.

About 800 acres of the lake are permanently inundated with water; another 400 acres are marsh. Because the terrain is very flat, the lake's levees have created a very shallow body of water. Much of its surface has been covered by water plants, and bald cypresses and other water-loving trees have taken root. Because the lake is small and shallow, there are numerous navigation hazards and boat motors are limited to 10 HP. Boats are not allowed on the lake from November 1 to February 28, to protect waterfowl.

Primary activities are fishing, boating, and wildlife observation, with waterfowl viewing at its best between late November and early March. Alligators are frequently seen in addition to waterfowl. In the spring, several heron and egret rookeries thrive on a number of small islands in the lake. The park has an environmental education center with boardwalks, trails, and interpretive programs.

VISITOR INFORMATION

2,503 acres. Open all year. Hot and humid in summer. No camping. Boating, fishing piers, birding. Full visitor services available in Houston. For information: Sheldon Lake State Park, 14320 Garrett Road, Houston, TX 77044, (281) 456-9350.

Lush water plants on Sheldon Lake

Varner-Hogg Plantation State Historical Park

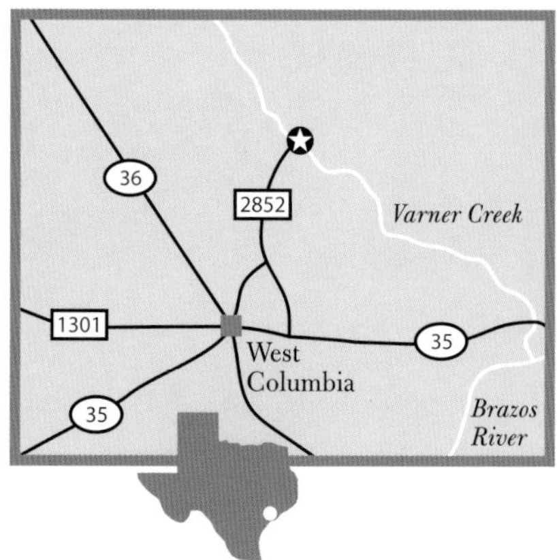

Martin Varner, a member of one of Stephen F. Austin's first colonizing families in Texas, known as the "Old Three Hundred," started the Varner-Hogg plantation in 1824. Varner's land grant of 4,605 acres on the Brazos River was the nineteenth of three hundred issued under Austin's first contract with the Mexican government. He built a small home on the site, planted corn and sugarcane, and raised livestock. He is believed to have produced the first rum in Texas.

In 1834, Varner sold the property to Columbus Patton and his parents. With time, the property became a large and prosperous sugar plantation with slave quarters and a sugar-processing building. The two-story main house was built using a regional variant of Greek Revival architecture. Brick made from Brazos River clay was used in its construction. To lessen the risk of fire, the kitchen was built in a separate building, as was common at the time.

Patton was declared insane in 1854, possibly because of a brain tumor, and died two years later. After Patton's stewardship ended, the plantation began to decline because of low sugar prices, the Civil War, and unfavorable weather. The property underwent a series of ownership changes in the latter half of the nineteenth century. Sugar and cotton continued to be produced, but the plantation never recovered its earlier level of prosperity.

In 1901, former Texas governor James S. Hogg purchased the property, initially as an investment, though he ended up using it as a second home and vacation retreat. Hogg believed that oil lay under the land and, before his death in 1906, drilled several unsuccessful wells in an effort to find it. His belief was corroborated in 1920, when the West Columbia Oil Field was discovered, adding greatly to the family's wealth.

In 1920, Governor Hogg's children undertook a major remodeling of the property. The architectural style was changed to Colonial Revival and the house was reoriented so that the front faced west instead of east. The kitchen building was enlarged and cement stucco replaced plaster on the exterior. The home remained in the Hogg family until 1958, when daughter Ima Hogg presented the furnished home and surrounding historic structures to the state for a park. The furnishings include many Hogg family heirlooms, period furniture, and other historic items and documents. Today, tall magnolias and pecans shade the historic home, an excellent example of an antebellum plantation house.

VISITOR INFORMATION

66 acres. Open for tours Wednesday through Sunday all year. Day use only; call for hours. Historic structures and exhibits, picnicking, interpretive trail. Full visitor services available in West Columbia and Lake Jackson. For information: Varner-Hogg Plantation State Historical Park, P.O. Box 696, West Columbia, TX 77486, (979) 345-4656.

Varner-Hogg home

Hill Country

Many of Texas' favorite state parks lie in the hilly, rocky terrain of the Hill Country in the center of the state. Although most of the parks in this region share a similar ecosystem and geologic underpinning, the many sites are distinguished from one another by a considerable variety of attractions. Several parks, such as Garner, Guadalupe River, and Pedernales Falls, contain sections of clear, cool Hill Country rivers; Kickapoo Cavern and Longhorn Cavern offer tours deep into the limestone heart of the land; the ruins of Fort McKavett stand watch over the western edge of the Hill Country, once the Texas frontier; the rugged canyons of Lost Maples State Natural Area have some of the best fall color in the state; and other parks offer everything from lake recreation to a living history farm.

Most of the Hill Country shares a similar geologic history. About 100 million years ago, thick layers of limestone and other sedimentary rocks were deposited in horizontal layers on the bottom of a Cretaceous sea. Between 10 and 20 million years ago, a large area of Central Texas was uplifted about 2,000 feet along the Balcones Escarpment, a long, curving fault that stretches from north of Austin southwest to San Antonio and west to the Del Rio Area. The rock layers were raised upward with little deformation and formed a relatively high, flat-surfaced area, the Edwards Plateau. During the many millennia since the uplift, erosion has carved the plateau into hilly terrain, especially along the eastern and southern margins.

Bigtooth maples bring brilliant color to Lost Maples State Natural Area in the fall.

The thick limestone layers were conducive to cave formation and hundreds of known caves lie hidden under the surface. Many are large and beautiful, and a number have been opened to the public both in state parks and in private sites. The sedimentary rocks of the Hill Country are also known for fossils and dinosaur tracks.

Although Cretaceous limestones underlie most of the Hill Country, a unique group of rocks lies in the center of the region. In an area centered around Llano, pink granite domes and twisted masses of schist and gneiss lie in sharp contrast to the surrounding whitish limestones. The overlying Cretaceous layers have been eroded away, exposing these metamorphic and igneous rocks that are more than a billion years old—the oldest in Texas. The gneiss and schist are the remains of ancient mountain ranges that were eroded into sediment that was heated and pressured to such an extent that it formed metamorphic rocks, visible today at Inks Lake State Park and other sites.

Masses of molten rock, or magma, rose within these rock layers and slowly cooled and solidified into large masses of granite. This high-quality stone is quarried at several Hill Country sites for use in buildings, monuments, jetties, and other construction projects. Not only does the durable stone provide a good building material, its sheer faces attract rock climbers to Enchanted Rock State Natural Area.

The Hill Country has a distinct ecosystem, shaped by its soils, slopes, elevation, and climate. Thick woodlands of live oaks, red oaks, Ashe junipers, and cedar elms are interspersed with open grasslands. Along permanent streams and rivers, lush riparian woodlands of bald cypresses, sycamores, and pecans thrive. The broad floodplain at South Llano River State Park is noted for its large, mature pecan bottomland forest. In areas such as Lost Maples State Natural Area, deep canyons provide shelter from sun and wind and allow trees such as the colorful bigtooth maple and black cherry to grow.

A number of Hill Country parks are notable for their wildlife. Most have good populations of white-tailed deer, armadillos, raccoons, opossums, and other mammals. A number of parks host endangered species, such as the black-capped vireo and the golden-cheeked warbler. A large flock of wild turkeys roosts in the pecans at South Llano River in winter. A number of Hill Country caves, including those at Kickapoo Cavern State Park and Devils Sinkhole State Natural Area, harbor large colonies of Mexican free-tailed bats.

Last but not least, the parks of the Hill Country offer a broad range of recreational opportunities, from water sports at Inks Lake and Guadalupe River to rock climbing at Enchanted Rock. Horse owners like the miles of trails at Hill Country State Natural Area, while mountain-bikers can pedal through the backcountry at Pedernales Falls. At Colorado Bend, visitors can tour a wild cave and walk to a waterfall tumbling over a fern-and-moss-covered cliff.

Hill Country

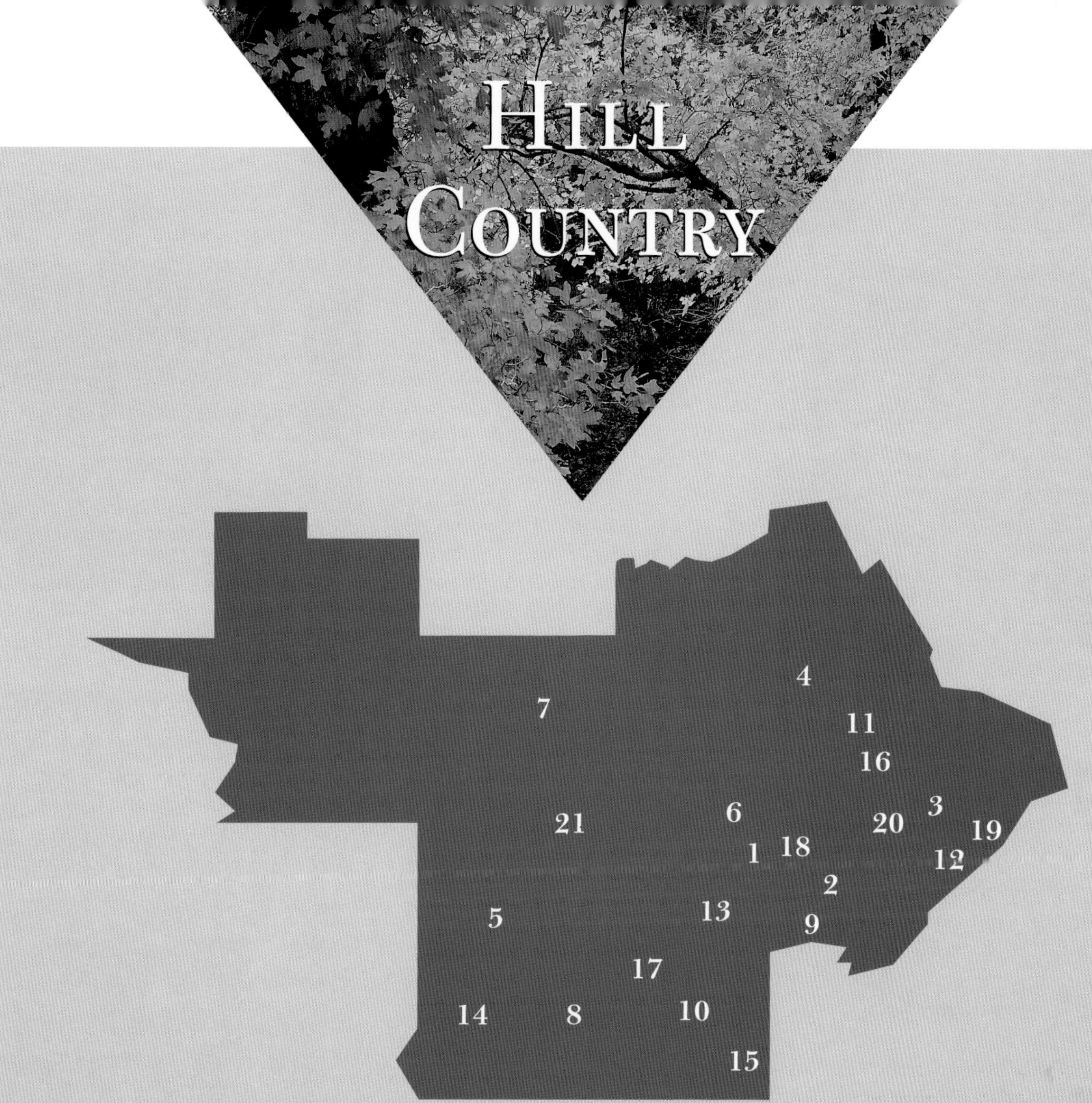

1 Admiral Nimitz Museum and Historical Center
2 Blanco State Park
3 Bright Leaf State Natural Area
4 Colorado Bend State Park
5 Devil's Sinkhole State Natural Area
6 Enchanted Rock State Natural Area
7 Fort McKavett State Historical Park
8 Garner State Park
9 Guadalupe River State Park • Honey Creek State Natural Area
10 Hill Country State Natural Area
11 Inks Lake State Park
12 John J. Stokes San Marcos River State Park
13 Kerrville-Schreiner State Park
14 Kickapoo Cavern State Park
15 Landmark Inn State Historical Park
16 Longhorn Cavern State Park
17 Lost Maples State Natural Area
18 Lyndon B. Johnson State Historical Park
19 McKinney Falls State Park
20 Pedernales Falls State Park
21 South Llano River State Park

Admiral Nimitz Museum and Historical Center

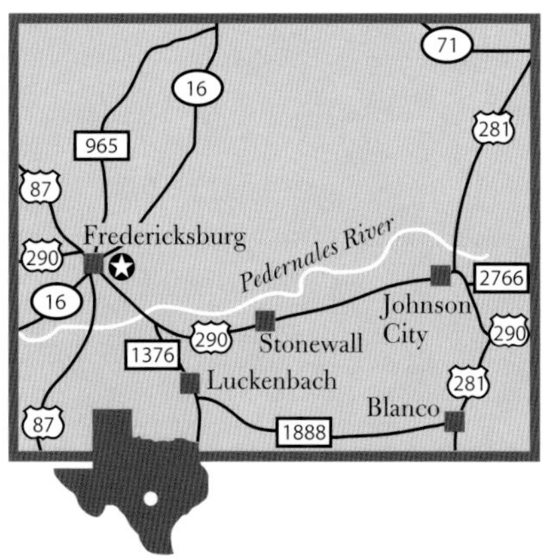

On February 24, 1885, Chester Nimitz was born in a modest home in the sleepy Hill Country town of Fredericksburg. In December 1941, Nimitz, by then an admiral in the U.S. Navy, became Commander-in-Chief Pacific after the Japanese attack on Pearl Harbor. Under his command were thousands of ships and aircraft and millions of people, more military power than had ever before been assembled under one man. Under the skilled leadership of Nimitz and his staff, the United States fought and won a long, brutal war in the Pacific.

Using a strategy of island hopping, the American forces led by Nimitz slowly defeated the Japanese, island by island. Massive sea battles, such as Midway and Coral Sea, and bitter land battles, such as Guadalcanal, Iwo Jima, and Saipan, were extremely costly on both sides in terms of lives and equipment lost. Finally, by mid-1945, the Japanese had been driven back to their homeland, but were unwilling to surrender. An invasion of well-defended Japan might have cost several million lives before the Japanese military was subdued. The agonizing decision was made to drop atomic bombs on Hiroshima and Nagasaki to end the war quickly. Five days after the bombs were dropped, the Japanese surrendered. Admiral Nimitz signed the Instrument of Surrender on the battleship *Missouri* in Tokyo Bay on September 2, 1945, formally ending World War II.

The Steamboat Hotel, on Main Street in Fredericksburg, was built in the mid-nineteenth century by Charles Nimitz, Chester Nimitz's grandfather. Because Chester's father died before he was born, his grandfather was a very important influence in his life. Over the years, the hotel had many famous guests, including

World War II plane

Admiral Nimitz Museum

Ulysses S. Grant, Robert E. Lee, and the notorious Jesse James. Today, it hosts the Museum of the Pacific War, dedicated to all who served under Admiral Nimitz in the Pacific. The museum's exhibits detail the life and career of Nimitz, along with the story of the Pacific war. Adjacent to the hotel is the large, newly opened George Bush Gallery of the Pacific War housing exhibits containing over 800 World War II artifacts.

Behind the hotel is the Garden of Peace, built using money raised by the people of Japan as a symbol of friendship between the United States and Japan. Within the classic garden is an exact replica of the study of Admiral Togo, the leader of the Japanese fleet. Although he was on the opposing side, Nimitz always had great respect for Togo.

Two blocks from the hotel is the History Walk of the Pacific War. A trail winds through a re-created Pacific Island battlefield. Exhibits include airplanes, tanks, guns, parts of ships, and even a bomb casing identical to that of the atomic bomb dropped on Nagasaki.

The exhibits of the park chronicle the life of Chester Nimitz and the events of the Pacific theater of World War II, but the Garden of Peace symbolizes the hope of the people of the United States and Japan that such a bloody conflict might never occur again.

VISITOR INFORMATION

4.5 acres. Open daily, 8 A.M.–5 P.M., except Christmas Day. Indoor and outdoor museums with elaborate exhibits. Full visitor services available in Fredericksburg. For information: Admiral Nimitz Museum, P.O. Box 777, Fredericksburg, TX 78624, (830) 997-4379.

BLANCO STATE PARK

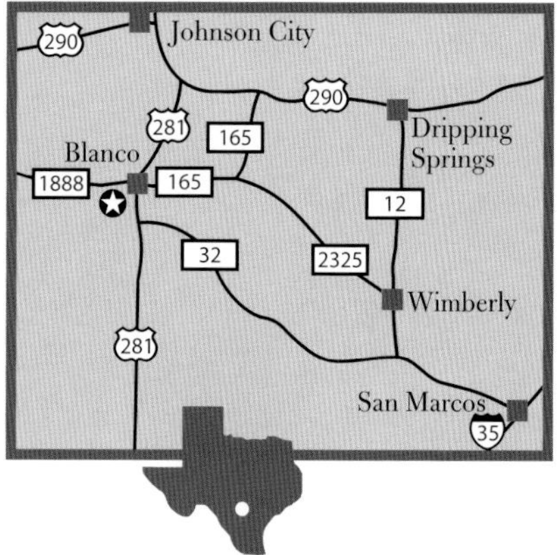

and create a stair-step topography in the surrounding hills.

Dinosaurs roamed the shores and mudflats lining the ancient seas and left their tracks to harden into stone. Although no tracks are exposed within the park, there are many in central Texas, including some on private land around Blanco. The best display in the state is located in Dinosaur Valley State Park, near the town of Glen Rose.

The Blanco River flows through typical Hill Country terrain—rolling rocky hills dotted with live oaks,

Blanco River

Blanco State Park may be small, but it provides a quiet, pleasant, and accessible Hill Country retreat from the nearby cities of Austin and San Antonio. The park, on the south side of the small town of Blanco, contains about a mile of the sparkling Blanco River. The river is fed by springs and seeps in the limestone hills to the west.

Within the park, the river flows over Glen Rose Limestone dating from about 100–120 million years ago, during the Cretaceous period, when shallow seas covered much of central Texas. The rock has alternating layers of soft marl and hard limestone that erode at uneven rates

Spanish oaks, Ashe junipers, and various shrubs. Trees that need more moisture, such as bald cypresses, sycamores, and pecans, thrive along permanent streams and rivers such as the Blanco. Commonly seen wildlife includes nutria, armadillos, squirrels, raccoons, and rabbits.

Like many Texas state parks, Blanco was originally developed by the Civilian Conservation Corps in the 1930s. Among other facilities, the corps built two small, low-water dams in the river that create a popular swimming area. While kids play in the cool water, anglers can pursue crappie, bass, catfish, perch, and, in winter, even stocked rainbow trout.

The small town of Blanco lies just outside the state-park boundary. It was founded in about 1853, but hostilities between settlers and Indians slowed development for about 20 years. The Blanco County seat was first located in Blanco, but was moved to Johnson City in 1891 after a bitter battle between the two towns. After more than 100 years, Blanco's striking stone courthouse, although no longer used as such, still dominates the center of town.

VISITOR INFORMATION

105 acres. Open all year. Hot in summer. Small campground with partial and full hookups and showers. Swimming, fishing, picnicking, seasonal paddleboat rental, limited canoeing. Full visitor services available in Blanco. For information: Blanco State Park, P.O. Box 493, Blanco, TX 78606, (830) 833-4333.

Bright Leaf State Natural Area

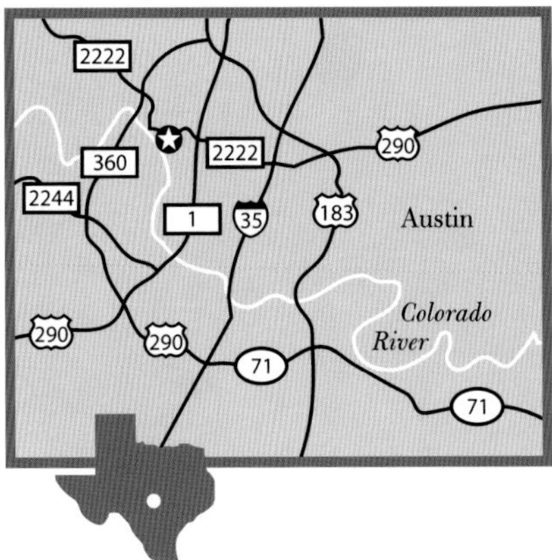

One of the state's newest parks was acquired as a donation. Georgia B. Lucas of Austin died on August 27, 1994, at the age of 76 and bequeathed her property, Bright Leaf, to the Texas Parks and Wildlife Department, in part to prevent future development of the property. Bright Leaf is a 216-acre tract located high in the hills above Lake Austin on the west side of the city. Because of its location and development potential, it has a very high value. It is one of the largest undeveloped pieces of land within Austin.

A series of canyons and ridges densely wooded with second-growth oaks and junipers crosses the hilly property. It rises almost 400 feet above Lake Austin and has views of the lake and surrounding hills, but does not have any water frontage. The presence of Ashe junipers gives the property good potential for harboring the endangered golden-cheeked warbler. Once careful studies have been done there, a number of other rare creatures and plants may also be found to exist on the property.

As of early 1996, the park could be entered only by special arrangement. However, the Parks and Wildlife Department planned to allow access in the near future—initially, probably for guided trips, interpretive programs, and educational activities with schools. In keeping with the donor's wishes, development will probably be limited to little more than hiking trails and an entrance area with parking.

VISITOR INFORMATION

216 acres. New park; accessible only by special request. Initial public access will probably be for interpretive and educational programs. Future hiking trails. Full visitor services available in Austin. For information: Bright Leaf State Natural Area, 4400 Crestway Drive, Austin, TX 78731, (512) 459-7269.

Bright Leaf

Colorado Bend State Park

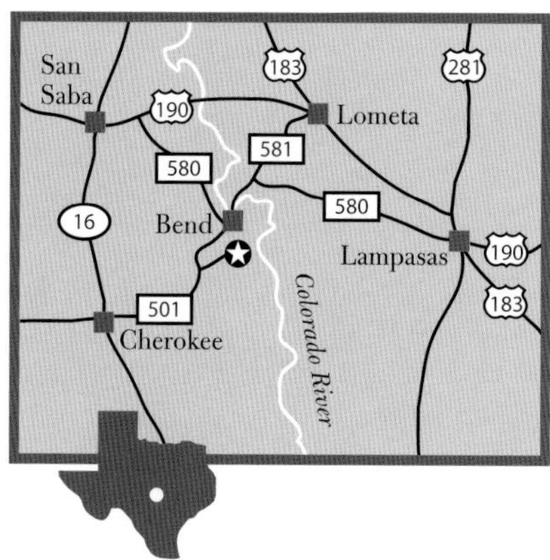

Hidden away in the far reaches of the Texas Hill Country, Colorado Bend State Park is one area in which the Colorado River still flows undammed. For many miles upstream from Austin, the river has been harnessed and tamed by a series of dams, with the upper end of each resultant lake reaching almost to the next dam. Colorado Bend lies at the most upstream end of Lake Buchanan, the first of the chain of Highland Lakes. Here, the Colorado River appears as it once did throughout its length. It flows through a deep canyon rimmed with limestone bluffs not flooded by lake waters. Large oaks, pecans, willows, and elms tower over the narrow floodplain on the canyon bottom, thriving in the deep, moist soil. Spring-fed creeks tumble down to the river as waterfalls and cascades, depositing travertine. Wildlife is undisturbed; even bald eagles winter at the park.

Above the river lies typical Hill Country terrain—rolling country dotted with live oaks, Ashe junipers, and other trees and shrubs. Since livestock grazing ended when the area became a park, grasses have recov-

TOP:
Hiker
MIDDLE:
Gorman Cave
BOTTOM:
Bikers on Lake Buchanan

ered well and now blanket open areas of the uplands.

The weathered, grayish rock shaping the hills is limestone that was laid down in ancient seas. Within the limestone lie many caves, forming one of the park's less obvious assets. The largest and best-known cave, Gorman Cave, tunnels 3,000 feet into Ellenburger Limestone. Guided tours of the undeveloped cave are offered on weekends. Although most of the route followed on these tours is in a passage in which easy walking is possible, a small stream and pools of water in the long tunnel mean wet feet for visitors. Tours are also offered of other caves in the park that require crawling and other strenuous activities. Because the caves are both fragile and dangerous, unescorted entry is not allowed. Hidden dangers in some of the caves include pits and bad air.

Gorman Falls is a small Hill Country paradise within the park. A spring-fed stream creates the large waterfall when it tumbles over a cliff lining the Colorado River canyon. The calcium-carbonate-rich water has deposited some of its contents at the falls in the form of travertine, creating many small dams and other formations. Moss and maidenhair ferns cover the travertine, sprayed constantly from the falling water. Tall elms and other trees shade the cool, moist environment at the base of the falls. Because the falls were damaged by heavy trampling in the past, access is now allowed only on guided tours on Saturdays and Sundays.

Birders will especially enjoy the park. The rare golden-cheeked warbler builds its nests in thick stands of Ashe juniper in the hills above the river, and the black-capped vireo inhabits patches of brush containing a variety of plant species. In winter, bald eagles migrate south from northern states to fish in the river.

Gorman Falls

The park is still relatively primitive, with a gravel entry road subject to flooding. The undeveloped campground along the river has several water taps, picnic tables, fire rings, and chemical toilets, but no other facilities. A boat ramp at the south end of the park allows access to the upper end of Lake Buchanan. Canoeists often put in at Flat Rock, just upstream of the town of Bend, and paddle downstream to take out in the park.

The white bass run attracts anglers to Colorado Bend between February and April. The fish swim upriver from Lake Buchanan in large numbers to spawn every spring. Other fish that draw anglers to the park include striped bass, crappie, and catfish.

Hikers enjoy trails along the river, as well as along Spicewood Creek and in the rolling uplands. Some of these same trails are also open to fat-tired mountain-bikes. Be it bicycling or hiking, caving or fishing, Colorado Bend State Park offers opportunities for a wealth of activities.

VISITOR INFORMATION

5,328 acres. Open all year, except during public hunts. Hot and humid in summer. Busiest during spring white-bass run. Relatively undeveloped, with gravel roads and chemical toilets. Campground area is undeveloped, without designated sites; operated on first-come, first-served basis. Tables, fire rings, water taps, chemical toilets, fish cleaning station. Boating, boat ramp, picnicking, mountain-biking, hiking trails, fishing, swimming. Guided tours of caves, Gorman Falls; call ahead for dates and times. Some food available in Bend; full visitor services in Lampasas, Llano, and San Saba. For information: Colorado Bend State Park, P.O. Box 118, Bend, TX 76824, (915) 628-3240.

Devil's Sinkhole State Natural Area

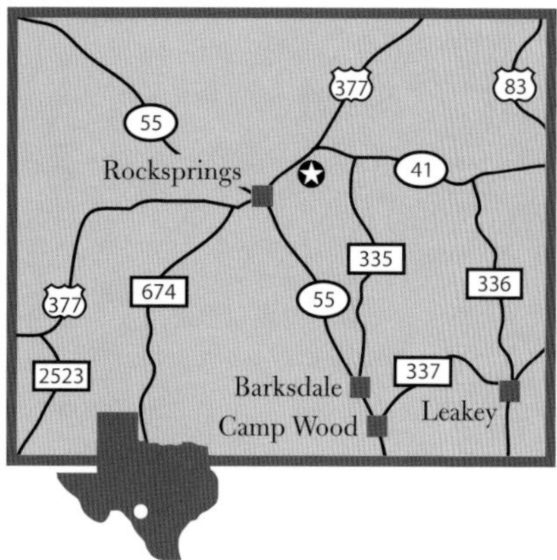

There is little to warn first-time visitors of the awesome, gaping pit of Devil's Sinkhole as they enter the park in the rolling Hill Country terrain near Rocksprings. Live oaks and junipers dot the rocky limestone hills as in most of the Hill Country, although this part of the Hill Country is drier than the eastern areas closer to Austin and San Antonio.

The entrance to the sinkhole comes as a surprise. It lies on a relatively flat upland part of the natural area. The entrance drops precipitously into a massive cavern from an oval entrance of about 40 feet x 60 feet. The opening quickly bells outward into a large chamber, so that the lip of the sinkhole is only a thin ledge overhanging the deep pit.

The sinkhole formed when underground water, made acidic with atmospheric carbon dioxide, slowly dissolved a huge underground cavern. Eventually, as the chamber enlarged and the ground surface above eroded away, the ceiling became too weak to support itself and collapsed, creating an opening to the outside world. The collapsing ceiling formed a large, cone-shaped pile of rubble in the chamber. From the surface down to the top of the rubble pile is an unobstructed drop of about 150 feet. The deepest parts of the sinkhole lie 350 feet below the surface, around the base of the rubble pile.

The sinkhole supports an important colony of more than a million Mexican, or Brazilian, free-tailed bats.

Devil's Sinkhole

In spring, the bats migrate north from Mexico to the sinkhole and other Hill Country caves to live and raise young until cold weather in fall again sends them south. Because these large bat colonies eat huge quantities of insects, they are very important ecologically. Although individual members of this species are small, they eat roughly half their weight in insects every night. A colony of a million bats, such as that at the sinkhole, eats as much as seven million pounds of insects annually.

Devil's Sinkhole State Natural Area is only open, by reservation, on scheduled guided tours. Most tours are in the evening, to allow visitors to watch the impressive flight of the bats as they emerge in the evening to begin their nightly hunt. Before the bat flight starts, be sure to crawl to the edge of the sinkhole and peer down into the vertigo-inducing abyss.

VISITOR INFORMATION

1,801 acres. Open for reserved guided tours only. The entrance road is rough; a high-clearance vehicle is required. Wildlife observation—bat colony. Full visitor services available in Rocksprings. For information: Devil's Sinkhole State Natural Area, P.O. Box 678, Rocksprings, TX 78880, (830) 683-3762.

Enchanted Rock State Natural Area

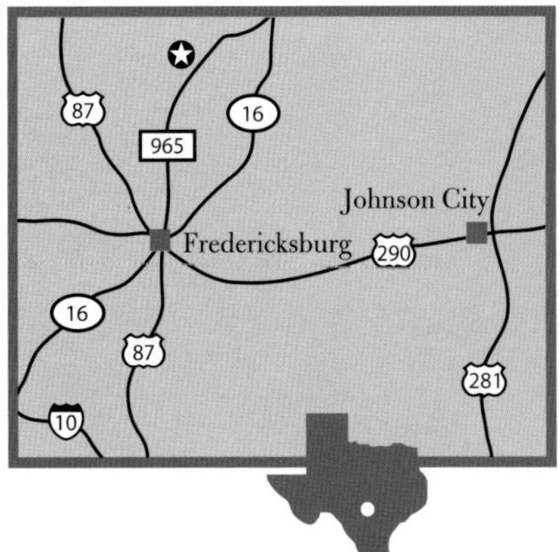

swirling around the dome that led to its being named Enchanted Rock early in the nineteenth century.

In 1978, the site, as Enchanted Rock State Natural Area, came under Texas Parks and Wildlife Department stewardship. Since pioneers moved into the Hill Country, the rock has been an important landmark and tourist attraction. As a state natural area, it continues to increase in popularity. The natural area contains several smaller peaks and domes in addition to Enchanted Rock, an enormous curving dome of pinkish granite that towers 400 feet above Sandy Creek. The smaller peaks and

Legends surround Enchanted Rock, the massive granite dome that lies in the center of the Texas Hill Country. Early settlers, including Stephen F. Austin, told of Indian ceremonies being held at Enchanted Rock because it was considered sacred. Many Indians feared the rock, believing it to be haunted, and would not climb to its summit. Tales were even told of human sacrifices made by the Comanches, and pioneers reported odd noises emanating from the rock and strange fires on its summit. It was these many stories

domes surrounding the main rock include Little Rock, Turkey Peak, Freshman Mountain, and Buzzard's Roost.

The domes within the natural area are but a small part of the Enchanted Rock batholith that is exposed to the surface over an area of more than 60 square miles. The batholith formed when molten rock, or magma, intruded into rock layers below the surface. It cooled slowly and crystallized into granite. Over time, the area was uplifted and erosion removed the concealing layers of rock, exposing

ABOVE:
Ferns and granite
BELOW:
Enchanted Rock from a distance
OPPOSITE PAGE:
Hiker at Enchanted Rock

the batholith. The granite is ancient—approximately a billion years old—and it has been buried by new rock layers and re-exposed more than once as seas have come and gone in past geologic ages.

When the batholith was exposed to the surface, erosion shaped it into its present form. Geologists call Enchanted Rock an exfoliation dome because of the way plates of rock break off the dome, or exfoliate, in thin curving layers, similar to the layers of an onion. Freezing and thawing water helps split the rocks off the dome. The strange noises reported at Enchanted Rock may be nothing more than creaks made as the rock heats and cools with temperature changes between day and night.

Other granite domes in the area have been heavily quarried for the beautiful granite of the Enchanted Rock batholith, although, fortunately, Enchanted Rock itself, the largest granite dome in Texas and the second largest in the United States, escaped such a fate. Buildings, monuments, and other structures throughout the country have used the durable, attractive stone. Prominent uses in Texas include the state capitol building in Austin and jetties along the Gulf Coast.

From a distance, much of the rock appears bare and devoid of life. Closer inspection reveals plant communities thriving in pockets of soil eroded from the dome. Colorful lichens grow on the rock itself, while mosses, grasses, ferns, and flowers blanket smaller pockets of soil. In deeper soils, prickly pear cacti and even oak trees find a toehold. Some of the moist shady crevices hold rare plants, such as the rock quillwort, the basin bellflower, and even a tropical fern. Around the base, cedar elms, mesquites, pecans, hickories, and oaks grow in deep soils.

The strong, well-consolidated granite of Enchanted Rock draws rock climbers from all over Texas. The only other place in the state offering such excellent climbing is Hueco Tanks State Historical Park in far West Texas. On pleasant spring and fall weekends, climbers tackle everything from boulders at the base of the rock to the high cliffs on the northwest side of the main dome. A trail system circles Enchanted Rock and some of the smaller domes, and leads to several primitive backpacking campsites. A cave near the summit is also a popular site with park visitors. It was formed when boulders roofed over a deep crack in the dome.

Most people visit simply to make the irresistible climb to the summit, a short but steep walk. Lie back on the smooth granite and enjoy the view, one of the best in the Hill Country. Gentle breezes cool you as they blow, unobstructed, across the bare summit. Vultures circle high overhead, attracted by rising thermals and good roosting sites. As the sun sets to the west and darkness descends, listen for sounds of the rock and imagine the ancient Indian ceremonies once held there.

VISITOR INFORMATION

1,644 acres. Open all year. Hot and humid in summer. The developed campground is small, with walk-in tent sites only; no RVs. Showers. Primitive backpacking sites require hiking to reach. Due to limited day use capacity, park often fills on weekends; call ahead. Reserve campsites well ahead on spring and fall weekends. Picnic area. Watch children closely near cliffs. Climbers must register at park headquarters. No bolts, pitons, or other rock-damaging equipment allowed. Lights and hardhats are recommended when visiting the cave near the summit. Full visitor services available in nearby Fredericksburg and Llano. For information: Enchanted Rock State Natural Area, 16710 RR 965, Fredericksburg, TX 78624, (915) 247-3903.

Wildflowers at Enchanted Rock

Fort McKavett State Historical Park

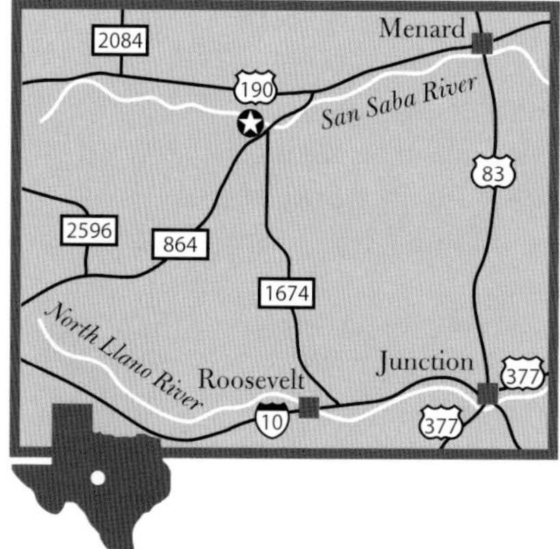

Fort McKavett was established in 1852 to protect settlers on the western frontier and travelers on their way farther west. A Comanche war trail passed near the fort and both Comanches and Lipan Apaches were common in the area. The fort was built on a hill above the San Saba River and was initially named Camp San Saba. The following year, it was renamed in honor of Captain Henry McKavett, a hero of the battle of Monterrey in the Mexican-American War. The fort was built using native limestone, oak, and pecan, along with finished lumber freighted in from San Antonio. After some initial problems were resolved, the post was well maintained and stocked and received good reviews from inspecting officers.

The fort was abandoned in 1859 when problems with the Indians lessened in that area and moved farther north. Settlers moved into the buildings during the following years. By the end of the Civil War, however, Indian raids had become more frequent once again, and in 1868 the post was reactivated. The facilities had fallen into ruin and were rebuilt under the leadership of Colonel Ranald S. Mackenzie. Much of the

TOP:
Fort McKavett ruins
BOTTOM:
Restored barracks

work was done by black "buffalo soldiers" stationed at the fort. Construction was frequently interrupted by military actions and scouting expeditions, but official inspectors and civilian visitors alike were impressed with Fort McKavett. It was "the prettiest post in Texas," said General William Tecumseh Sherman, after an inspection in 1871.

As the years passed, the frontier moved farther west and the need for Fort McKavett once again declined. The main body of troops was reassigned in the fall of 1882, and by June 30, 1883, the remaining soldiers had completed their official duties. The flag was taken down and Company D of the 16th Infantry marched away for the last time.

Local settlers again moved into some of the post's buildings and the military installation became the town of Fort McKavett. In 1968, the fort was acquired by the state and managed as an historic site. Today, visitors see a mix of restored fort buildings and ruins. The visitor center, located in the former post hospital, contains displays and exhibits detailing the fort's history. Reenactments, with men and women dressed in authentic clothing, periodically bring Fort McKavett back to life as a busy post on the western frontier.

VISITOR INFORMATION

82 acres. Open daily 8 A.M.–5 P.M. Closed Christmas. Picnicking, museum in visitor center, interpretive trail. Full visitor services available in Menard, Junction, and Sonora. For information: Fort McKavett State Historical Park, P.O. Box 68, Fort McKavett, TX 76841, (915) 396-2358.

Garner State Park

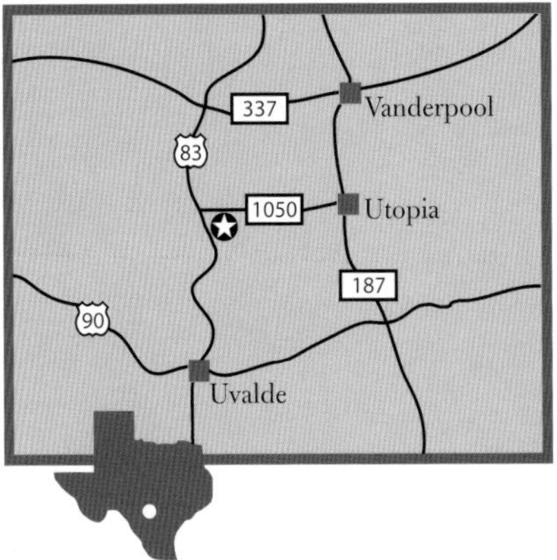

Frio River

Garner State Park is one of the classic state parks of Texas, as evidenced by its enduring popularity. The clear, cold Frio River tumbles and cascades over boulders as it flows past the park's wooded slopes. It swirls and eddies as it washes over smooth, polished limestone bedrock. Tall bald cypresses line the banks below rocky bluffs covered with live oaks, cedar elms, and Ashe junipers.

The park lies on the southwestern edge of the Hill Country, north of Uvalde. Millions of years ago, the Edwards Plateau was formed when a huge block of land was uplifted along a curving fault that stretched from north of Austin southwest to San Antonio and westward, to north of Uvalde. The plateau was uplifted approximately 2,000 feet and has been eroded ever since. Along the southwestern side of the Hill Country in the Garner area, rivers and streams such as the Frio have cut the once-flat plateau into a particularly rugged land of hills and canyons.

Garner State Park was named after John Nance Garner, vice-president under Franklin Roosevelt and former resident of nearby Uvalde. The park was developed during the 1930s to preserve a section of the Hill Country for public use and to put unemployed young men to work during the Depression. In 1935, the Civilian Conservation Corps (CCC) set up camp at the park site and began construction. The CCC workers used native materials, such as cypress, oak, and limestone, to build many of the park facilities that are still in use today. Among these is the large, central concession building, with its adjoining open-air pavilion, that is the park's premier building. Using excellent craftsmanship, the CCC built it in the French-Alsatian style

OPPOSITE PAGE:
Garner State Park from above

Saturday night dances were started by the CCC in the 1930s and have grown in popularity since then. On summer evenings, as many as several hundred people congregate at the outdoor pavilion by the concession building to dance to jukebox music or live bands. The dances attract a mix of young and old, both newcomers to Garner and those who have been returning for years to one of the most popular destinations in Texas.

VISITOR INFORMATION

1,420 acres. Open all year. Very busy park, especially in summer and on spring and fall weekends. Large campgrounds with partial hookups; reservations recommended, especially in summer. Cabins, screened shelters. Swimming, tubing, canoeing, fishing, picnicking, hiking, cycling, and nature trails, seasonal park store, paddleboat rental, 18-hole miniature golf course. Limited visitor services available in Leakey; full services in Uvalde. For information: Garner State Park, HCR 70, Box 599, Concan, TX 78838, (830) 232-6132.

LEFT:
Bald cypresses along Frio River
BELOW:
Camping at Garner

with stone walls and massive exposed wooden beams. The corps also built cabins, roads, and trails in the park.

Garner State Park officially opened in 1941 and has been welcoming increasing numbers of visitors ever since. That it is the most popular camping park in the state-park system is evidenced by its enormous campgrounds. Many people return year after year, drawn by the rugged hills and sparkling Frio River. Water-oriented activities are most popular, with swimmers, tubers, and canoeists filling the river on summer weekends. Cyclists pedal along park roads, while hikers climb the heights of Mount Baldy for spectacular views.

Guadalupe River State Park • Honey Creek State Natural Area

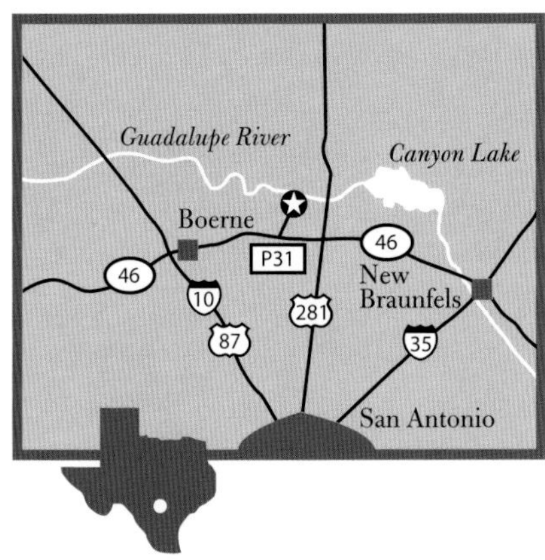

The cool, sparkling waters of the Guadalupe River drain from a large area of the central Texas Hill Country. The river has cut deeply into the limestone hills of this region, carving narrow canyons and broad valleys. Tall bald cypresses thrive in the wet soils of the river's banks and grow into massive trees that line the waterway. Guadalupe River State Park provides access to an upper section of what may be the quintessential Hill Country river.

The Guadalupe River rises in the hills west of Kerrville, fed by a series of springs. The river flows eastward through the Hill Country, slowly gaining in volume. Well before it reaches the state park, it usually has enough volume to attract canoeists, kayakers, and tubers. Occasional rapids punctuate long calm stretches of the river in and near the state park. Because most land along the river is privately owned, the state park has become a popular site to put in and take out canoes and other small watercraft. Fortunately, however, this section of the river does not have the crowds—nor their attendant problems—that are experienced along the lower section of the river below Canyon Lake.

Guadalupe River State Park lies on the Edwards Plateau, a large area of central Texas that was uplifted about 2,000 feet roughly 10 million years ago. The plateau was raised up along the Balcones Fault, a long series of faults that starts north of Austin, continues southwest to San Antonio, and curves west toward Del Rio. Most of the surface rock of the Edwards Plateau is Cretaceous limestone, formed in ancient seas that once covered much of Texas. Because the limestone was formed in the ocean, in large part from the skeletons of marine creatures, fossils are common in the Hill Country limestone. Some of the limestone is quite hard and durable and forms large cliffs, such as those found along the river within the park. Rivers, such as the Guadalupe, have slowly carved downward into the plateau, creating the canyons, valleys, and hills of the Hill Country.

Vegetation typical of the Hill Country blankets the state park. Upland areas are covered by a mix of grasslands and extensive groves of

Bald cypresses on Guadalupe River

Ashe juniper and live oak. Plants that favor more moisture, such as cypresses, sycamores, pecans, and other trees, thrive along creeks and on the river bottomland.

The cool waters of the Guadalupe attract most of the park visitors. Canoeists, tubers, swimmers, and waders all flock to the park during the heat of summer. Although the river is usually calm and quiet, occasional floods sweep down the Guadalupe with surprising ferocity. A tremendous flood in 1978 crested at 63 feet above normal levels, uprooting trees and washing out river banks. The flow volume was at least 240,000 cubic feet per second (cfs), far more than the 150–200 cfs usually found at the park. Fortunately, adequate upstream warnings of impending floods usually prevent any danger to people within the park. Such floods are rare in any case, and are unlikely to deter prospective visitors to Guadalupe River State Park, one of the Hill Country's outstanding parks.

In the dry, rocky Hill Country adjoining Guadalupe River State Park lies one of the hidden gems of the state-park system. The sparkling spring waters of Honey Creek tumble down a narrow canyon lined with tall bald cypresses and sycamores, to reach the Guadalupe River. The clear stream bubbles over small cascades and calms in long, deep pools dotted with spadderdock, a pond lily. With Spanish moss draping the trees and palmettos dotting the banks, the creek seems almost more typical of East Texas than of the Hill Country. The picturesque stream and the surrounding uplands form Honey Creek State Natural Area.

Various Indian tribes used the land until the middle of the nineteenth century, when the area was settled by German immigrants. The land was used as a ranch by a succession of owners until it was purchased by the Texas Nature Conservancy in 1980. Later, it was conveyed to the Texas Parks and Wildlife Department, and since that time, efforts have been made to restore the land's original live-oak grassland.

Like Guadalupe River State Park, Honey Creek lies on the Edwards Plateau. Three major sedimentary rock formations of the Cretaceous period make up the hills of the natural area. The most important is the Glen Rose Limestone, a rock well known for its many caves. Honey Creek Cave is the longest known cave in Texas. One particularly notable geological feature of the natural area is an igneous dike, formed when molten rock squeezed into vertical cracks in the Glen Rose Limestone. It hardened into a hard, black basalt of uncommon composition.

White-tailed deer, armadillos, wild turkeys, raccoons, and opossums are common within the natural area and adjoining state park. Of particular interest are rare species such as the golden-cheeked warbler and the Honey Creek Cave salamander. The creek contains several species of fish, including the native Guadalupe bass.

Because the creek environment is very fragile, access is limited to guided tours offered by park personnel and volunteers. The guides are knowledgeable and offer an excellent opportunity to see a beautiful, undisturbed Hill Country stream.

VISITOR INFORMATION

Guadalupe River State Park: 1,938 acres. Open all year. Hot in summer. Large number of campsites, from walk-in tent sites to partial-hookup sites, with showers. Canoeing, tubing, swimming, fishing, hiking, picnicking.

Honey Creek State Natural Area: 2,294 acres. Open for guided tours only. Tours are offered on most weekends throughout the year, and at other times. Call ahead for specific dates and times. Day use only.

Full visitor services available in Boerne. For information: Guadalupe River State Park/Honey Creek State Natural Area, 3350 Park Road 31, Spring Branch, TX 78070, (830) 438-2656.

OPPOSITE PAGE, TOP:
Honey Creek
OPPOSITE PAGE, BOTTOM:
Hiker on Honey Creek
TOP:
Guadalupe River canoeist
ABOVE:
Rainbow over Guadalupe River

Hill Country State Natural Area

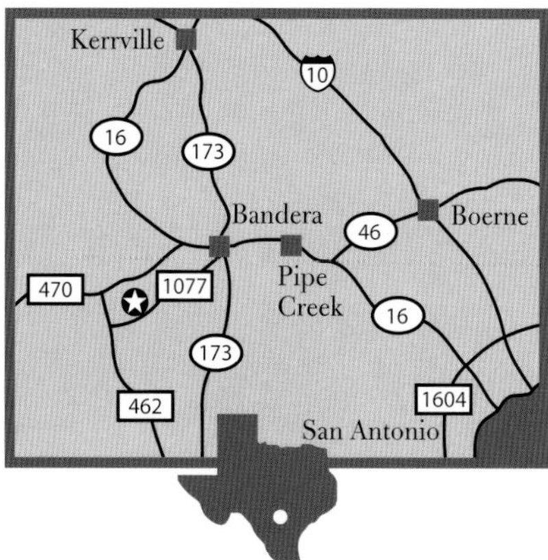

Tucked away in the rugged terrain southwest of Bandera is the Hill Country State Natural Area, a secluded retreat little known outside the equestrian community. Horse lovers have discovered its 35 miles of dirt roads and primitive trails that wind up grassy valleys, cross spring-fed streams, and climb steep limestone hills.

The Merrick Bar-O-Ranch that became the natural area was originally part of a Spanish land grant. It was registered during the republic period in 1840, but the State of Texas first deeded the land to William Davenport in 1877. He and his family worked the ranch until 1925, when it was sold to the next in a succession of owners. In 1945, the land was purchased by S. E. Lindsey, who, the following year, conveyed the property to his daughter, Louise Lindsey Merrick. She and her husband operated the ranch for the next 29 years. During its years of operation, the ranch was known for its productivity.

After her husband died, Merrick decided to donate the 4,753-acre property to the state. As an avid horsewoman who enjoyed riding across her property, she wanted Texans to have a public place where they could ride their horses across a large tract of undeveloped land. Her deed stated that the ranch was "to be kept far removed and untouched by modern civilization, where everything is preserved intact, yet put to a useful purpose." The state took over full ownership in 1982, purchased an adjoining tract of land, and opened the site as a natural area in 1984.

The Parks and Wildlife Department has left the ranch undeveloped. The natural area lies on the Edwards Plateau, a large uplifted area of land in central Texas. Over the course of millennia, erosion has carved steep hills and broad valleys out of the limestone plateau. A mix of grasslands and scrubby woods of live oak, Ashe juniper, and Texas oak covers the hills. Along West Verde Creek and other watercourses, large sycamores, cedar elms, and oaks arch over clear pools.

An extensive complex of old dirt roads and trails creates miles of paths for equestrians, hikers, and mountain-bikers. Novice riders, hikers, and cyclists may want to stay on the easier main routes in the valley bottoms. Several backcountry camp areas offer primitive campsites to backpackers and equestrians. Facilities at these campsites are minimal and food, water, and camping gear must be carried in.

Dead juniper trunks and sotol plants

Hill Country State Natural Area is a quiet, undeveloped site with few amenities in one of the most rugged parts of the Hill Country. To challenge visitors even more, it lies on an unpaved county road not even shown on many maps. The extra effort leaves the crowds behind and makes the scenic Hill Country park even more appealing.

Prickly pear cactus flowers

VISITOR INFORMATION

5,370 acres. Park open daily March–October. Occasionally closed from November through January for wildlife management purposes; call ahead before visiting. Hot and humid in summer. Primitive camp area near headquarters has an equestrian area and 10 walk-in tent sites near swimming holes, with tables, fire rings, and chemical toilets. Portable stalls and nearby water for horses. Several primitive campsites for backpackers and equestrians in backcountry. Group lodge. Extensive hiking, mountain-bike, and horse trails. To get there, take Tx Hwy 173 south of Bandera less than a mile, turn right on FM 1077, and follow it about 8 miles until the pavement ends. Continue on the county gravel road to the natural area. Full visitor services available in Bandera. For information: Hill Country State Natural Area, RR1, Box 601, Bandera, TX 78003, (830) 796-4413.

ABOVE:
Hill Country sunset
RIGHT:
Inks Lake tributary

Inks Lake State Park

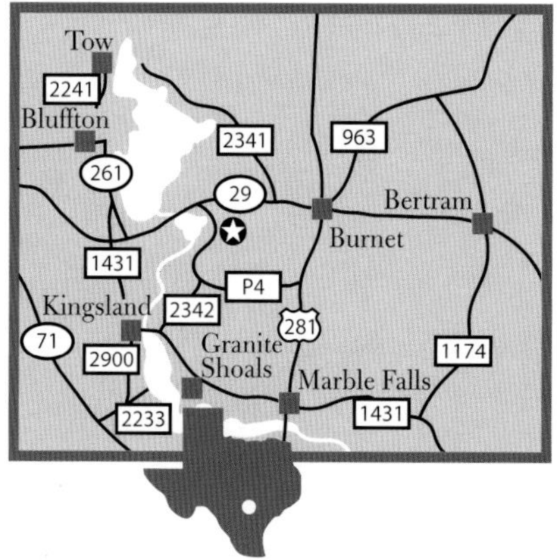

In the 1930s, periodic flooding by the Colorado River led to widespread calls for the river to be dammed. Llano businessman and mayor Roy Inks worked hard promoting the dam project, but it was a calamitous flood in 1935 that finally spurred the federal government to approve it. Ultimately a series of six dams was constructed, from upstream of Inks Lake to Austin; the reservoirs thus created became known as the Highland Lakes. Unfortunately, Roy Inks did not live to see the projects built; a ruptured appendix combined with a bout of pneumonia ended his life in August 1935. The Lower Colorado River Authority named the second dam and its reservoir in his honor.

Inks Lake State Park lines much of the eastern shore of Inks Lake on a solid bed of pinkish Valley Spring gneiss. The hard metamorphic rock resembles the pink granite of nearby Marble Falls and Enchanted Rock. The gneiss formed when volcanic rocks were recrystallized by heat and pressure. The rock is more than a billion years old and possibly the oldest in Texas. Outcrops of it are common throughout the area.

Vegetation cloaks the rocky hills of the state park. Ashe juniper, live oak, and mesquite are common on the rocky slopes; cedar elm, pecan, and hickory prefer the deeper, moister

TOP:
Sunrise on Inks Lake and ancient gneiss
LEFT:
Bluebonnets

soils along the creek bottoms. In spring, arrays of bluebonnets, Indian paintbrushes, and Indian blankets splash color across the open fields and hills.

Wildlife thrives at Inks Lake, and some of the wild animals there are almost tame. White-tailed deer roam the campgrounds, searching for deer corn and other handouts. At night, raccoons brazenly raid food carelessly left out by campers. Wild turkeys, armadillos, opossums, and other animals also frequent the area.

Fishing piers and a boat ramp make access easy for anglers wanting to pursue striped bass, white bass, catfish, and other species. Inks Lake even hosts a rarity in the Texas state park system—a 9-hole golf course. The course borders the lakeshore, providing a large water hazard for golfers who have not refined their strokes. More than 7 miles of trails wind through hills of gneiss to overlooks and a primitive camping area. Although the lake is relatively small, it welcomes waterskiers and sailboats. The extensive recreational opportunities draw many thousands of people to Inks Lake State Park every year, making it one of the state's most popular parks.

VISITOR INFORMATION

1,202 acres. Open all year. Very popular in spring and summer, especially on weekends. Hot and humid in summer. Large campgrounds in several areas, with partial hookups and showers. Screened shelters. Primitive camp area for backpackers. Fishing, boating, waterskiing, swimming, hiking, picnicking. Park store and canoe and paddleboat rental. Full visitor services available in Burnet, Marble Falls, and Llano. For information: Inks Lake State Park, 3630 Park Road 4 West, Burnet, TX 78611, (512) 793-2223.

John J. Stokes San Marcos River State Park

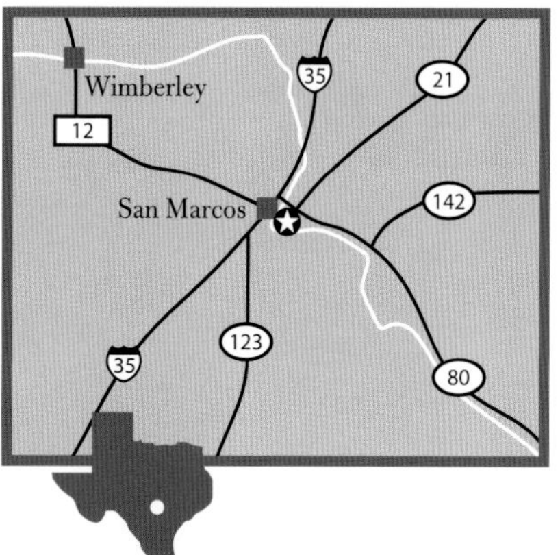

provide power when water levels were low. The plant was used to mill grain and to gin and bale cotton. Over the years the mill burned and was rebuilt more than once. Now, the small mill dam, an old warehouse, and some concrete foundations and ditches are all that remain of it. Today the park provides an undeveloped access point to the river for canoeists and swimmers.

San Marcos River

The John J. Stokes San Marcos River State Park is a small, undeveloped park operated by the City of San Marcos. The park is located on the river, a short distance east of Interstate 35 in San Marcos. Close by, the cold, clear waters of the San Marcos River bubble up from the Edwards Aquifer at Aquarena Springs, in the center of town.

The park is lushly wooded along the banks of the river. The site was originally used for a mill that was built by William Thompson in 1850. In 1867, Thompson's son constructed a new dam to raise the water level for the mill. After the latter died in 1913, the mill was sold to John Cape, who proceeded to rework the mill and to add a steam plant to

VISITOR INFORMATION

5.6 acres. Open all year. Day use only. Hot in summer. Historic mill site, swimming, fishing, canoeing. To get there, take the Seguin exit from IH 35 in San Marcos and go east on Tx Hwy 123 toward Seguin. Go about a block and turn left on River Road. Look for the park signs when you cross the river. Full visitor services available in San Marcos. For information: John J. Stokes San Marcos River State Park, c/o Texas Parks and Wildlife Department, Fountain Park Plaza, 2900 IH 35 South, Suite 206, Austin, TX 78704, (512) 444-1127.

Kerrville-Schreiner State Park

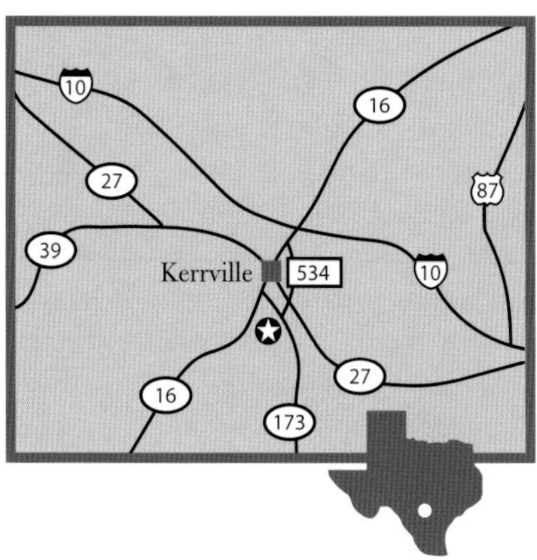

The rolling hills and clear, running rivers of the Hill Country draw people year-round to Kerrville-Schreiner State Park and the surrounding region. The park is a pleasant Hill Country site on the banks of the Guadalupe River on the southeast side of the town of Kerrville. The park is split into two segments by Texas Highway 173. The north side borders the clear, rushing Guadalupe River, one of the Hill Country's largest watercourses. Here, campgrounds, screened shelters, and a picnic area lie on the flat floodplain above the river, shaded by large pecans and other trees.

The south side of the park, across Texas Highway 173 from the river section, is much larger. It climbs up and out of the river floodplain into typical Hill Country terrain wooded with Ashe junipers, Spanish red oaks, live oaks, and cedar elms. Shrubs such as sumac, mountain laurel, and redbud are mixed in with the trees and add colorful blooms in spring or splashes of color in the fall. Wildlife found in the park includes armadillos, raccoons, coyotes, jackrabbits, foxes, and white-tailed deer that at times seem almost tame.

As in most of the Hill Country, a bedrock of limestone underlies the park, and is exposed in rocky ledges. The limestone was laid down in ancient seas that covered central Texas millions of years ago during the Cretaceous period. Later, a large block of the Earth's crust, now known as the Edwards Plateau, was uplifted about 2,000 feet along a large fault. Creeks and rivers such as the Guadalupe have carved the plateau into a land of rolling hills and valleys.

More campgrounds, screened shelters, and picnic areas lie in the large southern section of the park, but part of it has been left undeveloped. Several miles of hiking trails wind through the hilly terrain, leading from wooded creek bottoms to bare hilltops.

The river is probably the most popular destination in the park, especially on hot summer days. Swimmers, anglers, and canoeists are all attracted to the clear, cool waters. The popular vacation town of Kerrville lies just upstream along the river. The community was first settled in 1846 by Joshua Brown, who set up a shingle mill using bald cypresses that lined the river. Indians quickly ran him off, but he returned again in

TOP:
Fishermen
RIGHT:
Guadalupe River banks

1848. The town grew slowly, hindered by Indian attacks and depredation by livestock rustlers and other outlaws.

Charles Schreiner, a former Texas Ranger and Civil War veteran, led much of the town's growth after the war. He opened a mercantile company and bank and built up an enormous 600,000-acre ranch that specialized in sheep raising. In 1887, the railroad arrived after Kerrville competed heavily with Fredericksburg for it. Although ranching is still important in the Kerrville area, tourism is now the largest contributor to the local economy.

VISITOR INFORMATION

517 acres. Open all year. Hot in summer. Large number of developed campsites with partial or full hookups and showers in several areas of the park. Screened shelters. Boat ramp, canoeing, fishing pier, hiking trails, picnicking. Full visitor services available in Kerrville. For information: Kerrville-Schreiner State Park, 2385 Bandera Highway, Kerrville, TX 78028, (830) 257-5392.

Kickapoo Cavern State Park

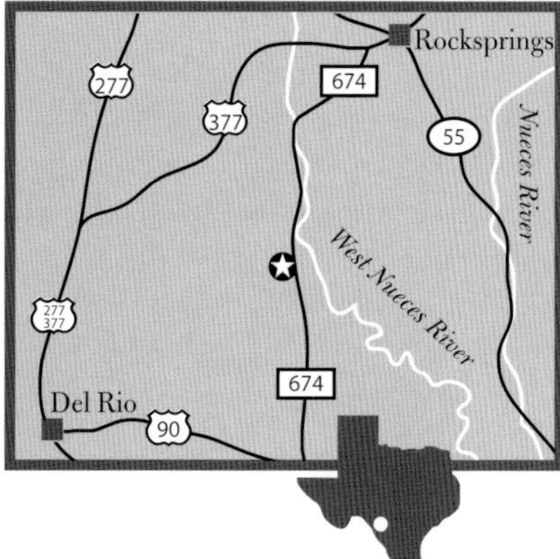

Kickapoo Cavern State Park lies in the far southwestern part of the Hill Country. Steep, rocky hills rise above dry, boulder-strewn washes in the former ranch. Because of its far western location, it is relatively dry. However, although vegetation is more sparse than in areas to the east, much of the plant life is typical of the Hill Country. Live oaks and Ashe junipers are common, along with papershell pinyon pines, small, hardy pines found in the southwestern part of the Hill Country, and related to several other species of pinyon found in the mountains of West Texas, Mexico, and the southwestern United States.

The rocky hills of the park conceal the namesake attraction, Kickapoo Cavern. The 1,500-foot-long cave is known for its sizable chambers and large calcite formations, including several massive floor-to-ceiling columns. Another cave, Green Cave, hosts a colony of approximately one million Mexican free-tailed bats from spring through fall. Except during stormy weather, the bats make a dramatic exit flight from the cave every evening to forage for insects.

LEFT:
Stalactites and helictites
BELOW:
Green Cave bat flight

Green Cave, Kickapoo Cavern, and other smaller caves are found in the Devils River limestone of the natural area. The limestone of the Hill Country was deposited in ancient seas that once covered the area. Later, a large section of central Texas now known as the Edwards Plateau was uplifted along the Balcones Fault and exposed to erosion. Over the course of millions of years, water eroded the relatively flat plateau into rolling hilly terrain.

Water carrying small amounts of carbon dioxide from the atmosphere is slightly acidic, giving it the ability to dissolve limestone and create caves. This slow dissolving action of the water formed the caves at Kickapoo and many other Hill Country areas. Later, dripping water deposited some of the dissolved limestone, or calcium carbonate, on cavern surfaces, creating stalactites, stalagmites, and other formations.

Although the two large caves are the main attractions of the natural area, other features draw visitors. Kickapoo harbors one of the state's largest nesting populations of the endangered black-capped vireo. Other avian species of interest include the Montezuma quail and the varied bunting. The pinyon pine thrives here, but does not grow in the wetter, more heavily visited eastern areas of the Hill Country; in the fall, it produces a large, tasty nut popular with wildlife as well as with local residents.

The natural area has changed considerably from its original appearance because of brush clearing and heavy livestock grazing, but it is slowly recovering its original character. Reservations for guided tours of Kickapoo Cavern and observation of the Green Cave bat flight are available. Advance arrangements are also required for other activities, such as birding and overnight lodge use.

ABOVE:
Kickapoo Cavern
LEFT:
Limestone hills

VISITOR INFORMATION

6,368 acres. Open all year by reservation only, as detailed above. Hot in summer. Campground with showers. Cave tours, bat-flight observation, birding, hiking. Full visitor services available in Brackettville and Rocksprings. For information: Kickapoo Cavern State Park, P.O. Box 705, Brackettville, TX 78832, (830) 563-2342.

Landmark Inn State Historical Park

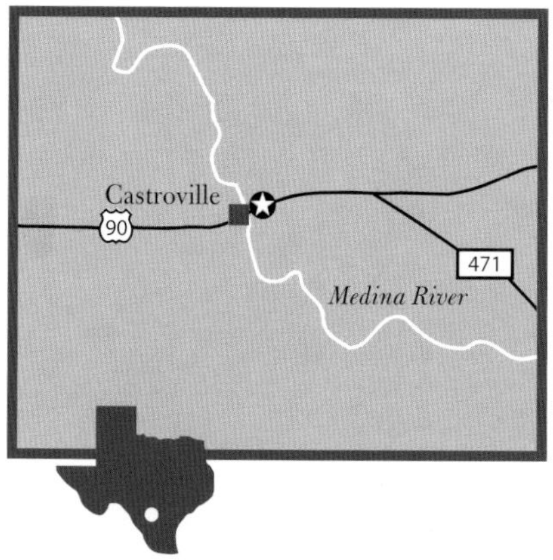

The history of Landmark Inn began shortly after Texas gained independence from Mexico, when the government authorized large land grants to colonists willing to settle in Texas. In 1842, Henri Castro, a French entrepreneur, obtained a colonization contract; his first settlement was Castroville, founded in 1844. Colonists were recruited from Germany, Switzerland, and France. The buildings are outstanding examples of indigenous Texas architecture common to Bexar and Medina Counties in the mid-nineteenth century.

In 1849, Cesar Monod bought two lots along the Medina River in Castroville and constructed a plastered stone building that he used as a general store and residence. In 1853, John Vance purchased the property and through the years expanded it. Castroville was located on the busy San Antonio–El Paso road, inspiring Vance to rent rooms to travelers and also to outfit them with supplies. In the 1870s the store was expanded and a hotel was added to the property. He built a bathhouse and a separate residence for his family to increase the available room.

In 1854, Vance sold the riverfront part of his property to George Haass and Laurent Quintle. By constructing a small dam on the Medina River, Haass and Quintle were able to build a water-powered grist mill that allowed local farmers to mill their grain in Castroville, instead of having to ship it to San Antonio for processing. Joseph Courand purchased the mill in 1876 and adapted it to also mill lumber and gin cotton. In 1899 his son purchased the hotel.

Jordan Lawler purchased the entire property in 1925 and converted the mill to a small hydroelectric plant that provided Castroville's first electricity. With his sister, Ruth Curry Lawler, he reopened the hotel as the Landmark Inn. In 1974, it was donated to the Texas Parks and Wildlife Department.

Today the inn still provides overnight guests with attractive whitewashed rooms decorated with antiques, and with a continental breakfast in the morning. In keeping with the historic nature of the property, no phones or televisions are in the rooms; however, unobtrusive air-conditioning units have been installed in some rooms in deference to the warm Texas climate. Day visitors may tour the inn and landscaped grounds, including the partially restored mill.

VISITOR INFORMATION

4.7 acres. Rooms are available all year from Wednesday through Sunday night, and daily during March spring break. Group rentals available. To protect historic furnishings, pets and smoking are not allowed. The grounds are open to day-use visitors during the daytime. Historic structures with exhibits, interpretive trail, picnicking, fishing. Full visitor services available in Castroville. For information: Landmark Inn State Historical Park, 402 Florence Street, Castroville, TX 78009, (830) 931-2133.

ABOVE:
Landmark Inn room
LEFT:
Landmark Inn

Longhorn Cavern State Park

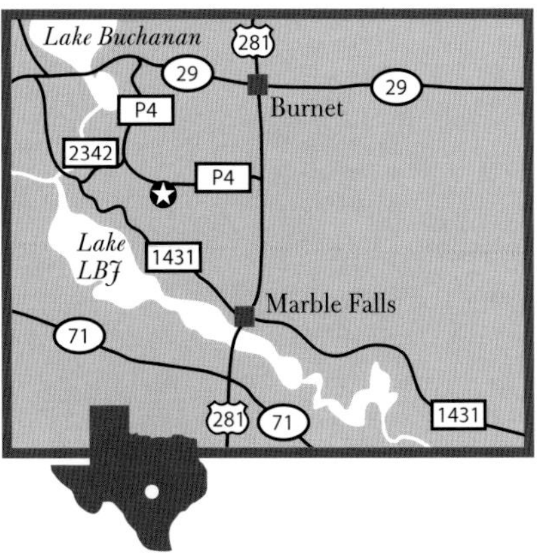

For many millennia, rainwater has been carving Longhorn Cavern from thick beds of Ellenburger Limestone. The cave lies on top of Backbone Ridge, a wedge of sedimentary rocks surrounded by billion-year-old igneous and metamorphic rocks. The limestone was laid down almost 500 million years ago in ancient seas that once covered central Texas. In West Texas, the deeply buried Ellenburger rock is an important natural gas and oil reservoir.

Rain picks up small amounts of carbon dioxide as it falls and becomes slightly acidic. As rainwater percolated through cracks and faults in the limestone of this area, it slowly dissolved chambers and passages. Later, flowing underground streams enlarged the passages, eroding them with suspended sand and silt. The water table fell and eventually the cave dried out. Unlike many caves, conditions in Longhorn Cavern were not right for large quantities of stalactites, stalagmites, and other dripstone decorations to form. However, large masses of sparkling calcite crystallized in some areas of the cave and the erosive action of the water left smoothly sculptured, marble-like walls as it receded.

Fossil evidence indicates that the Hill Country cave was used by now-extinct carnivores that preyed on and dragged in creatures such as prehistoric camels, giant bison, and mammoths. Later, Native Americans of early hunting cultures used the cave as a shelter. More recently, Comanches camped in the cave and even, according to stories, battled with Texas Rangers in one of its chambers. During the Civil War, Confederate soldiers manufactured black powder in Longhorn Cavern.

Later, it was rumored to be a hideout for outlaws, including the notorious Sam Bass, who, legend has it, hid a fortune in gold somewhere in or near the cave.

By the turn of the century, the Comanches had been defeated and the outlaws routed. A local rancher constructed a wooden dance floor in the cavern and created a popular local gathering place there. At various times the cave has served as a dance hall, a church, a nightclub, and a restaurant.

Longhorn Cavern

The state of Texas acquired the cavern and dedicated it as a state park in 1932. During the Depression, the Civilian Conservation Corps (CCC) made many improvements to the new park. With great workmanship, the CCC used native limestone and timber to construct buildings, retaining walls, and an observation tower. The workers excavated 2.5 million cubic yards of sediment from cavern passages and chambers, built trails, and installed an electric lighting system. The CCC projects were built well and most are still in use today. Interpretive exhibits, housed in the corps' old administrative building, describe the work of the CCC.

VISITOR INFORMATION

639 acres. Open all year, except Christmas Eve and Christmas Day, for guided tours only. Hours are longer on weekends and in summer; call for tour times. Cave is a constant 64°F, so a sweater may be desired on tours. Wear comfortable, rubber-soled walking shoes. Interpretive exhibits, picnicking, hiking, nature trail. Full visitor services available in Burnet and Marble Falls. For information: Longhorn Cavern State Park, Route 2, Box 23, Burnet, TX 78611, (877) 441-CAVE.

TOP:
CCC administrative building
RIGHT:
Bigtooth maple leaves

Lost Maples State Natural Area

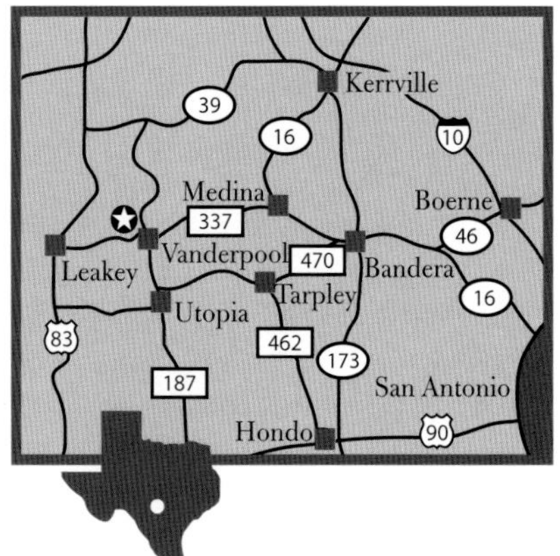

Some people believe that fall color in Texas is a contradiction in terms. However, hidden deep in an area of remote Hill Country canyons lies a fall color display that rivals any found in New England. Lost Maples State Natural Area contains some of the most scenic of these canyons.

Some of the most rugged terrain in the Texas Hill Country lies along the southern margin of the Edwards Plateau, a large piece of the earth's crust uplifted along the ancient Balcones Fault. Rivers, such as the Sabinal, the Frio, and the Medina, along with their tributaries, have cut deep canyons into the southern edge of the plateau near the towns of Leakey, Vanderpool, and Medina. Because these canyons are deeper and more steep-walled than those in

most other areas of the Hill Country, they provide more shelter from the sun and drying winds. Within this moist environment grows a unique community of plants, the most famous being the bigtooth maple.

Bigtooth maples grow in the Rocky Mountains, from Idaho through West Texas, and into the mountains of northern Mexico. Biologists believe that the trees at Lost Maples are relicts left from the last ice age. During this cooler and wetter time, the trees migrated eastward across Texas. When the climate became more hot and dry, the trees retreated west, surviving only in isolated pockets, such as the canyons of the natural area, where they receive extra shade and moisture. Small numbers of the maples also survive in two other eastern sites—Fort Hood and the Wichita Mountains of Oklahoma.

The fall color at Lost Maples is dependent on weather conditions during the preceding months. A combination of sunny days, cool fall nights, and adequate rainfall will spark a blazing display of gold, scarlet, and orange foliage from mid-October to mid-November. During good years, two other trees that favor the deep, moist canyons of Lost Maples, the black cherry and the red oak, add their share of color, too.

Other rare and interesting plants found at Lost Maples include American smoketree, sycamore-leaf snowbell, common witchhazel, and canyon mockorange. One particularly interesting tree, the Texas madrone, thrives here. It boasts a distinctive smooth, thin, peeling bark that ranges in color from cream to maroon, complemented by bright red berries and evergreen leaves.

Other more common trees grow with the maples in the canyon bottoms, including sycamores, pecans, oaks, and hackberries. Dense woodlands of Ashe juniper, red oak, and Lacey oak cloak the upper slopes, and are mixed with a sprinkling of Texas ash, black cherry, and other trees and shrubs. Grassland blankets most of the more exposed upland areas, along with scattered mottes of live oak, juniper, and other trees. One shrub, the mountain laurel, thrives here, blooming with fragrant purple flowers every year. Because the evergreen shrub is hardy and attractive, it has become a popular native landscaping plant in Texas.

Wildlife thrives in the rugged, undeveloped terrain. White-tailed deer are abundant, along with other mammals, such as armadillos, raccoons, opossums, fox squirrels, and striped skunks. Bobcats, gray foxes, and ringtails are common, but rarely seen. Bears and wolves are very rare or extinct in the area, but

TOP:
Hikers in Sabinal Canyon
ABOVE:
Fall color
OPPOSITE PAGE:
Maples and cherries along Sabinal River

mountain lions are occasionally seen. Many bird species flourish at Lost Maples, including the endangered black-capped vireo and golden-cheeked warbler.

Early peoples lived in the area possibly as much as 12,000 years ago. These early groups were nomadic and lived by hunting and gathering. In the eighteenth century, Apaches and Comanches moved into the area from the north and west. In 1762, the Spaniards established two short-lived, unsuccessful missions west of what is now the natural area, near Camp Wood. The first Anglo settlers arrived in the middle of the nineteenth century; they cut cypresses for shingles, grew crops in the flat river bottoms, and raised livestock in the rugged hills. Like visitors to the natural area today, the Indians and early pioneers probably also enjoyed the brilliant fall color of the bigtooth maples.

VISITOR INFORMATION

2,174 acres. Open all year. Very crowded mid-October to mid-November, especially on weekends. Small, developed campground with partial hookups and showers, along with primitive campsites for backpackers. Small museum and store at headquarters. Picnic area, nature trail, 10 miles of hiking trails for extensive back-country exploration. Fall color usually occurs between mid-October and mid-November, but quality varies from year to year. To avoid crowds during fall, go on weekdays if possible. Arrive early and reserve campsites well ahead of time. Limited food, lodging, and gas available in Vanderpool, Leakey, and Utopia; more extensive visitor services in Kerrville, Bandera, and Uvalde. For information: Lost Maples State Natural Area, HC01, Box 156, Vanderpool, TX 78885, (830) 966-3413.

TOP:
Hikers at Hale's Hollow
RIGHT:
Onions in smokehouse at Sauer-Beckmann Farm

Lyndon B. Johnson State Historical Park

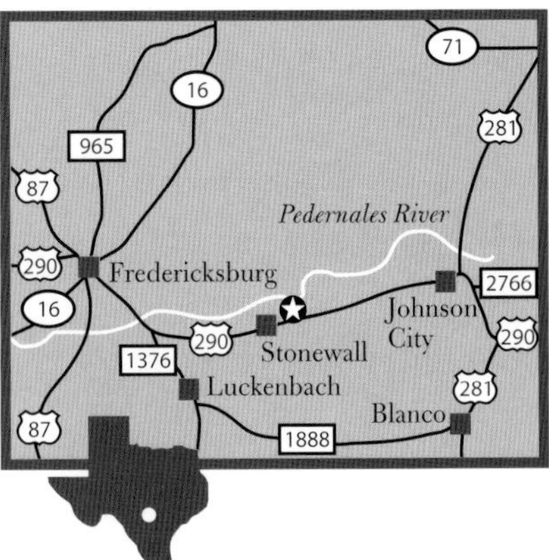

Lyndon B. Johnson State Historical Park had its beginnings when friends of President Johnson raised money to buy the land for the state across the Pedernales River from his ranch. The Texas Parks and Wildlife Commission accepted the land in 1967 and created the park to honor President Johnson as a "national and world leader."

Johnson, the 36th President of the United States, reigned during a turbulent period of American history, marked by bitter disputes over the Vietnam War, civil rights, and expansion of government power. Exhibits in the visitor center describe the president's life in the Hill Country and display presidential mementos and items given to Johnson by heads of state and others during his period in office. A restored two-room dogtrot cabin built in the 1870s by Johannes Behrens is attached to the visitor center.

Another cabin in the park was built in the middle of the nineteenth century by Casper Danz, among the first of many German immigrants to settle in the Hill Country. The rustic wood-and-stone dogtrot cabin faces U.S. Highway 290 just west of the park entrance. In spring, fields of bluebonnets, Indian paintbrushes, and phlox surround the cabin, making it a popular subject for photographers.

The Sauer-Beckmann Living History Farm, a working historical farm where Park employees recreate Hill Country farm life of about 1915, is probably the most interesting feature of the park. The staff members wear period clothes and operate the farm as it was at that time. They raise livestock, till a garden, can fruit, milk cows, butcher animals, make soap, smoke meat, and do the many other chores that were necessary to sustain a farm back then. The farm was originally built by Johan Sauer and his family in the late nineteenth century, and was added to after the turn of the century by Herman Beckmann and his sons.

The park also offers a number of recreational facilities, including a swimming pool, tennis courts, and a baseball field. Fishing is permitted in the Pedernales River, which borders the back side of the park along Ranch

TOP:
Sauer-Beckmann Farm
RIGHT:
Separating cream at Sauer-Beckmann Farm

ABOVE: *Pantry at Sauer-Beckmann Farm*

BELOW: *Milking cow at farm*

Road 1. Fenced pastures contain bison, longhorn cattle, and white-tailed deer.

The state park lies in the heart of the Hill Country, between Johnson City and Fredericksburg. The Hill Country's landscape was created when a large piece of the Earth's crust, now called the Edwards Plateau, was uplifted about 2,000 feet. Erosion of this plateau by creeks and rivers such as the Pedernales created a land of rolling limestone hills, broad valleys, and clear running streams. A scrub forest dominated by live oaks, Ashe junipers, Spanish oaks, and cedar elms covers the slopes. The moist, deep soils along watercourses nourish bald cypresses, sycamores, pecans, and other trees. A nature trail connecting the visitor center and the Sauer-Beckmann Living History Farm identifies and describes many Hill Country plants and animals.

Lyndon B. Johnson National Historical Park lies across the river from the state park and is operated by the National Park Service. The national historical park contains the LBJ Ranch and house, the Junction schoolhouse (where Johnson first attended school), a reconstruction of the former president's birthplace, and the Johnson family cemetery. Tour buses that visit these sites start from the state park's visitor center. The National Park Service also manages another unit of the park in nearby Johnson City.

VISITOR INFORMATION

733 acres. Open all year. No camping. Historic structures and exhibits, living history farm. Bookstore in visitor center, nature trail, picnicking, swimming pool, fishing, tennis courts, baseball field. Limited visitor services available in Stonewall; full services in Johnson City and Fredericksburg. For information: LBJ State Historical Park, P.O. Box 238, Stonewall, TX 78671, (830) 644-2252.

McKinney Falls State Park

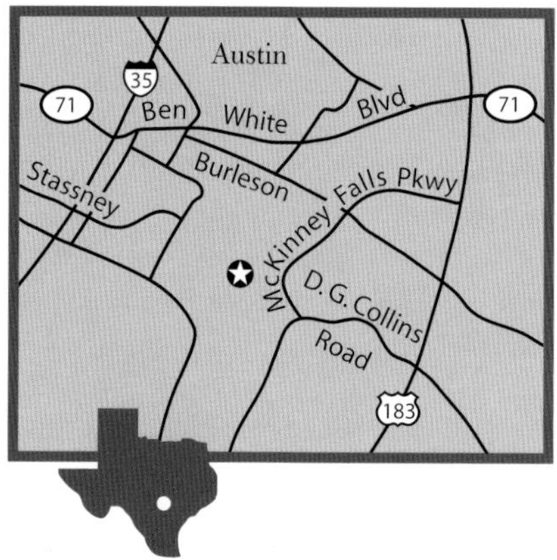

Two small waterfalls pour off limestone ledges and tumble into deep pools in Onion Creek not far from the center of Austin. They are part of McKinney Falls State Park, which provides a quiet, natural retreat from the noisy, busy city just beyond the park boundary. The highlights of the park, the upper and lower falls, were created when hard layers of limestone resisted erosion by the water of Onion Creek better than the other layers of softer rock. Eventually, the softer rocks eroded away, leaving higher ledges over which the water pours in cascades and falls.

Although the landscape around McKinney Falls is quiet today, at one time it was quite violent. The limestone layers exposed by Onion Creek were deposited in a shallow Cretaceous sea about 80 million years ago. Later, fractures broke the Earth's crust in this area, and hot molten rock, or magma, worked its way to the surface through these cracks. When the lava hit wet sediments and sea water, massive steam explosions erupted, forming craters around the vents and eventually islands in the shallow sea. Pilot Knob, the hill just to the south of the park, was one of these volcanoes. After the volcano became dormant, reefs built up around its edges. Wave action ground up shells and crumbled the rock, and later sediments then buried the debris and compressed it into the reef-beach rock that can be seen today at the falls.

Today, Onion Creek and its tributary Williamson Creek wind peacefully through the countryside, supporting a lush riparian woodland of bald cypresses, sycamores, pecans, and oaks. On the drier uplands away from the water, live oaks, Ashe junipers, prickly pears, and mesquites thrive. In the spring, open areas often boast patches of wildflowers such as bluebonnets, Indian blankets, Indian paintbrushes, and many other species.

In several places, the flowing waters of the creek have carved out large shelter caves from the limestone. Archeologists have found extensive remains of prehistoric and historic

ABOVE:
Mountain-biker
RIGHT:
Lower McKinney Falls

Native American peoples in the shelters, which, apparently, were favored camping sites for many years.

In 1832, Santiago del Valle bought a large area around McKinney Falls from the Mexican state of Coahuila y Texas and became the site's first landowner. Later, in 1839, Thomas McKinney, one of Stephen F. Austin's original three hundred colonists, bought part of the land from Michel Menard. McKinney was a prominent man who aided Texas during the war of independence, cofounded Galveston, and helped start the Texas Navy. He loved horses, and retired to the McKinney Falls land to raise them. The ruins of his homestead, horse-trainer's cabin, and grist mill lie within the park. Sadly, the Civil War and poor investments destroyed his wealth, and after he died his widow sold the land to pay creditors.

Ultimately, the land was acquired by the Parks and Wildlife Department and opened as a state park in 1976. The rushing waters of Onion Creek are still the main attraction as they course through channels of sculptured limestone and pour over the two small waterfalls. Swimming and fishing engage many park visitors, while others take the interpretive trail through one of the late-prehistoric historic rock shelters. Cyclists enjoy the paved trail that winds through the campground and upland areas. Volcanoes may be part of McKinney Falls' past, but today the park provides a tranquil escape from the hustle and bustle of the nearby city of Austin.

VISITOR INFORMATION

641 acres. Open all year. Hot and humid in summer. Relatively large campground with partial hookups and showers. Interpretive center, hiking, cycling, swimming, fishing, picnicking, nature trail. Full visitor services available in Austin. For information: McKinney Falls State Park, 5808 McKinney Falls Parkway, Austin, TX 78744, (512) 243-1643.

Pedernales Falls State Park

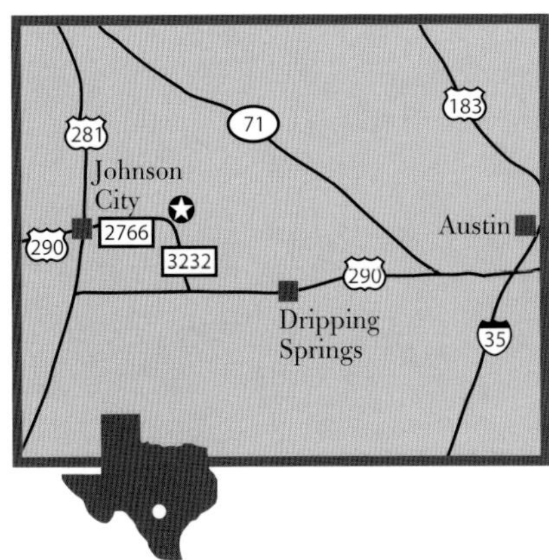

Crystal clear water rushes over rocks and into deep pools, bubbling and foaming. It races through polished limestone chutes and cascades over ledges, drawn by gravity toward the sea. Within the heart of the Texas Hill Country, the Pedernales River drops rapidly through a series of waterfalls and cascades in Pedernales Falls State Park, for many reasons one of the Hill Country's jewels.

The Pedernales River originates in the rolling hills west of Fredericksburg, but owes its fame to the section that flows through the ranch of former President Lyndon B. Johnson. Some miles downstream from LBJ Ranch, the Pedernales flows into the state park. It enters a rocky canyon and runs into tilted beds of durable Marble Falls limestone. The Pennsylvanian period limestone was laid down about 300 million years ago and then was tilted in the succeeding period of Ouachita Mountain building. Overlying rocks of the later Cretaceous period were then laid down flat on top of the tilted Pennsylvanian rocks. Erosion of the Cretaceous rocks led to the exposure of tilted Pennsylvanian Limestone ledges. The falls and cascades of the river are formed as the water tumbles down over these ledges.

Below the falls, the river calms and continues flowing downstream at a slower pace. Bald cypresses line the banks, although most are relatively small or stunted because of past floods. The Pedernales River is notorious for sudden, violent floods, making it difficult for streamside vegetation to become well established. One of its most famous floods occurred in September 1952, when as much as 26 inches of rain fell on the watershed in three days. Massive flooding ensued, uprooting trees and washing out river banks. A highway bridge upstream in Johnson City trapped debris, temporarily damming the river. When it broke, the resulting torrent did serious damage downstream in the park and elsewhere. Large sand deposits below the falls and the broken-off tops of cypress trees still exist as reminders of the flood of '52. Since then, sirens have been installed along the river section of the park to warn people of impending floods. If the sirens sound, all visitors should leave the river area and climb to higher ground.

The park lies in typical Hill Country terrain—a hilly landscape wooded with a scrub forest of live oaks, red oaks, and Ashe junipers.

OPPOSITE PAGE:
Pedernales Falls
BELOW:
Mountain-biker

Dry land plants, such as prickly pears and mesquites, are also common. Before the area was heavily grazed and natural fires suppressed, the Hill Country was grassier than it is today and trees were less dominant. The Ashe juniper in particular has spread widely; it now blankets entire hillsides of the park. Juniper bark is a crucial nest-building material for the endangered golden-cheeked warbler. Areas with a mixture of such shrubs as mountain laurel, agarita, shin oak, and Mexican persimmon are favored by another rare bird, the black-capped vireo.

The canyons of the river and its tributaries support plant life that is more lush. Pecans, sycamores, American elms, and bald cypresses thrive in the deeper, moister soils of the canyon bottoms. These areas are more protected from the sun and dry wind than are upland areas. The short Pedernales Hill Country Nature Trail introduces visitors to many of the plants and animals of the park. The highlight of the trail is an observation platform that overlooks the confluence of Bee and Regal creeks, two small tributaries of the river. Tiny cascades tumble into a fern-lined pool in the canyon bottom, shaded by towering bald cypresses unaffected by the 1952 flood. Because the site was heavily damaged by trampling in the past, entry is no longer allowed into this area. It is still possible, however, to enjoy the view from above.

Plenty of recreational pursuits are possible at the park, including swimming and tubing in a designated area 2.5 miles below the falls. When the river is high, schools of shad sometimes make their way upstream to the falls, and fishing is allowed with a single pole or rod and reel.

Hikers and backpackers will enjoy the developed 8-mile Wolf Mountain Trail. It leads to a primitive back-country camping area, viewpoints, historic sites, and the river. Mountain-bikers can also enjoy the broad, relatively easy route. More adventurous hikers who are good at route-finding may want to try the primitive trail system across the river. Horseback riders can also enjoy 12 miles of trail set aside for their use.

VISITOR INFORMATION

5,212 acres. Open all year. Hot in summer, but river is cool and pleasant. Busy on spring, summer, and fall weekends. Moderate-sized campground with partial hookups and showers. Primitive campground for backpackers. Swimming and tubing allowed, beginning 2.5 miles below the falls. Fishing, picnicking, hiking, mountain-biking, horseback riding. Full visitor services available in Johnson City. For information: Pedernales Falls State Park, 2585 Park Road 6026, Johnson City, TX 78636, (830) 868-7304.

South Llano River State Park

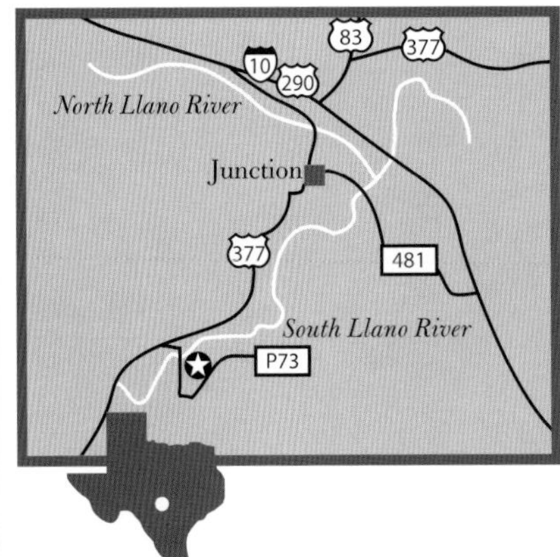

cedar elms, live oaks, American elms, and chinkapin oaks.

The pecan bottomland of the park and adjoining properties is one of central Texas's largest and oldest winter roosting sites for the Rio Grande turkey. Although the wild turkeys frequent the park all year, in winter as many as 500 or more of the birds congregate in the floodplain. Because of the roost's importance, most of the bottomland is closed to visitors from October 1 through the end of March to prevent disturbance of the turkeys. However, the campground remains open, along with other facilities, including a blind that

The clear, cool waters of the South Llano River wind through a broad valley a few miles upstream from the confluence with the North Llano River at the town of Junction. For a mile and a half in this broad valley, the South Llano River forms the north boundary of South Llano River State Park. Most of the park lies in the broad floodplain, a lush, shady area thickly wooded with large, majestic pecan trees and lesser numbers of

allows observation of the large, impressive birds. During the rest of the year, easy trails allow hikers and mountain-bikers to travel through the open woodland, along the river bank, and by two small oxbow lakes where anglers can try their luck.

The headwaters of the South Llano River rise some miles to the southwest in Edwards County. Water levels fluctuate depending on rainfall, but permanent springs ensure that the river always flows. In the warm months, the cool water attracts canoeists and tubers. Various access points allow trips of differing lengths, both within the park and on adjoining sections of river. In shallow areas, where the water flows over gravel bars, canoes may scrape bottom, but overall, the river offers easy, enjoyable float trips.

Additional recreational opportunities exist in the adjoining Walter Buck Wildlife Management Area. In 1977, Walter Buck donated this area, along with what is now the state-park land, to the state for wildlife protection and enjoyment by the public.

The 2,123-acre wildlife management area begins at the south side of the state park, at the edge of the valley bottom. Unlike the broad, relatively flat bottomland of the state park, it consists of rugged, hilly terrain typical of the Texas Hill Country. Along with a blanket of grasses, stunted Ashe junipers and live oaks dot the hills. The small ravines and canyons are more lushly vegetated with larger trees and thicker grasses. Wildlife, in the form of white-tailed deer, turkeys, rabbits, and armadillos, is common. The rare black-capped vireo can sometimes be seen.

Several miles of old ranch roads provide access to the wildlife management area for mountain-bike riders and hikers. One short, steep hike leads to a scenic overlook that gives tremendous views of the park bottomlands and river valley. At various times of the year, the wildlife management area may be partially or completely closed because of wildlife-management activities or endangered-species protection.

Through the generosity of Walter Buck, the state park and wildlife management area, in combination, protect an important wildlife habitat and also offer a broad range of recreational activities.

VISITOR INFORMATION

523 acres. Open all year; some areas may be closed at various times, as described above. Hot in summer. Moderate number of campsites with partial hookups and showers. Small number of walk-in tent sites. Wildlife viewing, hiking, mountain-biking, fishing, canoeing, tubing, picnicking. Canoe and tube rental from local businesses. Full visitor services available in Junction. For information: South Llano River State Park, HC-15, Box 224, Junction, TX 76849, (915) 446-3994.

LEFT: *Native pecan grove*
OPPOSITE PAGE: *South Llano River*

Panhandle Plains

Although a large part of the Panhandle is flat and treeless, as is much of the adjoining Rolling Plains region to the east, the area contains a number of parks that are scenic and historic jewels, including Palo Duro Canyon, arguably the best-known state park in Texas. Other parks in the area contain the ruins of frontier forts and some of the earliest traces of humans in Texas.

The High Plains, also known as the Llano Estacado, covers much of the Panhandle. The very flat grassy plains are the smooth surface of a broad sheet of debris washed eastward from the slopes of the Rocky Mountains of New Mexico and southern Colorado. Eventually the Pecos River cut its way headward through these plains in eastern New Mexico and into northern New Mexico, and intercepted the mountain streams that had been depositing sediment in the Panhandle. The Pecos cut a broad valley, leaving the High Plains as a large, isolated, eastward-tilting plateau. The sediment layers have become an important water-bearing aquifer, the Ogallala.

Erosion continues to gnaw away at the edges of the High Plains. Tributaries of the Pecos River continue to cut into the western edge of the plains, while the Red, Canadian, and Brazos rivers carve their way into the eastern margin. Only the Canadian has managed to cut its way through the High Plains into northern New Mexico, but eventually the other rivers too will slice all the way across the plains.

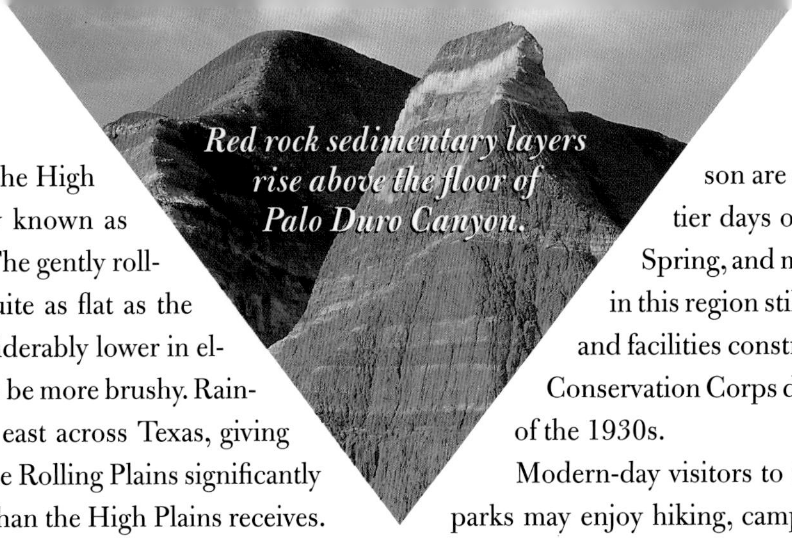

Red rock sedimentary layers rise above the floor of Palo Duro Canyon.

The area east of the High Plains is commonly known as the Rolling Plains. The gently rolling terrain is not quite as flat as the High Plains, is considerably lower in elevation, and tends to be more brushy. Rainfall increases to the east across Texas, giving the eastern part of the Rolling Plains significantly more precipitation than the High Plains receives.

A steep escarpment creates a dramatic division between the High Plains and the Rolling Plains. Deep, sheer-walled canyons, mostly tributaries of the Red River, cut westward into this escarpment, exposing colorful walls of red, ocher, and lavender sandstones and shales. The most spectacular example is 800-foot-deep Palo Duro Canyon. Other rugged canyons lie within Caprock Canyons State Park.

Several state parks preserve important historical sites in this part of Texas. Lubbock Lake Landmark contains the only known site in North America with a continuous archeological record of all the human cultures of the region, from the ice-age nomads to the early pioneers. The ruins of Fort Griffin and Fort Richardson are remnants of the frontier days of Texas. Abilene, Big Spring, and many other state parks in this region still utilize the buildings and facilities constructed by the Civilian Conservation Corps during the Depression of the 1930s.

Modern-day visitors to the Panhandle Plains parks may enjoy hiking, camping, picnicking, and visiting historical museums. A unique feature at Caprock Canyons is the 64-mile-long Caprock Canyons Trailway. Hikers, mountain-bikers, and equestrians enjoy the former railroad grade as it descends from the High Plains to the Rolling Plains down canyons, across high trestles, and through a long tunnel.

Fishing and water sports are popular at lake parks in the eastern part of the region. Two of the parks, Possum Kingdom and Lake Brownwood, are far enough east to share some of the ecological characteristics of the adjoining Hill Country and Prairies and Lakes regions. Scrubby oaks, cedar elms, and Ashe junipers dot the hills of these parks, unlike the treeless areas farther west.

Panhandle Plains

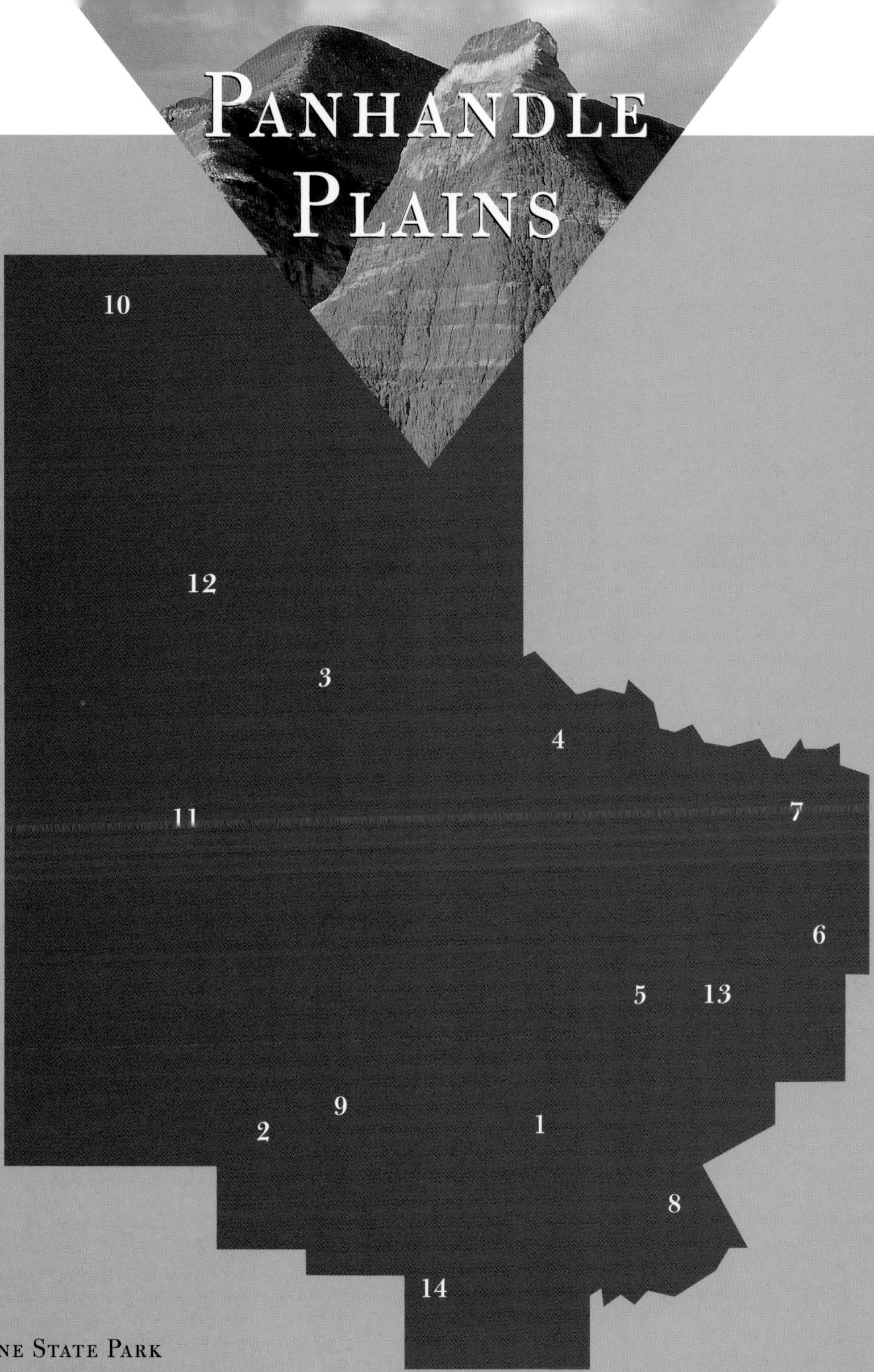

10
12
3
4
11
7
6
5 13
9
2
1
8
14

1 Abilene State Park
2 Big Spring State Park
3 Caprock Canyons State Park
4 Copper Breaks State Park
5 Fort Griffin State Historical Park
6 Fort Richardson State Historical Park
7 Lake Arrowhead State Park
8 Lake Brownwood State Park
9 Lake Colorado City State Park
10 Lake Rita Blanca State Park
11 Lubbock Lake Landmark State Historical Park
12 Palo Duro Canyon State Park
13 Possum Kingdom State Park
14 San Angelo State Park

Abilene State Park

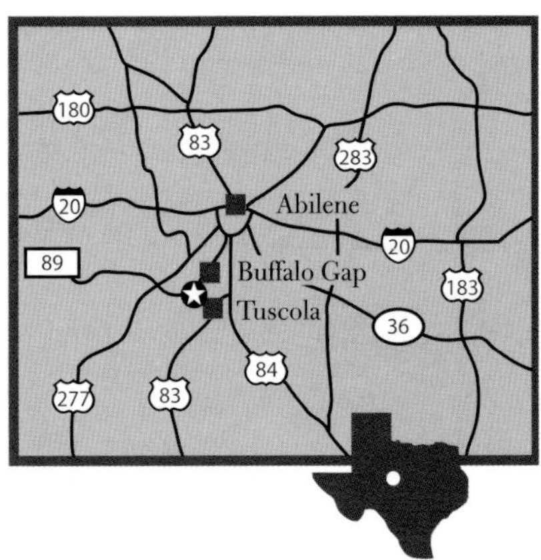

Much of the country surrounding the city of Abilene is rolling grassland dotted with mesquite. The weather is hot and dry much of the year, and first-time visitors to Abilene State Park may be surprised to find a wooded oasis on the banks of Elm Creek. The park lies in a valley surrounded by the low limestone hills of the Callahan Divide, south of the city of Abilene. The divide is an area of higher country that separates the watersheds of the Brazos and Colorado rivers. The hills are sparsely wooded with mesquites and stunted Ashe junipers, but Elm Creek waters a lush ribbon of woodland.

Pecans, live oaks, red oaks, willows, hackberries, and elms provide a thick canopy of shade in the creek's floodplain. People have

BELOW: *Elm Creek*

ABOVE: *Park swimming pool*

long been attracted to the site; Comanches, Tonkawas, and many other Indian groups camped in the shade of the thick woodland lining Elm Creek before the area was settled by American pioneers.

The Civilian Conservation Corps was responsible for much of the early development of the park. The organization was created in the 1930s to employ young men during the hard times of the Depression. The most prominent reminder of their labors here is the stone water tower and swimming pool complex, still the centerpiece of the park today. The workers used a rust-red sandstone quarried locally for construction material. As well as being attractive, the masonry arches and intricate stonework of the pool complex have proved also to be durable. A roofed observation platform on top of the concession building gives an overview of the pool and the surrounding hills.

The area surrounding the park is also important historically. From prehistoric times to the present, the woods and waters of Elm Creek have attracted people from the surrounding semi-arid country. A few miles north of the park lies the small town of Buffalo Gap, the first county seat of Taylor County. It is located in a break in the hills of the Callahan Divide that is also known as Buffalo Gap. The gap created an easy travel route through the hills and, in their heyday, it was used by thousands of buffalo during their seasonal migrations. Indians also used the gap as a travel route and later it was used by cattle drives and by the Butterfield Stage.

Today, the area is enjoyed by those involved in recreational pursuits. Kids splash in the large pool and campers relax in the shade of the bottomland forest, while Lake Abilene, adjoining the park to the west, offers fishing and boating opportunities.

VISITOR INFORMATION

529 acres. Open all year. Swimming pool open Memorial Day weekend through Labor Day weekend; call for exact schedule. Hot in summer. Large number of campsites with partial hookups and showers. Group trailer area. Screened shelters. Hiking, picnicking, Texas longhorn herd. Limited visitor services available in Buffalo Gap; full services in Abilene. For information: Abilene State Park, 150 Park Road 32, Tuscola, TX 79562, (915) 572-3204.

TOP:
CCC-built swimming complex
RIGHT:
Limestone rimrock at Big Spring State Park

Big Spring State Park

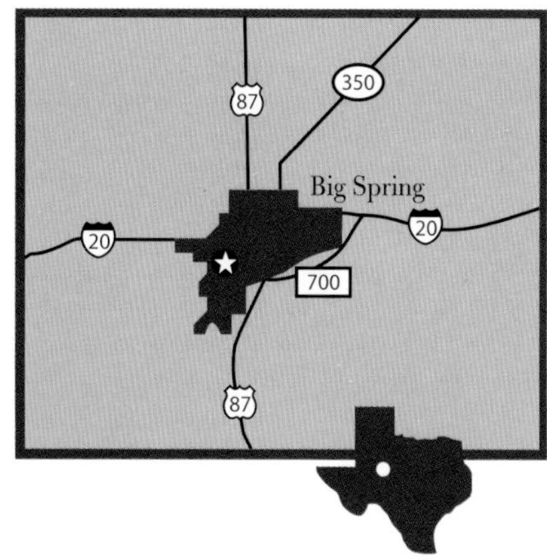

Much of west-central Texas is a relatively flat, dry region noted for its geographic monotony. At Big Spring State Park, however, the northern limit of the Edwards Plateau is reached, culminating in a series of bluffs rising 200 feet above the Rolling Plains. The Edwards Plateau is a vast, relatively flat upland area stretching as far southeast as Austin and San Antonio. Thick beds of Lower Cretaceous limestone form the plateau, deposits of an ancient sea that once covered much of Texas. The eastern and southern parts of the

plateau have been cut by rivers and streams into hilly terrain known as the Hill Country.

Big Spring State Park caps one of the limestone bluffs at the northern edge of the plateau. Below the bluff, known as Scenic Mountain, sprawls the town of Big Spring, named for a large spring that once flowed nearby. As happened to many West Texas springs, excessive groundwater pumping ended its flow.

Vegetation typical of the semiarid region blankets the park. Bigger plants include mesquites, scrubby shin oaks, and redberry junipers.

Prickly pears and other cacti are common on the rocky slopes of the park. Wildlife, in the form of cottontails, jackrabbits, and roadrunners, is common, particularly early or late in the day. Even a small prairie dog town lies in a little valley on the south side of the park.

In the past, Comanches and earlier Indian groups frequently visited the park area, probably attracted by the permanent source of spring water. Spaniards may have first visited the area as early as 1768, but the first recorded mention of the spring occurs in an October 3, 1849, entry in the journal of Captain R. B. Marcy.

The park was acquired by the state in 1934 and developed shortly thereafter by the Civilian Conservation Corps, created during the Depression to employ young men unable to find jobs. Using limestone quarried on the site and quality workmanship, the corps built the pavilion, headquarters, and restroom. Its biggest project was the 3-mile drive that loops around the mountain. Retaining walls for the drive were built using large blocks of limestone—some weighing as much as two tons—and mortarless masonry techniques.

The loop road built by the corps is the highlight of the park. Most of the route follows the edge of the limestone rimrock capping the bluff. Early in the morning, before park gates open to cars, the loop is used by joggers, walkers, and cyclists from the city of Big Spring, who circle it, enjoying the dramatic views as they exercise. Later, others drive the loop, enjoying the same views as the early-morning visitors. Today, the city of Big Spring sprawls out across the valley below and Interstate 20 transports high volumes of traffic east and west across Texas. It was not so long ago, however, that Comanches visited the spring and U.S. cavalry troops trekked across the empty country.

VISITOR INFORMATION

382 acres. Open all year. Hot in summer. Limited number of campsites with barbecue grills and shaded picnic tables; two sites with electricity. Pavilion may be reserved for group functions. Picnicking, nature and hiking trails, Fourth of July fireworks display, combined scenic drive and walking route. Full visitor services available in Big Spring. For information: Big Spring State Park, #1 Scenic Drive, Big Spring, TX 79720, (915) 263-4931.

TOP:
CCC-built pavilion
LEFT:
Prickly pear

Caprock Canyons State Park

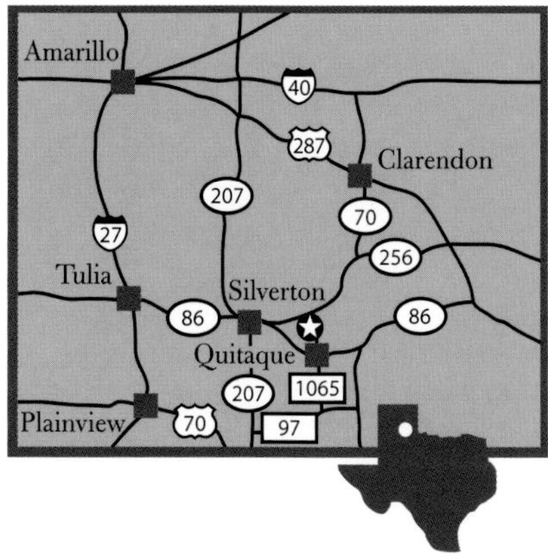

Caprock Canyons State Park provides a startling contrast to the flat plains that make up most of the Texas Panhandle. Within the park, the flat, high plains of the Llano Estacado give way to the lower Rolling Plains in a long, serrated, red-rock escarpment as much as 1,000 feet high.

About a million years ago, the High Plains of the Panhandle had a smooth surface, consisting of material eroded from the southern Rocky Mountains and washed eastward along a very gentle slope. The Pecos, Canadian, and Red rivers slowly cut valleys upstream into the High Plains, in a process called headward erosion. In time, the Pecos and Canadian rivers cut all the way through the plains and diverted flow from across them. The High Plains were left as an isolated plateau.

The Red River, too, continued to cut into the Llano Estacado, but was slowed by thick beds of red sandstone. Erosion by the river cut deep, narrow canyons in the durable rock rather than the broad valleys carved by the Pecos and Canadian rivers. Interestingly, the 1,300-mile-long Red River is one of the longest rivers in North America that does not originate in mountains. It continues to erode the Llano Estacado today, the narrow fingers of its canyons and tributaries slowly cutting westward from the lower plains to the east. The most prominent canyon is Palo Duro, but Caprock Canyons State Park contains two impressive smaller canyons, the North Prong and the South Prong of the Little Red River.

Humans arrived at least 10,000 years ago and built campsites near what is now Lake Theo, as well as in other areas. The earliest documented people, members of what is known as the Folsom culture, are identified by the distinctive design of their projectile points: a large flake was carefully chipped from the base of each side of the point, which was then mounted on a spear and used to kill large animals. These early people were nomadic and followed game across the High Plains, as did many later groups. Contrary to modern myth, these hunter-gatherer groups did not leave the land undisturbed. They used fire to encourage grassland growth and to help with hunting. Many archeologists now believe that they contributed to the extinction of many Pleistocene mammals, including the mammoth, the giant bison, and a type of camel.

More recent cultures utilized pottery and the bow and arrow to improve their standard of living.

Sandstone formations

Starting about a thousand years ago, some groups established permanent settlements and began cultivating crops of beans, corn, and squash. The Spaniards first appeared in 1541, with Francisco Vásquez de Coronado's epic journey across the High Plains. The Comanches arrived from the north in the early eighteenth century, establishing a nomadic culture centered around bison hunting using horses acquired from the Spaniards. In the late nineteenth century, Anglo settlers founded towns and vast cattle ranches across the High Plains.

The state park preserves a large area of rugged canyons on the eastern margin of the High Plains. Some of

the plants tucked away in the deep canyons, such as the Rocky Mountain juniper, are at the limit of their range. Bison, wolves, and black bears no longer roam the canyon country, but mule deer, bobcats, coyotes, porcupines, jackrabbits, and many other animals are common. Aoudads, sheep native to northern Africa, were introduced nearby in 1957 and have thrived. Although they are an interesting addition to the rugged canyon country of the Red River, they compete for food directly with the native mule deer.

The park offers one of the most unique features of any state park. A recently abandoned railroad line that passes by the park was converted into a combination hiking, biking, and equestrian trail. The 64-mile route traverses rugged Quitaque Canyon, goes through a long railroad tunnel, and crosses many tall trestles as it climbs its way up from the Rolling Plains onto the High Plains. With several access points, trips of many different distances can be arranged. At times, shuttles are provided to take visitors to the west end of the trail up on the High Plains. This allows those desiring a less arduous hike to enjoy a one-way, mostly downhill run into Quitaque through the most scenic section of the trail.

In addition to the converted railroad trail, hikers are attracted to the many miles of trail that climb up the North Prong and South Prong canyons to spectacular viewpoints on Haynes Ridge. Two backcountry campsites allow overnight stays along the hiking trails. A large loop trail draws equestrians to another section of Caprock Canyons. Small Lake Theo, fed by Holmes Creek on the south side of the park, offers fishing and boating opportunities. The rugged state park, one of the largest in Texas, provides a welcome change from the flat terrain of most of the Panhandle.

VISITOR INFORMATION

15,161 acres. Open all year. Hot in summer during day, but cools off pleasantly at night. Occasional snowstorms in winter. Developed campground with partial hookups and showers. Undeveloped walk-in tent campground in attractive setting in mouth of South Prong Canyon. Primitive backcountry campsites for backpackers and equestrians. Picnicking, fishing, limited boating. Outdoor pavilion with interpretive exhibits. Limited visitor services available in nearby Quitaque; full services in Plainview. For information: Caprock Canyons State Park, P.O. Box 204, Quitaque, TX, 79255, (806) 455-1492.

ABOVE:
Railroad tunnel on Caprock Canyons Trailway
OPPOSITE PAGE, TOP:
Caprock's rugged margin
OPPOSITE PAGE, BOTTOM:
Railway trestle on trailway

Copper Breaks State Park

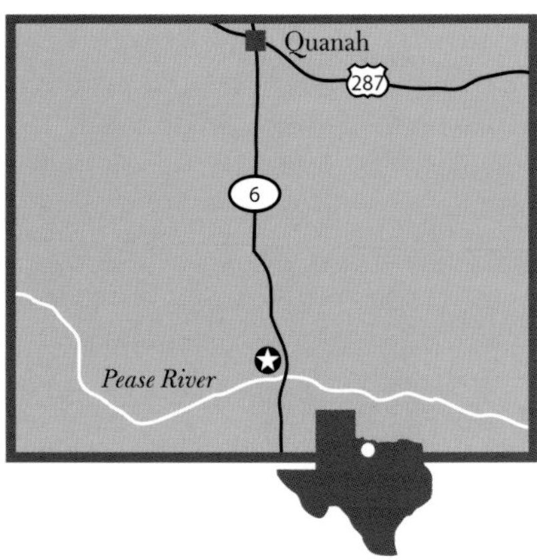

Copper Breaks State Park provides an excellent introduction to a remote part of Texas, far from any cities. It lies in the vast, lonely Rolling Plains north of Abilene, near the Red River. Grass and mesquite-covered mesas are broken up by low, reddish cliffs and juniper-covered escarpments along the Pease River. Old copper-mining activities in the area gave the park its name.

Comanches arrived in the Copper Breaks area in the eighteenth century, mounted on horses obtained from the Spaniards. For more than 150 years they followed a nomadic lifestyle of hunting bison and raiding. In 1860, some troops led by Captain Sul Ross caught a group of Comanches near the park and rescued Cynthia Ann Parker, a young white woman who had been captured 24 years earlier as a small child by a Comanche raiding party near Mexia. She had grown up with the tribe, and when she was reunited with her relatives, she did not adjust well to the white people's ways. She died only a few years later, supposedly of a broken heart. Her son, Quanah Parker, became the last great war chief of the Comanches.

The broken country along the Pease River consists of layers of shale, clay, and gypsum deposited more than 250 million years ago during the Permian period. In places, the rock and soil appear greenish, indicating copper mineralization. The prairie region once supported extensive grasslands, but many years of heavy livestock grazing and suppression of natural fires have encouraged invasion by mesquites, red-berry junipers, prickly pears, and other shrubby plants. In moist areas along the river, in canyon bottoms, and around ponds, cottonwoods, western soapberries, hackberries, and willows provide welcome shade. Commonly seen wildlife includes cottontails, hawks, roadrunners, mule deer, white-tailed deer, jackrabbits, raccoons, and many species of songbirds. More elusive creatures, such as beavers, porcupines, bobcats, coyotes, and even rare mountain lions, live in the dissected landscape.

The state park provides an excellent escape for local residents. The small 60-acre Lake Copper Breaks offers a sandy beach for swimming; no-wake boating is also permitted there, as well as fishing,

with largemouth bass, crappie, catfish, sunfish, and even rainbow trout (stocked in winter) challenging anglers. A smaller pond within the park affords additional fishing opportunities. Hiking and nature trails give access to the backcountry and lead from shady canyon bottoms to high viewpoints. An equestrian trail and campground allow horse owners to explore a system of old ranch roads on the north side of the park. The visitor center has excellent exhibits giving information about the human and natural history of the area, and is dominated by a large bronze sculpture of three bison.

VISITOR INFORMATION

1,889 acres. Open all year. Hot in summer. Developed campground with partial hookups and showers, in two areas. Separate developed equestrian campground. Primitive camp area for backpackers. Swimming, fishing, limited boating, volleyball court, hiking, equestrian and nature trails, longhorn herd, evening interpretive programs on summer weekends, exhibits in visitor center. Seasonal paddleboat rental, park store. Trout stamp required for trout fishing. Limited visitor services available in Crowell; full services in Quanah. For information: Copper Breaks State Park, 777 Park Road 62, Quanah, TX 79252, (940) 839-4331.

Fort Griffin State Historical Park

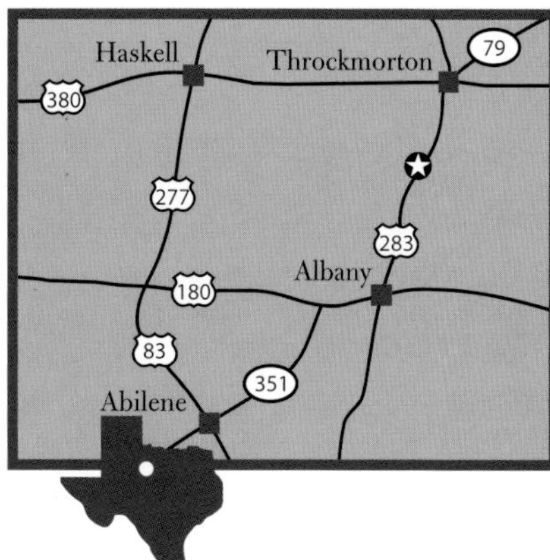

After the Civil War, the United States government re-garrisoned forts abandoned during the war and established new ones to protect travelers and settlers on the western frontier. Troops began building Camp Wilson on a high, mesquite-dotted bluff above the Clear Fork of the Brazos River to protect buffalo hunters, settlers, travelers, and cattle herds from raids by Comanches and Kiowas. The following year the post was renamed Fort Griffin in honor of the late General Charles Griffin.

The plans for this fort called for an elaborate structure consisting of solidly built stone buildings. However, the troops were away on various campaigns too often to complete much of the original plan. Only five stone buildings were completed; the rest of the fort consisted of tents and crude huts built of rough lumber. In winter, the accommodations were drafty, cold, and miserable.

Over the years, a number of cavalry and infantry units were stationed at the fort, including units of the black buffalo soldiers. The troops provided escort duty to travelers and conducted long campaigns in the High Plains in search of raiding Indian parties.

Fort Griffin was the primary supply point for units attempting to force the Comanches onto Oklahoma reservations. Ultimately, Colonel Ranald Mackenzie drove the last of the Indians from the High Plains in the 1870s, helped by the extermination of their primary food source, the buffalo. With the last of the Comanches defeated, Fort Griffin's reason for existence ended and it was abandoned in 1881.

Today, the only remaining structures are those built of stone.

LEFT:
Lake Copper Breaks
RIGHT:
Fort Griffin ruins

Of these, the bakery is intact; the others are in arrested stages of decay. Little remains of the other buildings but scattered foundations. A few of the old wooden buildings have been reconstructed.

Although the old fort is the main attraction, the park offers much more, including fishing in the Brazos River, camping, and hiking on the trails. Part of the official Texas longhorn herd grazes in park pastures.

VISITOR INFORMATION

506 acres. Open all year. Hot in summer. Small number of campsites with partial hookups and showers. Historic buildings, interpretive exhibits, hiking and nature trails, picnicking, fishing, longhorn herd. Full visitor services available in Albany. For information: Fort Griffin State Historical Park, 1701 N. US Highway 283, Albany, TX 76430, (915) 762-3592.

Fort Richardson State Historical Park

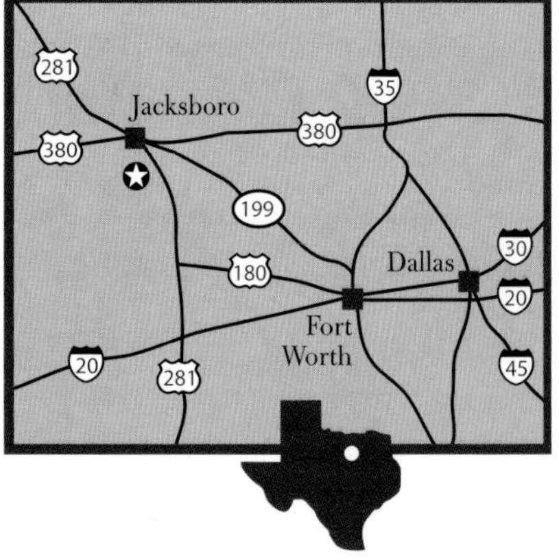

With the establishment of the fort, settlement of towns, farms, and ranches increased in the area. Jacksboro grew, partly as a supplier of services for the fort. Within the fort, many buildings were constructed around the central parade ground. By 1878, the Indian problems had ended and the fort, once a thriving community, was abandoned. Many of the buildings no longer exist, but nine structures remain, including seven of the original buildings. Of these, the most impressive is the large two-story hospital. Original and recreated furniture, beds, cabinets, tables, supplies, and other items within the restored building show life as it was in the post hospital during the fort's active days. They show, too, how primitive medical techniques were back then, making visitors appreciative of modern medicine. Other remaining fort buildings include a reconstructed officers' barracks on the

Restored fort hospital

In 1867, the area around Jacksboro lay on the western edge of the frontier. Settlers and travelers were moving into the region, displacing Comanches, Kiowas, and other Indians. Violence and constant conflict resulted from the cultural clash, and had worsened in Texas during the Civil War when federal troops were withdrawn and the Confederacy was no longer able to effectively police the frontier. Fort Richardson was established as one of a line of outposts to protect people from the bloodshed.

south side of the parade ground. Today it houses an interpretive center.

Although the old fort is the main attraction of the park, other features also draw many people. The fort lies in flat-to-rolling prairie country, blanketed with grass and scattered mesquite trees. Hidden in a narrow valley behind the fort lies Lost Creek, a permanent stream shaded with a dense woodland of live oaks, cedar elms, post oaks, hackberries, and other trees. Several springs tumble out from underneath the limestone ledges lining the creek and feed it their cold, clear waters. From an area of the campground that is tucked into the creek bottom, a short trail leads to Rumbling Spring. Another short, very well-constructed nature trail follows the creek from the campground to the picnic area, a shady walk on a hot summer day. On cooler days, a longer trail can be taken that winds through the open upland area of the park.

The creek is not the only surprise for park visitors; behind the headquarters building, a former quarry has filled with water, providing opportunities for fishing. Anglers catch black bass, perch, and catfish from the small lake. Visitors may initially go to the park simply to see the fort, but other lesser-known attractions encourage longer stays.

VISITOR INFORMATION

396 acres. Open all year. Hot in summer. Small number of campsites with partial hookups and showers. Primitive camping area. Screened shelters. Historic structures and interpretive center, hiking and nature trails, fishing, picnicking. Full visitor services available in Jacksboro. For information: Fort Richardson State Historical Park, P.O. Box 4, Jacksboro, TX 76458, (940) 567-3506.

Lake Arrowhead State Park

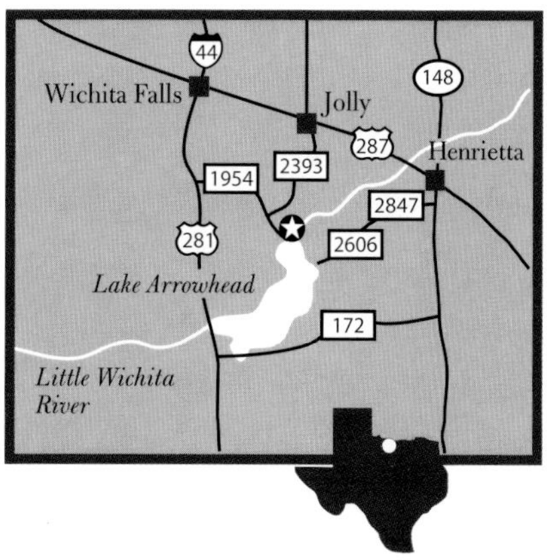

In the vast, flat prairies near Wichita Falls lies Lake Arrowhead, a magnet for local boaters and anglers. The reservoir, which was built in 1965 by damming the Little Wichita River, provides one of Wichita Falls' water supplies. The 3-mile-long earth-fill dam created a reservoir with a surface area of about 16,500 acres and a shoreline length of 106 miles. Because the terrain is relatively flat, the lake is shallow. Interestingly, a number of steel oil derricks dot parts of the lake surface, indicating petroleum reservoirs that lie deep under the lake waters.

The area is part of the Rolling Plains, a vast area that stretches from the eastern part of the Texas Panhandle to east of Wichita Falls. The gently rolling terrain is open prairie, except along creeks and rivers, where additional moisture allows woodlands to grow. Past grazing practices have allowed mesquite and other brushy plants to invade much of the rich grasslands. At the state park, grasses and mesquite are probably the most common plants.

Within the park, small animals, including raccoons, skunks, and prairie dogs, are the most commonly seen forms of wildlife. Waterfowl and wading birds frequent the lake, while crappie, catfish, bass, and perch swim through its waters. Fishing piers, a boat ramp, and a lengthy shoreline give anglers plenty of lake access. The waters around the oil derricks seem to favor good populations of fish and are popular fishing sites on the lake. Fishing and water sports, such as waterskiing, attract many people every year to Lake Arrowhead State Park.

VISITOR INFORMATION

524 acres. Open all year. Hot in summer. Moderate number of campsites with partial hookups and showers. Boating, waterskiing, fishing piers, boat ramps, picnicking, and hiking, nature, and equestrian trails. Seasonal park store and paddleboat rental. Full visitor services available in Wichita Falls. For information: Lake Arrowhead State Park, 229 Park Road 63, Wichita Falls, TX 76310, (940) 528-2211.

Picnic area at Lake Arrowhead

Lake Brownwood State Park

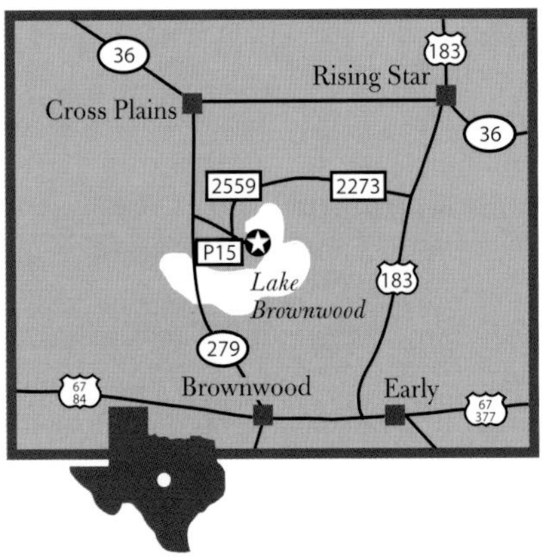

Popular Lake Brownwood State Park has drawn visitors to the North Texas area ever since it was developed in the 1930s. The park lies on the shore of Lake Brownwood, an 8,000-acre lake that was created when a dam was built at the confluence of Pecan Bayou and Jim Ned Creek. It was built in 1932 by the Civilian Conservation Corps (CCC), whose workers also built most of the basic facilities of the state park, including roads, cabins, and the notable recreation hall, constructed of locally quarried stone.

The park lies in an area of mixed habitats. Limestone bedrock in parts of the park encourages the growth of Hill Country species such as live oak and Ashe juniper. Cedar elms and post oaks are more reminiscent of the Cross Timbers country to the northeast, while mesquite trees are common in the drier Rolling Plains of the northwest.

The recreation hall is situated on top of a hill in the middle of the park; its rooftop observation deck gives a good view of the park, lake, and surrounding rolling hills. Other good viewpoints lie along the park hiking trail, especially at its terminus on Council Bluff, a high ridge overlooking the lake.

Lake Brownwood sunset

The park has many attractions for visitors. A fishing pier and boat ramp provide easy lake access for boaters, waterskiers, and anglers; the roads and trails attract hikers and cyclists; and historians are interested in the recreation hall, stone pavilions, and other buildings constructed by the CCC.

In the past, Comanches and earlier Indian groups frequented the banks of Pecan Bayou and Jim Ned Creek, drawn by water and abundant game. Settlers farmed the floodplains and ranched the hills around the lake. Today, people come to Lake Brownwood State Park to relax and escape the hectic pace of modern life.

VISITOR INFORMATION

538 acres. Open all year. Hot in summer. Large number of campsites with partial or full hookups and showers. Cabins and screened shelters. Hiking and nature trails, picnicking, fishing pier, boat ramp, waterskiing. Park store. Full visitor services available in Brownwood. For information: Lake Brownwood State Park, RR 5, Box 160, Brownwood, TX 76801, (915) 784-5223.

TOP:
Lake Brownwood
RIGHT:
Lake Colorado City shoreline

Lake Colorado City State Park

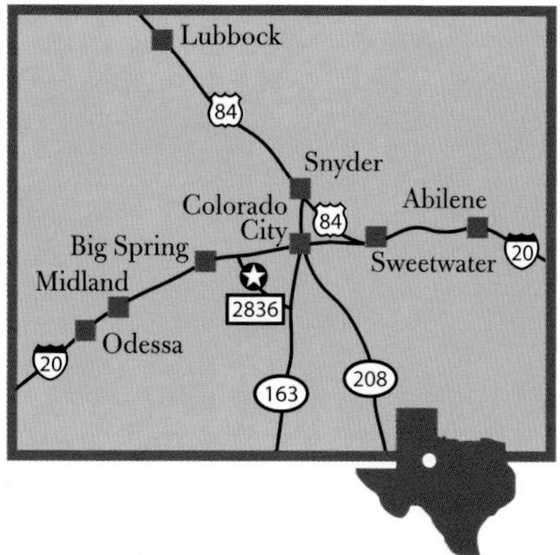

Lake Colorado City State Park lies on the southwest shore of Lake Colorado City, a small 1,600-acre lake built on Morgan Creek, a tributary of the Colorado River. The dam is just upstream of the confluence of the river and Morgan Creek. The lake was created in 1949 to supply cooling water to a Texas Electric Service Company power plant. The plant, fueled with natural gas produced from oil and gas fields in the area, is the largest in West Texas.

The lake lies in the slightly rolling plains of west central Texas. The climate is relatively dry, so the plains are generally treeless except along watercourses. Grasses and shrubs, particularly mesquite and juniper, cover the park uplands. Prickly pear and other cacti are also quite common.

The lake, together with the channels of blue water that wind upstream along Morgan Creek and several smaller tributaries, provides a welcome contrast to the surrounding plains. Waterskiers zip across the lake while small sailboats glide through the water, pushed by frequent West Texas breezes. Anglers pursue bass, redfish, and catfish from the rocky shoreline, from boats, and from park fishing piers.

Boaters

Because of the power plant, lake water stays warmer than normal for this area of the country. The warmer water extends the season for swimming and waterskiing, and also provides a longer growing and feeding season for fish.

The town for which the lake is named originated as a construction camp for the Texas and Pacific Railroad in 1880, although it had been a Texas Ranger camp earlier. After the railroad was completed, the town developed as a supply and shipping center for local farms and ranches. Later, after oil and gas were discovered in the area, the petroleum industry became the most important element of the local economy. Creation of the lake not only provided water for the power plant and the town, it also created recreational opportunities still enjoyed today at Lake Colorado City State Park.

VISITOR INFORMATION

500 acres. Open all year. Hot in summer. Large number of developed campsites with partial hookups and showers. Boating, boat ramp, waterskiing, picnicking, swimming, fishing piers. Full visitor services available in Colorado City. For information: Lake Colorado City State Park, 4582 FM 2836, Colorado City, TX 79512, (915) 728-3931.

Fishermen

Lake Rita Blanca State Park

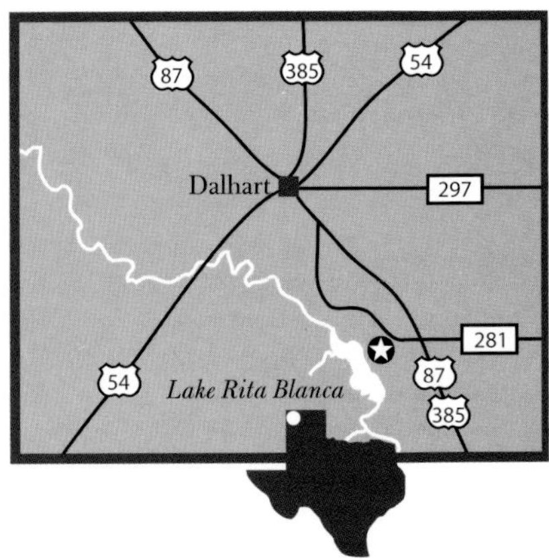

Located near Dalhart, Lake Rita Blanca State Park is the northernmost state park in Texas and, at an altitude of almost 4,000 feet, is exceeded in elevation by only a few parks in West Texas. It lies on the High Plains, a very flat part of the state that occupies much of the Panhandle. The level surface of the plains was created by sediment eroded off the Rocky Mountains to the west, in New Mexico and Colorado, and deposited in broad sheets. The High Plains, including the state park, is blanketed by a grassland dominated by blue grama and buffalo grass. Except along watercourses and broken terrain, trees are rare.

Lake Rita Blanca itself is a shallow, 150-acre body of water within the park. It was created by damming the small, meandering Rita Blanca Creek, the headwaters of which lie mostly to the northwest in New Mexico. Although the lake is small, every year thousands of ducks and geese winter there, making it one of the most important wintering sites in the Texas Panhandle on the bird-migration route known as the Central Flyway. From 40,000 to as many as 100,000 geese alone sometimes come to the lake. In spring and summer, a large number of migratory neotropical birds frequent the park. Also found at Lake Rita Blanca are mule deer, bald eagles, and red and gray foxes.

The park is set up for day use only and offers 9 miles of trails for hiking, mountain-biking, and equestrian use. Birding is another popular activity, especially when the winter waterfowl are in residence.

VISITOR INFORMATION

1,525 acres. Open all year. Day use only. Hiking, mountain-biking, and equestrian trails. Full visitor services available in Dalhart. For information: Lake Rita Blanca State Park, c/o Palo Duro Canyon State Park, Route 2, Box 285, Canyon, TX 79015, (806) 488-2227.

Lubbock Lake Landmark State Historical Park

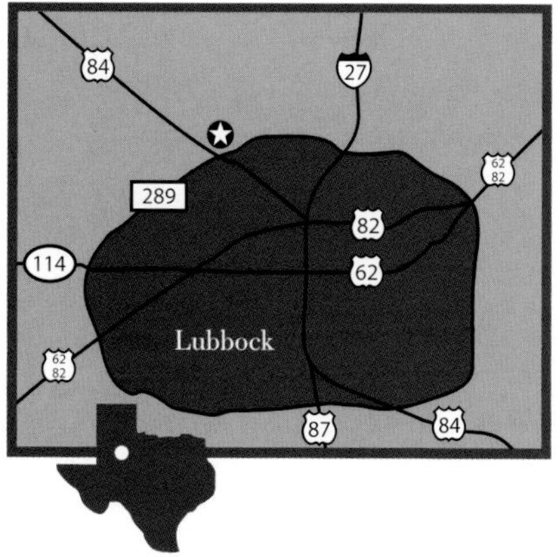

Lubbock Lake Landmark is an important archeological site, owing to its continuous human occupation for the last 12,000 years. No other known site in North America contains remnants of all the cultures known to have existed on the Southern Plains. Relics have been unearthed here that span the entire period from the nomadic hunters of the last ice age to the pioneers who settled the Lubbock area.

The site lies on a looping bend of Yellowhouse Draw, an upstream tributary of the Brazos River on the northwest side of Lubbock. Water has been available here for thousands of years and has attracted both animals and their human hunters. After local crop irrigation using wells lowered the water table in the 1930s, the site was dredged to rejuvenate some old springs. The digging exposed the bones of extinct animals and the remains of ancient human cultures. Excavations and research have been conducted at the site ever since.

The sediment deposits contain many layers denoting different ages, with the oldest on the bottom and newer layers added on top. Within these layers, scientists have found evidence of many different cultures and periods of occupation. Research indicates that the Lubbock area was once much wetter and cooler than it is today. Many animals that are now extinct, such as the mammoth and a type of camel, once roamed the plains and were hunted by early human groups. As the climate became drier and some creatures became extinct, the early peoples were forced to adapt.

The park is operated in partnership with Texas Tech University. Excavation continues at the park under the supervision of university

Museum exhibit at Lubbock Lake

archeologists who have studied animal remains and human artifacts from Lubbock Lake for years. Based on their findings, an interpretive center, filled with a series of fascinating dioramas and exhibits, details the history of Native American occupation of this unique site on the High Plains.

VISITOR INFORMATION

366 acres. Open all year, Tuesday through Sunday. Day use only. Large interpretive center with museum exhibits, hiking and interpretive trails through the site, picnicking. Full visitor services available in Lubbock. For information: Lubbock Lake Landmark State Historical Park, 2202 Landmark Lane, Lubbock, TX 79415, (806) 765-0737.

TOP:
Plains rainbows
LEFT:
Prehistoric bear

Palo Duro Canyon State Park

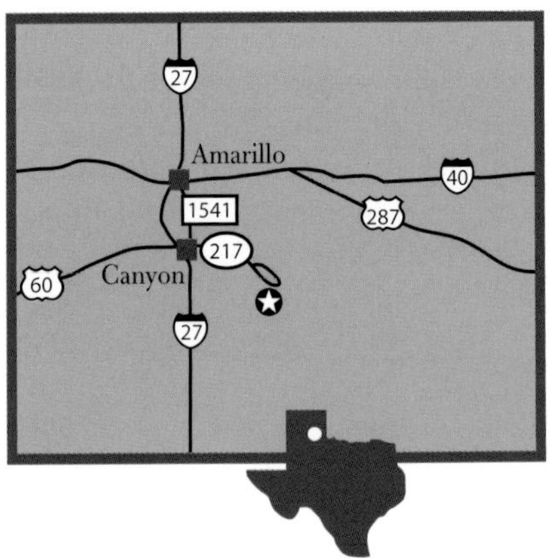

As you cross the High Plains south of Amarillo on the way to Palo Duro Canyon, the flat, treeless country inspires only drowsiness. The horizon stretches to infinity, broken only by occasional windmills and ranches. The hot air shimmers and mirages seem to form pools of water on the pavement. Before you enter the park, a small canyon on the right side of the road might cause a raised eyebrow or two, but it only foreshadows what lies ahead. Boredom vanishes after you enter the park and drive to the first overlook on the rim of the canyon.

In startling contrast to the surrounding country, a massive 800-foot-deep abyss appears below, the flat plains dropping away abruptly. Cliffs of red, yellow, and purple color the scene. Scrubby forests of gnarled junipers soften the slopes and add greenery. At the bottom, a tiny creek flows downstream, its waters nourishing a narrow ribbon of lush cottonwoods.

Without a doubt, Palo Duro Canyon is one of the most spectacular sights in the Panhandle and one of the premier state parks in Texas. At one time it was even considered by the federal government for national-park status. The common juniper trees gave the canyon its name: *palo duro* means "hard wood" in Spanish.

Visitors to the canyon are sometimes amazed that the tiny creek—the

little Prairie Dog Town Fork of the Red River—could have carved the deep, 60-mile-long canyon. However, in the past, the area received more rainfall, helping erosion to proceed more quickly. Anyone who has witnessed one of the canyon's notorious floods will not doubt the erosive power of the Prairie Dog Town Fork when filled with torrents of rushing water.

The colorful red rocks through which the creek has cut its canyon belong to several different geologic periods. The oldest rocks of the canyon, the bright red shales, clays, and sandstones of the Permian period, line the bottom and lower slopes of the canyon. These soft rocks, called the Quartermaster Formation, were formed about 250 million years ago in shallow waters on the edge of ancient seas. Slightly newer Triassic shales and sandstones, called the Trujillo and Tecovas, lie on top of the Permian rocks, and are distinguished by their multiple colors, often shades of yellow, pink, and lavender. The Trujillo, the top Triassic layer, is a hard sandstone that resists erosion better than the other rocks, so it forms cliffs, as well as capstones on such formations as the Lighthouse, the 75-foot-tall rock pinnacle that has become the canyon's trademark.

The Lighthouse

Above the Trujillo lies the Ogallala Formation, a mix of sandstone, siltstone, conglomerate, and caliche that is between 2 and 10 million years old. The Ogallala is very porous and permeable and is an important aquifer for the Panhandle. Fossils of many extinct species of mammals have been found in the formation. There is a gap in time of more than 200 million years between the Trujillo and the Ogallala layers. Either the intervening rocks eroded away or they never existed.

The flat surface of the High Plains resulted when sediment eroded from the uplifted Rocky Mountains to the west was carried east and deposited in sheets across the plains. With time,

the Pecos River eroded northward and "captured" mountain streams that had been flowing eastward across the plains. The Pecos ultimately cut a broad valley and the High Plains were left as a large, flat, eastward tilting plateau. The eastern edges of this plateau have retreated westward over time as streams flowing toward the Gulf of Mexico eroded headward, leaving today's canyon-riddled escarpment. Only the Canadian River has managed to cut entirely across the High Plains in Texas, but eventually the Prairie Dog Town Fork and other watercourses will erode westward and eventually cut canyons all the way through the plains.

Palo Duro Canyon is more than just a geologic wonder. Its broken country harbors a mix of eastern and western plant and animal species, including montane trees such as the Rocky Mountain juniper, that were left here after the Pleistocene ended and the climate warmed and dried. The Palo Duro mouse lives in the Red River canyonlands and nowhere else. Many different species of birds have been sighted here—almost 200 so far. Mule deer compete for browse with the introduced African aoudad, and before they were exterminated, wolves and bears haunted the canyon country.

Humans lived in the area as much as 12,000 years ago, hunting now-extinct ice-age animals such as the giant bison and the Jefferson's mammoth. Succeeding groups came and went, ending with the arrival of the Comanches in the eighteenth century. For many years, Palo Duro Canyon and the surrounding plains were the Comanches' domain, from which they ventured forth to hunt buffalo and raid other Indian tribes, as well as Mexicans and Anglos. The last major Indian battle in Texas, the Battle of Palo Duro Canyon, brought the Comanches' reign to a close in 1874.

Francisco Vásquez de Coronado was probably the first European to see the canyon when he made his epic journey through the Southwest and across the High Plains in 1541. Although hunting and trading parties ventured occasionally onto the plains, especially from New Mexico, the canyon area was not settled until after the Comanches were defeated. Charles Goodnight established the

first large cattle ranch in the area and was soon followed by others. Ranching and farming are still the predominant land uses in the area today.

The park offers much to visitors in addition to spectacular scenery. During the summer, a large cast presents the elaborate musical drama *Texas*. The outdoor performance has been very successful since it started playing in 1966, and has drawn more than 2 million visitors.

A mule-drawn wagon ride at the Old West Stables provides a unique way to visit part of the canyon. Horses can be rented in season to see another section of the park. A relatively easy hiking and mountain-bike trail leads to the spectacular Lighthouse pinnacle. The scenic loop drive also provides an excellent introduction to Palo Duro Canyon, one of the largest and most famous state parks in Texas.

TOP:
Canyon view from rim
LEFT:
The red Quartermaster Formation

VISITOR INFORMATION

16,402 acres. Open all year. Hot in summer during the day, pleasant at night; can be quite cold and occasionally snowy in winter. Heed any park warnings on flooding of creek; some serious floods do occur. *Texas* is performed nightly in summer, except on Sundays; call for exact dates, times, and prices. Relatively large number of campsites with partial hookups and showers, scattered in several locations. Primitive equestrian camp area. Horse rentals, miniature railroad, interpretive museum, picnicking, hiking, mountain-biking, and equestrian trails. Park store and snack bar. Full visitor services available in Canyon and Amarillo. For information: Palo Duro Canyon State Park, 11450 Park Road 5, Canyon, TX 79015, (806) 488-2227.

Possum Kingdom State Park

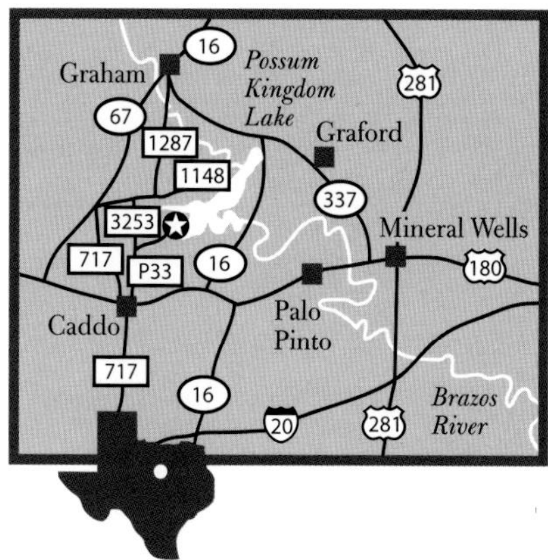

Congress authorized the building of Morris Sheppard Dam on the Brazos River after World War II. At the same time, it gave the large 20,000-acre reservoir that was backed up by the dam the name "Possum Kingdom Lake," because its legislation stated that the area was a "veritable paradise for opossums." The opossums still roam the hills of Possum Kingdom State Park, but today they are joined by thousands of people who come to enjoy the clear waters of the lake.

Unlike many Texas lakes, Possum Kingdom winds like a snake, following the course of the meandering Brazos River. Because of its long, sinuous course, it has more than 300 miles of shoreline. It provides excellent opportunities for boating, swimming, and waterskiing, and the clear waters attract local scuba divers. Anglers test their skill pursuing catfish, bass, crappie, and perch. The rocky shoreline provides a good habitat for black bass, which need such sites for spawning. Striped bass, the largest member of the bass family, is also a popular catch in the lake. Stripers normally live in salt water, but move up rivers and streams to spawn in fresh water. By accident, it was discovered that they could survive year round in fresh water, and as a result they have been stocked in many Texas lakes.

Possum Kingdom State Park is a great access point to Possum Kingdom

Lake and offers a relaxing escape from the nearby cities of Fort Worth, Wichita Falls, and Abilene. It lies on the west side of the lake on the edge of a relatively hilly area of North Texas known as the Palo Pinto Mountains. The rocks that make up the mountains, the canyons of the Brazos River, and the rocky lakeshore are limestones, shales, and sandstones. The most prominent is the Winchell Limestone, the white rock that makes up the towering cliffs at the dam and lower parts of the lake. The rocks were formed about 280 million years ago during the Pennsylvanian period, when an ancient sea filled the Permian Basin to the west. Rich deposits of petroleum, coal, and clay were created during this time, and many are still produced in the area today.

The park lies on the western edge of the Cross Timbers area, known for its thick woods of stunted Ashe juniper, cedar elm, oaks, and mesquite, interspersed with strips of prairie. Here at the drier, western side of the region, Ashe junipers seem to dominate. White-tailed deer and small mammals such as rabbits, raccoons, and, of course, opossums are common. Hell's Gate, a pair of tall cliffs that frame a narrow spot on the lake, hosts a noisy colony of cliff swallows.

VISITOR INFORMATION

1,529 acres. Hot in summer. Large number of campsites with partial hookups and showers. Cabins—very popular; reserve in advance. Boating, waterskiing, picnicking, swimming, boat ramp, lighted fishing pier, longhorn herd. Seasonal park store, boat and pop-up trailer rental. Full visitor services available in Breckenridge and Graham. For information: Possum Kingdom State Park, P.O. Box 70, Caddo, TX 76429, (940) 549-1803.

TOP:
Possum Kingdom Lake
BOTTOM:
Waterskier

San Angelo State Park

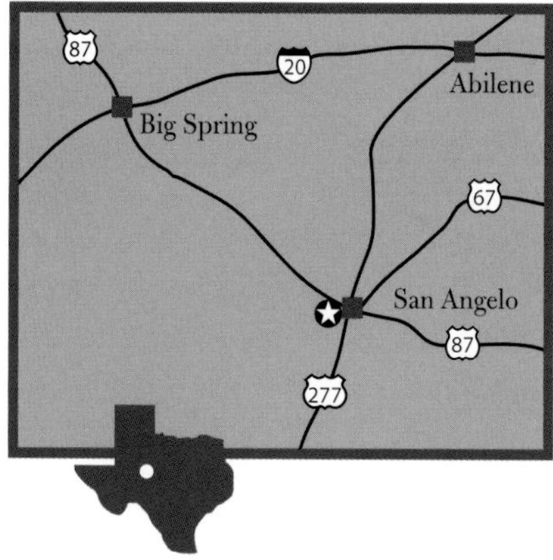

San Angelo State Park lies on the shores of O. C. Fisher Reservoir, just west of the city of San Angelo. The 5,440-acre lake was built by the U.S. Army Corps of Engineers in the 1950s by damming the north fork of the Concho River. The reservoir provides a means of flood control and water storage, as well as recreational opportunities.

The O. C. Fisher Reservoir lies just upstream from the North Concho River's confluence with the Middle and South Concho River forks. The river, ultimately a tributary of the Colorado River, drains a large area of country in a broad arc around San Angelo, from northwest to west to south of the city. The river takes its name from the Spanish word for shell, because of the plentiful freshwater mussels found in its waters. These mussels sometimes produce pearls prized for their iridescent colors, particularly purple.

The park contains a mix of habitats. It is located on the far western edge of the Hill Country, and has some of the plants and animals common to that part of the state. However, since the park is so far west, the climate is considerably drier there than it is in the Hill Country, and is greatly influenced by the deserts of the Trans-Pecos. The oaks, pecans, and cedar elms common in most of the Hill Country become scarce here and grow mostly only in moist bottomlands. Mesquite is probably the most common tree. The Rolling Plains and High Plains to the north also contribute some plant and animal species.

Various Indian groups once dominated the area. The Spaniards were the first Europeans to arrive as they attempted to extend their empire and convert the Indians to Christianity. Later, the area fell under the dominion, successively, of Mexico, the Republic of Texas, the Confederacy, and the United States. The first settlers in the area sustained themselves with farming and ranching. Fort Concho was established in 1867 to protect western travelers and settlers. It was decommissioned in 1889, but many of the original buildings still stand.

Today the park offers plenty of recreational opportunities. The many lake activities include bass and catfish fishing, swimming, and boating. The park was originally operated by the U.S. Army Corps of Engineers, but was taken over in 1995 by the Texas Parks and Wildlife Department. Under the new management, the development of more facilities is planned.

VISITOR INFORMATION

7,063 acres. Open all year. Hot in summer. Campground with partial hookups and showers. Fishing platform, swimming, waterskiing, boating. Over 60 miles of trails for hiking, biking, and horseback riding. Full visitor services available in San Angelo. For information: San Angelo State Park, 3900 Mercedes, San Angelo, TX 76901, (915) 949-4757 or (915) 947-2687; *Red Arroyo Campground:* (915) 949-8935; *Bald Eagle Creek Campground:* (915) 653-5551.

Sunrise over Lake O. C. Fisher

Pineywoods

A thick woodland of pines and hardwoods blankets the East Texas region known as the Pineywoods. Plentiful rain, usually 50 inches or more per year, fuels lush forest growth and creates a humid climate. In the southern part of the region, near Beaumont, the land is very flat and low lying. This area of southeastern Texas is dominated by the Big Thicket, a large ecological region that once covered 3.5 million acres but that is now reduced to less than 300,000 acres. The Big Thicket contains a variety of habitats, from cypress sloughs to grassy prairies to a climax forest of towering magnolias, beeches, and loblolly pines. The thicket is also the meeting place for an interesting mix of plants and animals from the east and west; yuccas, prickly pears, and roadrunners thrive only a few hundred feet from southern orchids and water tupelos. Much of the low-lying Big Thicket is wetland, with cypress sloughs, sluggish rivers, and palmetto flats. Two state parks, Village Creek and Martin Dies, Jr., lie in or on the edge of the Big Thicket.

To the north of the Big Thicket, the land begins to roll with gentle hills. Deep woods of oaks, sweet gums, longleaf and loblolly pines, hickories, and other trees stretch north to the Red River, interrupted by cleared fields and urban areas. Wildlife is plentiful, from white-tailed deer and wild turkeys to alligators. Black bears and red wolves once roamed much of East Texas, too, but they are gone now.

Lakes attract many people to the state parks in the Pineywoods region. Some of the parks, such as Huntsville and Tyler, have small no-wake lakes that are perfect for canoes and paddleboats. Quite a few others, including Lake Livingston and Lake Bob Sandlin, offer vast expanses of open water that are ideal for sailing and waterskiing. All of the lakes, whatever their size, attract anglers hoping to catch largemouth bass, stripers, crappie, catfish, and other species.

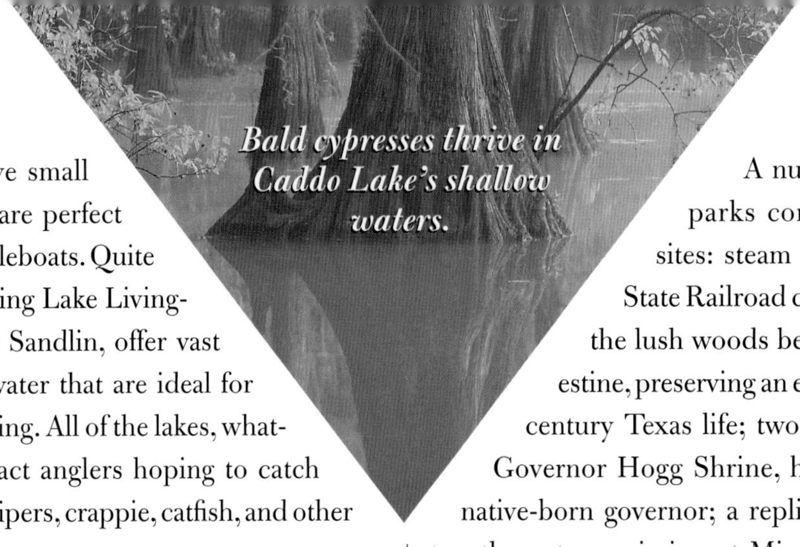

Bald cypresses thrive in Caddo Lake's shallow waters.

Caddo Lake State Park lies on the upper end of a particularly unique lake. Caddo Lake is the only significant lake in Texas that was formed naturally, although a dam now maintains the water level. A large logjam on the Red River downstream in Louisiana is thought to have created the lake in about 1800. The jam, which stretched for 100 miles and was as much as 25 feet high, is believed to have backed up enough water into Big Cypress Bayou to create Caddo Lake and a navigable waterway to Jefferson upstream of the lake. Steamboats plied the lake's waters until 1874, when the U.S. Army Corps of Engineers blew the logjam apart and lowered lake levels. Today, cypresses cloaked with Spanish moss grow from the lake, creating a mysterious, primeval atmosphere. Anglers find the most diverse fishing in Texas here, with 71 different species.

A number of Pineywoods parks commemorate historic sites: steam engines of the Texas State Railroad chug 25 miles through the lush woods between Rusk and Palestine, preserving an element of turn-of-the-century Texas life; two sites, Jim Hogg and Governor Hogg Shrine, honor the state's first native-born governor; a replica of an early seventeenth-century mission at Mission Tejas marks the unsuccessful Spanish effort to colonize East Texas; Camp Ford marks the site of a Civil War Confederate prisoner-of-war camp; and Caddo Indians built three ceremonial mounds at Caddoan Mounds, the most southeasterly site of the Mound Builder culture of the eastern United States.

The Pineywoods parks offer more than lake recreation and historic sites, however. Hiking and mountain-biking trails wind through the woods of many parks; most of them provide campgrounds and picnic areas; canoeing is possible on quiet creeks and cypress sloughs; and most years there is the chance to see good fall color dotting the woods of Daingerfield and cypresses that have turned burnt orange at Caddo Lake. For many reasons, then, the East Texas parks are always popular.

Pineywoods

1 Atlanta State Park
2 Caddoan Mounds State Historical Park
3 Caddo Lake State Park
4 Camp Ford State Historical Park
5 Daingerfield State Park
6 Davis Hill State Park
7 Fort Boggy State Park
8 Governor Hogg Shrine State Historical Park
9 Huntsville State Park
10 Jim Hogg State Historical Park
11 Lake Bob Sandlin State Park
12 Lake Livingston State Park
13 Martin Creek Lake State Park
14 Martin Dies, Jr. State Park
15 Mission Tejas State Historical Park
16 Starr Family State Historical Park
17 Texas State Railroad State Historical Park and Rusk/Palestine State Park
18 Tyler State Park
19 Village Creek State Park

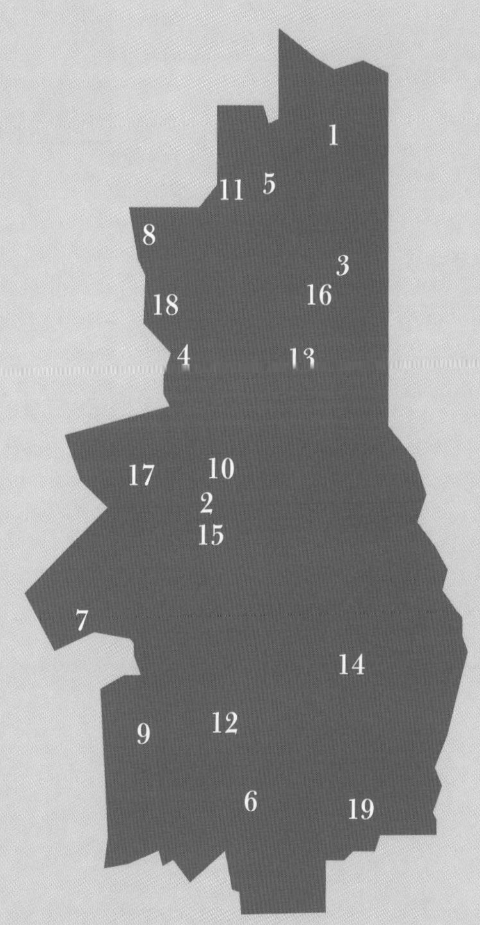

Atlanta State Park

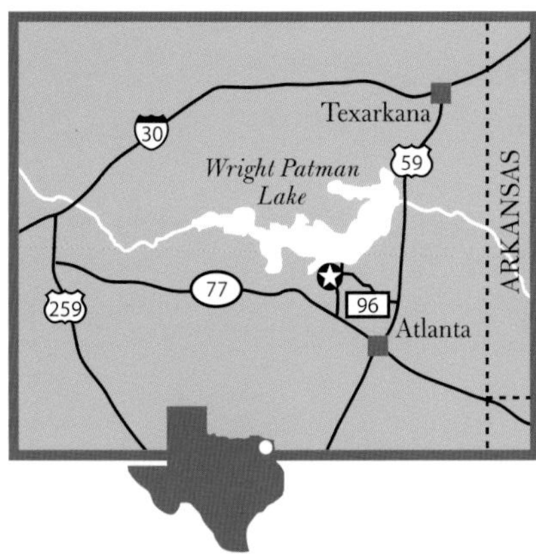

Atlanta State Park lies on the shores of Wright Patman Lake in far northeastern Texas. Hills wooded with thick stands of second-growth pines, oaks, and sweet gums tumble down to the sandy lakeshore. In fall, sweet gums, sumac, and other deciduous trees and shrubs add splashes of scarlet and gold to the dense forest.

Atlanta State Park was named for the nearby town of Atlanta, the principal city and commercial center of Cass County. In turn, Atlanta was named for the capital of Georgia, from where some of its earliest settlers had come. The town was established when the Texas and Pacific Railroad was built through the area in 1872. Farming and lumbering were the most important early economic activities, and were followed later by oil and gas production. Before Anglo settlers arrived in the area now comprising the state park, Caddo Indians, the most culturally advanced tribe in Texas, lived and farmed in northeastern Texas.

Wright Patman Lake is the most popular attraction of the state park. The U.S. Army Corps of Engineers built the 20,300-acre reservoir by damming the Sulphur River. The lake is popular for fishing, sailing, waterskiing, boating, and swimming. Although the reservoir is the main draw at Atlanta State Park, several miles of hiking and nature trails wind through the thick forest and add another recreational activity to Texas' most northeastern state park.

VISITOR INFORMATION

1,475 acres. Open all year. Hot and humid in summer. Campground with partial and full hookups and showers. Picnicking, hiking and nature trails, fishing, waterskiing, boat ramp. Full visitor services available in Atlanta and Texarkana. For information: Atlanta State Park, Route 1, Box 116, Atlanta, TX 75551, (903) 796-6476.

ABOVE:
Chameleon
LEFT:
Wright Patman Lake

Caddoan Mounds State Historical Park

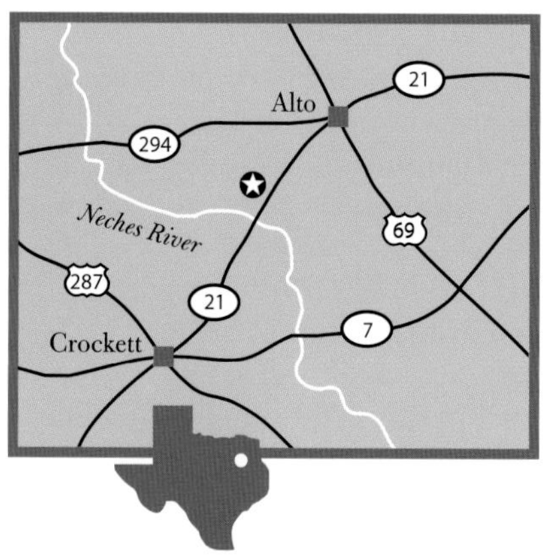

Over the course of more than 2,500 years, from about 1000 B.C. to A.D. 1500, the Mound Builder culture spread across the woodlands of eastern North America. In approximately A.D. 800, the Early Caddos, the westernmost group of Mound Builders, selected a site for a village and ceremonial center above the Neches River. The site was a frontier location for the Early Caddos, whose culture was centered farther east in the area around the Great Bend of the Red River in southwestern Arkansas. The village at what is now Caddoan Mounds State Historical Park proved to be the most southwesterly outpost of the Mound Builder culture.

The site was probably selected because it had good soil for agriculture, was level, had a supply of water in the nearby Neches River, and had abundant natural food sources in the mix of bottomland hardwoods and upland pine forests. Using wooden frames and bundles of cane for thatch, these early settlers built round, conical homes in the village area around the earthen mounds that give their culture its name.

Archeologists believe that the mounds were built as temple sites, for burials of members of the ruling class, and for religious ceremonies. Through careful excavation of the mounds and village sites, archeologists have learned much about the Early Caddos. They appear to have had an elite ruling class whose members lived in and around the temple mounds and had greater power and material wealth than the average villagers. The common people lived in outer areas of the village and in outlying farming settlements.

Excavations of the burial mound at this site uncovered remains of 14 individuals, from which archeologists infer that in total, about 90 people were interred in the mound. Group burials suggest that servants and/or family members were sacrificed upon the death of an important member of the ruling class.

At its peak at about A.D. 1100, the culture of the Early Caddos was the most highly developed prehistoric culture known in Texas, with a trade network that extended from central Texas to beyond the Mississippi River—artifacts found include Gulf Coast sea shells and copper from the Great Lakes region. The people of this culture were prosperous enough and had a strong enough social organization to devote massive amounts of labor to building the large mounds.

The Early Caddos abruptly abandoned the village in the thirteenth century, probably after the ruling class lost its influence and power. War does not appear to have played a role in the abandonment. The Late Caddo culture remained in the area until Europeans arrived and for some time thereafter, but it never reached the same level of material wealth and sophistication that the earlier culture had achieved.

Today, visitors can walk to the mounds along a short interpretive trail. The visitor center has exhibits on the Caddo culture and artifacts belonging to it.

Reconstructed Caddo hut before it was burned.

VISITOR INFORMATION

94 acres. Open all year, Thursday through Monday 9 A.M.–4 P.M. Day use only. Museum with exhibits and audio-visual program, short interpretive trail through mounds and village site. Limited visitor services available in Alto; full services in Rusk and Crockett. For information: Caddoan Mounds State Historical Park, Route 2, Box 85C, Alto, TX 75925, (936) 858-3218.

Caddo Lake State Park

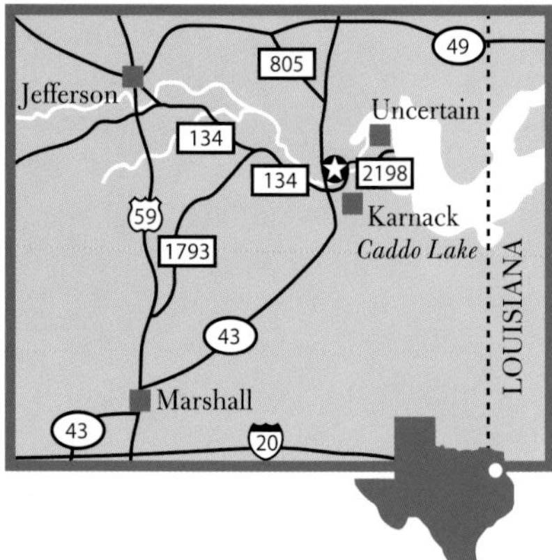

According to Caddo Indian legend, the large, mysterious body of water known as Caddo Lake had a violent beginning. After having a vision of impending disaster, a Caddo chief quickly moved his people to higher ground. The earth trembled and shook, rains fell, the ground sank, and floods drowned the tribe's former homeland. Caddo Lake was born.

The legend of Caddo Lake may be tied to the great New Madrid (Missouri) earthquake of 1811 that shook the United States from Texas to Illinois. Although the lake could have been created as a result of the earth subsiding and water filling the sunken area, researchers believe that it actually formed as a result of a huge logjam on the Red River.

Sometime around 1800, the logjam, called the Great Raft, is thought to have caused water to back up into Big Cypress Bayou and create the lake. The enormous logjam stretched more than 100 miles, from Natchitoches, Louisiana to north of Shreveport. Masses of trees piled 25 feet high and loosely cemented with roots, dirt, moss, and trees that were still growing blocked the river's flow. Pools of still water lay between sections of the jam. Some water flowed through the Great Raft, but most bypassed it on the Texas side, creating lakes and swamps. As the logjam grew upstream, it is thought to have blocked Big Cypress Bayou and formed Caddo Lake, the site of the present-day state park that bears its name.

After the Louisiana Purchase of 1803, the United States and Spain disputed their mutual boundary in the Caddo Lake area. In 1806, the countries agreed to declare the area neutral ground, and to ban settlement there. Instead, the unpoliced region became a no-man's-land and attracted all manner of outlaws and renegades. The area remained lawless and disputed after Mexico gained its independence from Spain in 1821. Nor did Texas's independence bring peace to Caddo Lake. From 1840 to 1844, a virtual civil war raged

RIGHT:
Bald cypresses
BELOW:
Lake canoeists

between two local factions, the Regulators and the Moderators.

The Regulator faction was a vigilante group organized to curtail lawlessness, but its members committed so many crimes themselves that an opposing group, the so-called Moderators, formed to curb the excesses. No one could remain neutral; all were forced to join one group or the other. At times, as many as a hundred men fought in pitched battles. Texas historian Henderson Yoakum wrote that the area was a place where "law was only a passive onlooker."

Finally, Texas president Sam Houston himself pleaded for the war to stop and sent in 500 militia. The fighting ceased at last and the Regulators and Moderators disbanded, although personal feuds persisted for years.

In the 1830s, Captain Henry Shreve of the U.S. Army Corps of Engineers cleared the Great Raft as far north as Shreve's Landing (later called Shreveport), but the jam reformed. However, steamboats found a way around the raft and through Caddo Lake and Big Cypress Bayou to Jefferson, which soon became Texas's second-largest port, with overland trade arteries branching out all over northeast Texas. Even though Jefferson was far inland, only Galveston boasted a greater volume of trade in the late nineteenth century.

Steamboats more than 200 feet long plied the shallow, hazardous waters of Caddo Lake, carrying as much as 4,500 cotton bales or 700 head of cattle in cargo. Roads leading into Jefferson were jammed with wagons. The town boomed and palatial houses sprouted along its streets. The first gas-powered street-lighting system in Texas was installed there and it boasted one of the world's first ice plants.

Jefferson's prosperity came to an abrupt end in 1874, when the U.S.

Army Corps of Engineers blasted loose the Great Raft, some say at the behest of railroad owners who wanted the trade that until then had been won by the steamboats. Water levels fell, steamboat traffic ended, and Shreveport took over as the premier Red River port. In about 1914, the army corps built a dam in Louisiana to maintain the lake's lower level.

The Regulators' bullets no longer fly and steamboat whistles no longer echo across Caddo Lake; today, people come to enjoy the lake's natural beauty. Its shallow waters support thick stands of bald cypress throughout, and water lilies, duckweed, lotus, and water hyacinths also thrive in the lake waters. When combined with the Spanish moss draping the cypresses, the plants give the lake an eerie, primeval, swamplike atmosphere.

The cypresses and other vegetation are so thick that much of the 32,700-acre lake is really more a maze of sloughs, bayous, and ponds than it is open-water lake. Because the twisting, intersecting channels confuse boaters, the Parks and Wildlife Department has marked a series of boat roads. Darkness or bad weather can make it especially easy to get lost; boaters who dawdle on the lake after the sun sets may get to spend the night on the water in the "Caddo Hotel," dreaming of Regulators and Moderators.

Caddo Lake State Park offers excellent access to the upper end of the lake. A boat ramp allows an easy put-in and a fishing pier provides the opportunity to fish without a boat. The lake offers the most diverse fishing in Texas, with 71 species of fish identified, including crappie, largemouth bass, and catfish. Here, too, the prehistoric-looking alligator gar grows to as much as eight feet in length.

The park was developed in the 1930s by the Civilian Conservation Corps (CCC). The entrance gates, cabins, pavilions, and other facilities were built of heavy timbers and stone by the corps. They are still in use today, a testament to the builders' craftsmanship.

Although most visitors come to the state park for lake-oriented activities, hiking and nature trails lead into backcountry areas of the park. Deep in woods of magnolia, oak, and loblolly pine, hikers can come across such finds as an old CCC-built pavilion hidden away in thick forest and almost forgotten. In fall, the bald cypresses of Caddo Lake turn burnt orange, providing visitors with a rare opportunity to see fall color in Texas. Caddo Lake has a long, sometimes violent history, but today makes a quiet escape from city life.

VISITOR INFORMATION

7,090 acres. Open all year. Hot and humid in summer. Busy on summer weekends. Small campground with both partial and full hookups and with showers. Screened shelters. Cabins are popular and are booked early on weekends. Picnic area, hiking and nature trails, small interpretive area in the headquarters building that introduces lake history and biology. Canoe rental in season. Limited visitor services available in Uncertain and Karnack; full services in Marshall and Jefferson. For information: Caddo Lake State Park, Route 2, Box 15, Karnack, TX 75661, (903) 679-3351.

OPPOSITE PAGE:
Fall color at Caddo Lake

Camp Ford State Historical Park

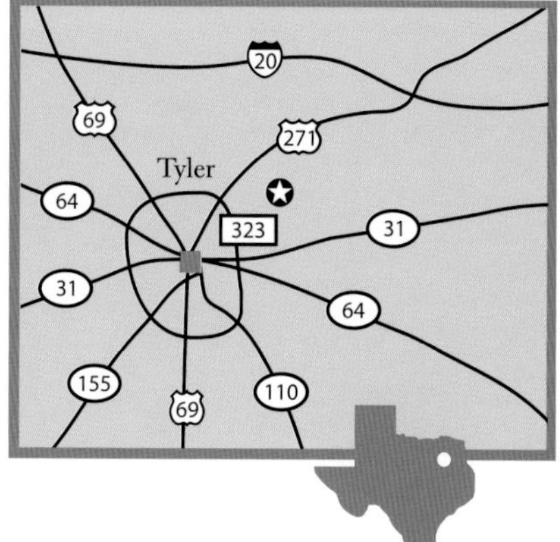

Camp Ford State Historical Park marks the site of a Civil War Confederate prisoner-of-war camp. From the summer of 1863 until its abandonment in the spring of 1865, it housed the largest number of Union prisoners west of the Mississippi River. The park contains the northern half of the once-stockaded area, although there are no visible signs of the camp today.

The park lies on the northeast side of Tyler in rolling country wooded with pines, oaks, and other trees characteristic of the Pineywoods. It is undeveloped and accessible only by special request. Once archeological studies have been conducted there, however, interpretive facilities may be built. This park is now managed by the Smith County Historical Society.

VISITOR INFORMATION

8.1 acres. Access by special request only. Undeveloped historical site. Full visitor services available in Tyler. For information: Smith County Historical Society, 125 South College Street, Tyler, TX 75702, (903) 592-3558.

Daingerfield State Park

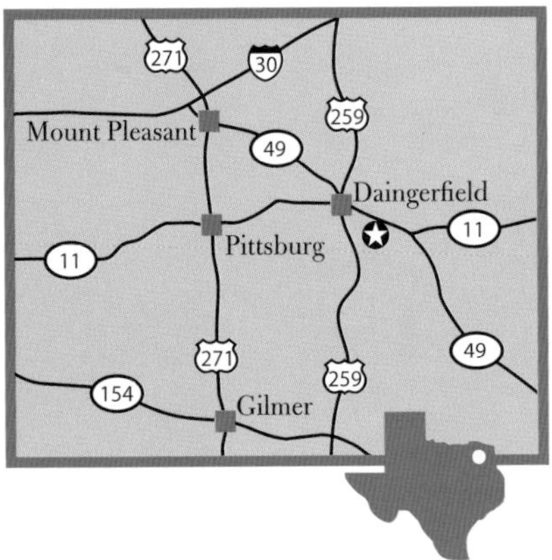

The dense mixed pine-and-hardwood forests of northeast Texas shelter popular Daingerfield State Park. In spring, masses of dogwoods adorn the forest with their white blooms, like some sort of strange late-season snowstorm. The forests resume their lush green appearance for the long days of summer, but in fall, as temperatures drop and days shorten, sweet gums and maples dot the park with splotches of orange and scarlet, an uncommon sight in most of Texas.

The park was founded in the 1930s and has been carefully protected since; as a result, the forest is mature, with towering loblolly pines, oaks, sweet gums, and other trees. The Civilian Conservation Corps (CCC) built many of the park facilities with its usual meticulous craftsmanship. Most of the buildings built by the corps, including the cabins, lodge, and bathhouse, are still in use today. The most obvious CCC project is the small lake around which the park is centered. The corps built an earthen dam to impound this spring-fed 80-acre reservoir.

Most park activities center around the small no-wake lake, especially in summer. In warm weather, people swim in its cool waters or lounge on the grassy banks. Canoes and small sailboats glide almost silently across it, while paddleboats churn through the water. Anglers pursue largemouth bass, crappie, chain pickerel, and both blue and channel catfish from the fishing pier, the shore, or small boats. Winter weather cools the water enough for even rainbow trout to be stocked periodically.

A 2.5-mile hiking trail circles the lake. One segment of the trail on the west side of the lake climbs to the top of a hill, of a respectable size for East Texas. Although from the top the view to the southwest is somewhat obscured by trees, it is quite expansive. On parts of the hike the rock and soil have a reddish color, having been stained by iron ore that, nearby, is rich enough to be mined and smelted for steel production.

If you can, take the hike on a quiet fall weekday. Autumn color dots the lakeshore beneath a deep blue sky. The cool, crisp air carries the distinctive, astringent smell of decaying foliage. Fallen leaves pile up on the trail, crunching noisily as you walk through them. A white-tailed deer takes flight, crashing through the brush, while a woodpecker hammers away at a tree trunk, searching for insects. Although you are still in Texas, you may feel like you have traveled to New England.

VISITOR INFORMATION

551 acres. Open all year. Hot and humid in summer, but mitigated by the lake. Very popular on weekends during warm part of year. Moderate number of sites in three campgrounds, with both partial and full hookups and showers. Three cabins and larger lodge. Picnic area, hiking trail, boating, fishing, swimming. Seasonal canoe, rowboat, and paddleboat rental. Concession sells camping supplies and food from April through October. Full visitor services available in Daingerfield and Mount Pleasant. For information: Daingerfield State Park, Route 3, Box 286-B, Daingerfield, TX 75638, (903) 645-2921.

TOP:
Lake shore
ABOVE:
Fall color

Davis Hill State Park

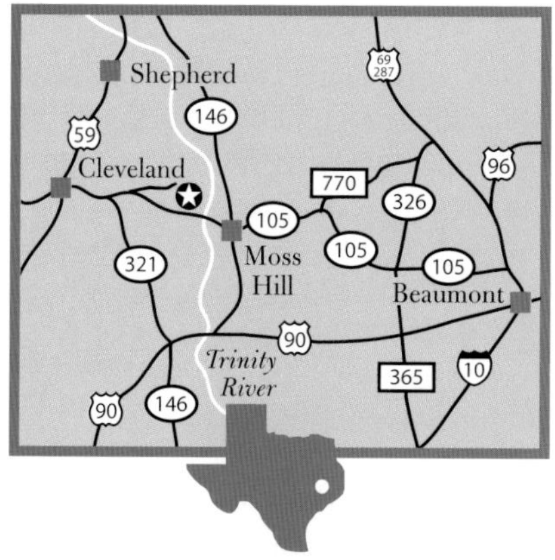

In the flat, low-lying coastal plain of Liberty County in Southeast Texas, Davis Hill stands out as quite a landmark. It was formed by an underground salt dome, deep in the earth, pushing up the overlying layers of sedimentary rock, creating a hill that rises 200 feet above the surrounding Trinity River floodplain. The hill weathered as it rose, but it is still the most prominent topographic landmark in this part of the state.

Erosion of the rising dome exposed different underlying rock and sediment layers and altered surface and subsurface water flows, resulting in a surprising variety of habitats. The plant and animal communities from three different habitats—the Pineywoods, the post-oak savannah, and the coastal prairies and marshes—are all represented here. Within a park measuring less than 3 square miles in area, cypress-tupelo swamps rub shoulders with sandy prairies, and deep, fern-lined ravines flow into flat, slow-moving bayous. So far, biologists have found 800 plant species, including 40 considered rare.

Fern gully

The hill is named for General James Davis, a veteran of the War of 1812. He came to Texas with his family from Alabama in 1834 and settled in the area. He was a friend of Sam Houston and served as field officer of the Army of the Republic, and was also a member of the 1848 Texas delegation to Washington. In about 1843, he began a plantation at Davis Hill which he called Lake Creek, a name stemming from the fact that Davis Bayou may have been dammed on the property to create a lake. It is said that Davis's house was a two-story structure on the east flank of the hill that looked out over cotton and corn fields to the Trinity River beyond. Apparently the plantation, which included a cotton gin, deteriorated soon after Davis's death in 1859 and the emancipation of the family slaves at the end of the Civil War. The hill has remained unoccupied since the departure of the Davis family at the end of the Civil War, leaving an archeological record consisting largely of just the antebellum cotton plantation.

The diverse habitats of Davis Hill have been preserved as a result of several other factors besides the absence of recent human residents. After the Spindletop well gushed vast quantities of oil from a salt-dome reservoir in 1901, oil companies drilled into and around salt domes all over the Gulf Coast, hoping to discover more large fields. A number of wells were drilled on the flanks of Davis Hill, but no large amounts of oil or gas were found. Because the hill was remote and steep, logging was prevented until a railroad spur was built into the area in 1909 or 1910. Logging was then done in sections, and apparently selectively, because there are still quite a few large, mature trees on the hill.

In the early 1980s, the state began to acquire the hill, because of its unique character, through donations and purchases. The state park includes most of the dome, as well as more than a mile of Trinity River floodplain. The park was not open as of late 1996, but at least limited access was anticipated as soon as the park is developed. Initial access will probably be in the form of guided tours or special public access days.

VISITOR INFORMATION

1,735 acres. The park was open only by special request as of late 1996; call for current status. For information: Davis Hill State Park, c/o Village Creek State Park, P.O. Box 8565, Lumberton, TX 77657, (409) 755-7322.

Fort Boggy State Park

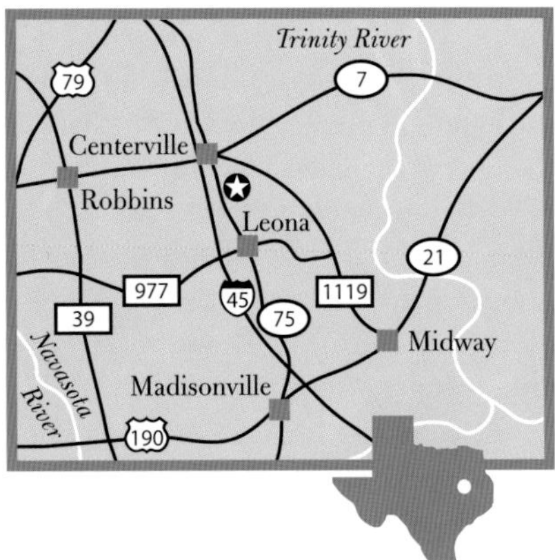

Fort Boggy State Park lies in East Texas on Boggy Creek near the small town of Centerville. The creation of the new park, which opened in 1985, was spurred by a land donation. It lies in an area of gently rolling, mostly wooded hills. The park is not quite far enough east to have pines, so the forest is dominated by oaks and other hardwoods.

Boggy Creek flows through the property, nurturing a large area of bottomland hardwoods. Beavers and their ponds are plentiful in the spring-fed creek, in addition to other park wildlife such as white-tailed deer, raccoons, opossums, and armadillos. The park is named for a fort that existed on or near the property in the nineteenth century.

Until it is developed, the park is open only for special tours. Plans for the park's future development, however, include standard park facilities such as campgrounds, picnic areas, fishing, and trails.

VISITOR INFORMATION

1,847 acres. Open only for reserved tours; call for information. No park facilities at present. Full visitor services available in Crockett. For information: Fort Boggy State Park, 4994 Highway 75 South, Centerville, TX 75831, (903) 536-1523.

Governor Hogg Shrine State Historical Park

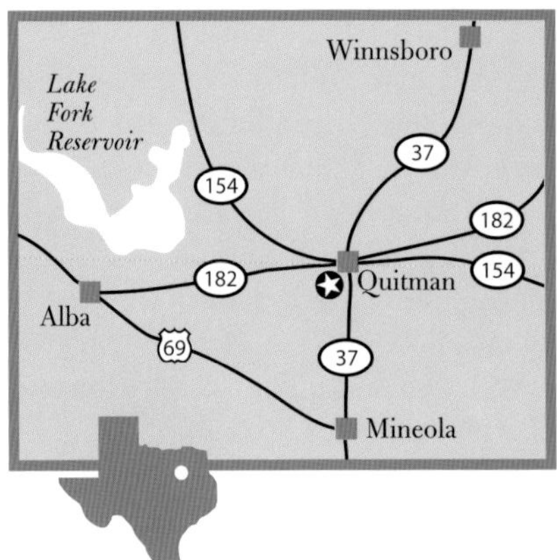

Governor Hogg Shrine State Historical Park contains the first home of Governor James Hogg and his wife, Sarah Ann Stinson Hogg, as well as the Stinson family home, the Miss Ima Hogg Museum, and the Old Settlers' Tabernacle. James Hogg was born in 1851 near Rusk at a site now preserved at the Jim Hogg State Historical Park. Hogg's first jobs as a youth were tied to the newspaper business, and one of them was at the local town of Quitman, where he worked on the *Clipper*. In 1869, he became a sharecropper on a small tract of land near Quitman. His views on law enforcement were shaped later by his involvement in a shooting incident: after Hogg had helped the county sheriff catch some outlaws, one of the captured men later shot him in the back. Hogg began studying law and returned to newspaper work to support himself. In 1873, he ran for the office of justice of the peace and won.

In 1874, Hogg married Sarah Ann (Sallie) Stinson at her family home, today one of the park's historic buildings. The next year his first son was born and he completed his law studies. During the following years he was elected county attorney, district attorney, state attorney general, and, on November 4, 1890, governor of Texas. Hogg was the first native Texan to attain the office of governor. His many accomplishments included regulation of corporations, introduction of antitrust laws, and creation of the Railroad Commission. Hogg left public office after two terms, and went on to establish an Austin law practice and pursue various oil

ventures. After he died in 1906, his four children managed the family affairs and became involved in many civic pursuits. His only daughter, Ima, long outlived her siblings and was well known for her many civic contributions.

Jim and Sallie Hogg's first home, the Honeymoon Cottage, was moved to the state park in 1952 and restored, in part through the assistance of the Hoggs' daughter, Ima. It is beautifully furnished with period furnishings and many items owned by the governor and his wife. The large Stinson family home was also moved to the site and is almost entirely original. It was furnished by Ima Hogg with period belongings of hers, her brother Will, and other items specifically acquired for the home. The Miss Ima Hogg Museum chronicles the history of Wood County and northeast Texas.

Before the site became a state park, it was the Wood County Old Settlers' Reunion Grounds. Except for an interruption during World War I, annual reunions have been held since 1902. The tabernacle, an open-air pavilion, was erected on the grounds in 1906, but has since been rebuilt. In addition to the museums, the park also contains a picnic area, camping with hookups, and a short hiking trail. Managed in part by the City of Quitman.

VISITOR INFORMATION

27 acres. Open all year, the grounds daily, the museums and homes Friday, Saturday, and Sunday by guided tour only. Historic buildings and museum, picnicking, nature trail. Full visitor services available in Quitman and Mineola. For information: Governor Hogg Shrine State Historical Park, 101 Governor Hogg Parkway, Quitman, TX 75783, (903) 763-4045.

LEFT:
The Honeymoon Cottage
RIGHT:
Lake Raven

Huntsville State Park

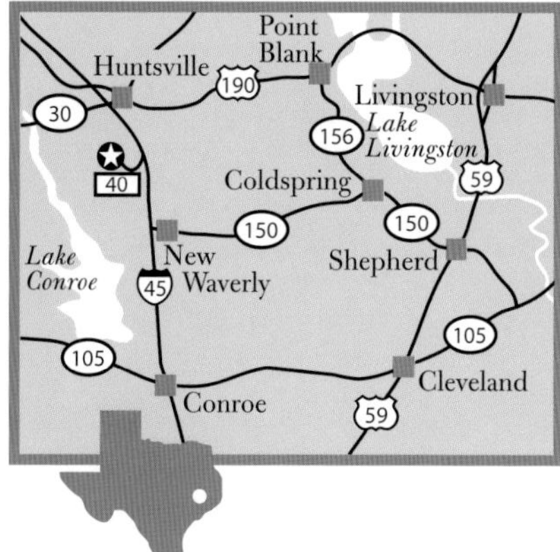

Loblolly and shortleaf pines tower over the shoreline of Lake Raven, a small impoundment that forms the heart of Huntsville State Park. As tall as the pines are, however, they are second-growth trees dating from early this century. In the period from 1880 to 1930, almost all harvestable trees were cut down in the South, including those in East Texas. Much of the land in the state park and surrounding Sam Houston National Forest was devastated. With time, the forest has regrown, forming dense pine woodlands, interspersed with hardwood trees—such as willow and water oak, American and cedar elm, black gum, black willow, and green ash—that are most commonly found in creek bottoms. Understory trees in the pine forests include red maple, dogwood, and sassafras.

The thick forest supports abundant wildlife. White-tailed deer, fox squirrels, raccoons, opossums, and armadillos are commonly seen. Creatures such as bobcats roam the woods also, but are reclusive and rarely observed. Occasionally alligators can be seen in the lake, floating motionless and almost completely submerged. Many species of birds flit through the forest canopy, especially during spring and fall migrations. Some birds make their presence obvious—crows squawking loudly over the lake, for instance, and pileated woodpeckers hammering away at tree trunks.

The park and the nearby town of Huntsville were named for Huntsville, Alabama, because an early trader and settler from there believed that the area resembled his home. Sam Houston, commander-in-chief of Texas forces during the war for

independence, first president of the Republic of Texas, and governor of the state of Texas, bought a plantation near Huntsville in 1844. Houston had grown up with neighboring Cherokees in Tennessee and later married a Cherokee woman. He named the plantation Raven Hill in reference to "Colonneh," the name given him by the Cherokees; *Raven* is the English translation of this name. Within the state park, Lake Raven, too, was named after Sam Houston, rather than after the raucous crows that frequent the area.

The park offers plenty of recreational opportunities. Canoes, sailboats, paddleboats, and small no-wake fishing boats float on the lake's three arms. Boats and fishing piers let anglers pursue largemouth bass, crappie, and flathead and channel catfish, and buoys mark off an unsupervised lake swimming area near the bathhouse. Onshore, miles of trails challenge hikers, cyclists, and mountain-bikers. Like many other Texas state parks, some of Huntsville's facilities were built during the Depression by the Civilian Conservation Corps, using durable native materials. Many of these buildings are still used today by park visitors seeking a quiet escape in the Pineywoods of East Texas.

VISITOR INFORMATION

2,083 acres. Open all year. Hot and humid in summer. Very popular, especially in summer and on spring and fall weekends. Large campgrounds with partial hookups and showers; reservations recommended during popular times. Screened shelters. Interpretive center and trail, trails for hiking, cycling, and mountain-biking, fishing, swimming, no-wake boating, fishing piers, and boat ramp. Seasonal park store and canoe, paddleboat, and flat-bottomed boat rental. Full visitor services available in Huntsville. For information: Huntsville State Park, P.O. Box 508, Huntsville, TX 77342, (936) 295-5644.

Swimmers at Lake Raven

Jim Hogg State Historical Park

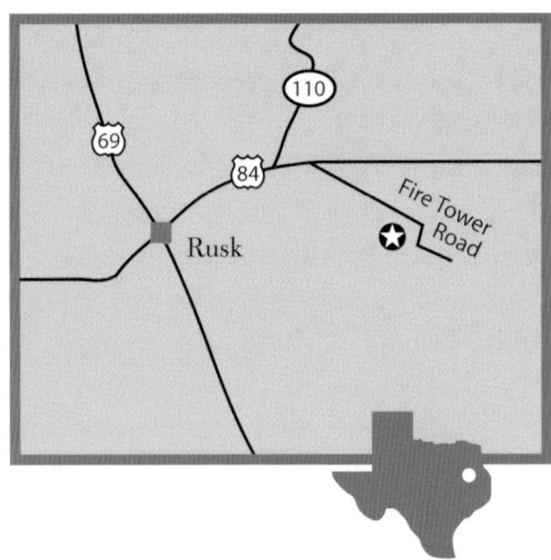

James Stephen Hogg was the first native Texan to hold the state office of governor. His father, Joseph Lewis Hogg, a respected lawyer, planter, and military leader, moved with his wife to Texas in 1838 and in 1846 carved out a plantation near Rusk in the tall woods of the site that is now the park. His son Jim was born here, at Mountain Home.

Sadly, Jim Hogg learned compassion firsthand through a series of tragedies that struck his family. His father died of dysentery near the battlefield of Shiloh in 1862 when Jim was only 11 years old. His younger brother, Richard, died of illness only a year later, followed shortly by his mother, Lucanda.

Jim Hogg supported himself and paid for a law degree by taking on a succession of jobs with newspapers and working as a sharecropper. In the late 1860s he moved to Quitman, where he met and married Sarah Ann (Sallie) Stinson. Eventually he became state attorney general, and then governor from 1891 to 1895. During his political life, he helped regulate industry and pushed for antitrust laws during the difficult transition from an agricultural to an industrial society. He also supported strong law enforcement, perhaps influenced by an incident in Quitman when he was shot in the back by an outlaw. His major achievement was the establishment of the Railroad Commission to regulate railroads' trade practices and their monopolistic power. Years later, the commission became the powerful regulator of the Texas oil industry.

After Hogg left the governor's office, he returned to his law practice and also participated in oil ventures. He was a partner in the company that was later to become Texaco. He died in 1906 and was buried in Austin's Oakwood Cemetery, at his request without a headstone. Instead, he asked that a pecan tree be planted at his head and a walnut tree at his feet, and that their nuts be distributed to the people of Texas for planting throughout the state.

The state park, at the site of Mountain Home, has a replica of the governor's birthplace with period furniture and artifacts. It also contains exhibits on the Hogg family—including a printing press and other items from Hogg's newspaper days—as well as on local, pioneer, and Indian history. The family cemetery lies on the park grounds next to the birthplace. In addition, there is a picnic area, a playground, and a 1.5-mile hiking and nature trail that winds through a lush forest of loblolly pines, oaks, dogwoods, and other trees, and past a historic iron-mining site.

ABOVE:
Replica of Governor Hogg's birthplace
RIGHT:
Sweetgum tree

VISITOR INFORMATION

178 acres. Open all year, Friday through Sunday. Hot and humid in summer. Day use only. Historical building with interpretive exhibits, research center for Hogg genealogy, picnicking, hiking and nature trail. Full visitor services available in Rusk. For information: Jim Hogg State Historical Park, Route 5, Box 80, Rusk, TX 75785, (903) 683-4850.

Lake Bob Sandlin State Park

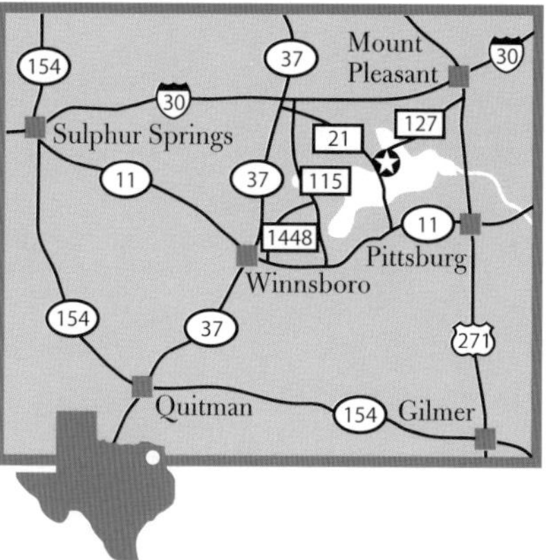

Lake Bob Sandlin State Park provides easy access to the great bass-fishing waters of Lake Bob Sandlin, a 9,460-acre reservoir in northeast Texas. The lake has a long, sinuous shoreline, with deep coves and bays. Two other small lakes, Cypress Springs and Monticello, adjoin Lake Bob Sandlin on two of its arms. The three are sometimes referred to as the Tri-Lake Area. A nearby power plant warms the waters of 2,000-acre Lake Monticello, improving its bass fishery.

Lake Bob Sandlin was created in 1977 by damming Lake Fork Creek and was named for a Mount Pleasant businessman who tirelessly lobbied for the construction of reservoirs in Titus County. In its early years the lake was heavily stocked with Florida

bass and channel catfish. A large amount of timber was left standing in its waters to provide habitat for small forage fish, and so provide food for the larger bass. Regular stocking, ideal habitat, and good reproduction have made Lake Bob Sandlin and the two adjoining reservoirs famous for their bass fishing.

Within the state park, a boat ramp, a lighted fishing pier, and the shoreline offer good access for anglers. Swimmers, waterskiers, and boaters also enjoy the open lake waters away from the areas of flooded timber. Inland from the lake, most of the park is heavily wooded with a mixed forest of loblolly pines, sweet gums, black hickories, and various species of oaks. Wildlife includes armadillos, white-tailed deer, bobcats, and opossums, as well as many other creatures. Several miles of hiking trails wind through the lush forest, past two ponds and several primitive campsites. A small cemetery in the day-use area is a remnant of Fort Sherman, built in the 1840s to protect settlers from Indian attack.

In spring, wildflowers blanket open fields in the park, while in fall, sweet gums and other trees add splashes of color to the woods. Lake Bob Sandlin State Park offers a quiet escape in East Texas for anglers, campers, and other outdoor enthusiasts.

VISITOR INFORMATION

641 acres. Open all year. Hot and humid in summer. Campground with partial hookups and showers. Backpacking campsites. Shelters with closable windows in addition to screens. Fishing pier, boat ramp, hiking, picnicking, boating, waterskiing, swimming. Full visitor services available in Mount Pleasant. For information: Lake Bob Sandlin State Park, Route 5, Box 224, Pittsburg, TX 75686, (903) 572-5531.

TOP:
Small park pond
BOTTOM:
Picnic area

Lake Livingston State Park

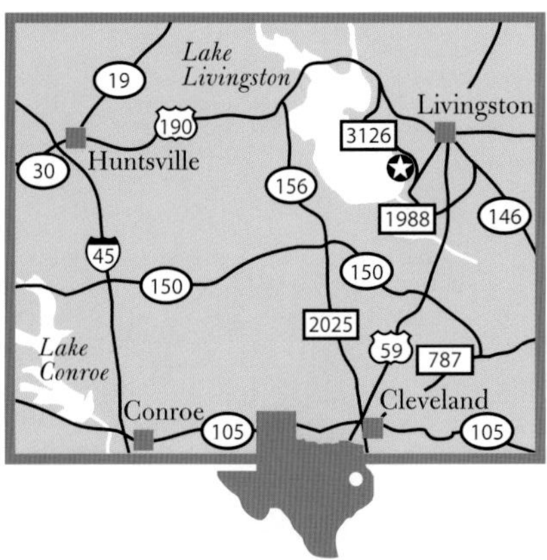

The shores of Lake Livingston provide the setting for Lake Livingston State Park. The huge, 84,800-acre reservoir was created in 1969 by damming the Trinity River. The lake sprawls across four counties and has a 450-mile-long shoreline. The state park contains about 2.5 miles of the lakeshore.

Lake Livingston lies in the thick East Texas Pineywoods, about 75 miles north of Houston. Tall loblolly pines and water oaks shade the lakeshore park, and are mixed with bottomland hardwood species such as willow oak and elm. Park wildlife is typical for East Texas: white-tailed deer, swamp rabbits, and raccoons roam the park woodlands, browsing plants and brush or searching for prey; pileated woodpeckers hammer away at tree trunks, hunting for grubs; and frogs and other amphibians favor the moist areas along creeks and around ponds.

Fish are probably the most popular wildlife attraction at the state park. Boat ramps and fishing piers attract anglers year-round. Native and Florida largemouth bass have long been popular at the lake, but the white bass spawning run is probably its most famous fishing-related attraction. Every spring, the white bass swim up the Trinity River from the lake, attracting thousands of fishermen. Not only are the bass plentiful, they are particularly large, sometimes weighing as much as four pounds.

Another popular fish is the striped bass, an introduced saltwater fish that does well in the fresh water of the lake. Flathead, channel, and blue catfish thrive in the lake as well. In 1976, a 114-pound flathead catfish was pulled from the lake, setting a state record.

Other attractions include more than 4 miles of nature and hiking trails that wind through the backcountry and developed areas of the state park. There is also a swimming pool with bathhouse, allowing visitors to cool off on hot summer days. Finally, an observation tower offers great views of the park and the sprawling waters of Lake Livingston, one of the largest reservoirs in Texas and a popular escape for residents of Houston and other cities.

VISITOR INFORMATION

636 acres. Open all year. Hot and humid in summer. Large number of developed campsites with partial hookups and showers, scattered across several areas. Screened shelters. Fishing piers, boat ramps, boating, waterskiing, picnicking, swimming, and nature, hiking, and mountain-bike trails. Seasonal park store. Full visitor services available in Livingston. For information: Lake Livingston State Park, Route 9, Box 1300, Livingston, TX 77351, (936) 365-2201.

ABOVE, LEFT:
Boaters on Lake Livingston
ABOVE, RIGHT:
Park shoreline

Martin Creek Lake State Park

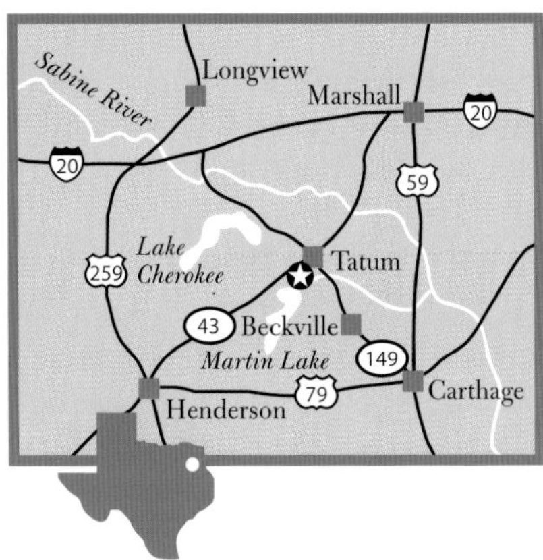

The site of Martin Creek Lake State Park, deep in the forests of East Texas, has been popular with humans since prehistoric times. Although the park itself does not have any significant archeological sites, the Caddo Indians occupied villages in the area long before the first settlers arrived.

In the late seventeenth century, Spanish explorers began crossing the area. By the end of the eighteenth century, European immigrants moving west had begun to displace Cherokees, Choctaws, Chickasaws, and other tribes from their eastern homelands, and some of them moved to East Texas. The Caddos also gave up their eastern lands and moved westward into their remaining lands in East Texas. Part of present-day Rusk County had been a land grant promised to the Cherokee Nation by the Mexican government. After Texas gained its independence from Mexico, President Sam Houston granted land rights in the area to the Cherokee tribe, but despite his insistence, the Texas Senate did not ratify the treaty. In 1838, Mirabeau B. Lamar, the newly elected president of the Texas republic, initiated an effort to remove the Indians from East Texas. While Sam Houston was away in 1839, Lamar sent troops to remove the Cherokees and their allied tribes from Texas. The action led to a period of hostilities and to the displacement of the Indians.

An historic trail, Trammel's Trace, is still visible in the park near the fishing pier. It was initially created by local Indians who used it as a travel route. Later it was widened into a wagon path and became an important route used by settlers traveling into Texas from Arkansas.

Martin Creek, formerly known as Hogan's Bayou, was renamed for Daniel Martin who, in 1833, settled with his family near the bayou. Martin's lands included the present-day park and most of the area now occupied by the reservoir. He and John Irons built a small fort and made a living through trade and hunting.

A small town named Harmony Hill was established near the park entrance in the mid-nineteenth century. The settlement prospered as a farming and trading center until 1882, when it was bypassed by a railroad. The town quickly declined, leaving little more than a cemetery and a building or two today.

Martin Creek Lake was created in the 1970s to provide cooling water for a Texas Utilities power-generating plant. The 5,000-acre lake is relatively shallow, so boaters and waterskiers need to watch for tree stumps and other hazards. The power plant warms the lake in winter,

attracting swimmers as well as providing fine year-round fishing for crappie, largemouth bass, sunfish, and channel catfish. Two boat ramps and a lighted fishing pier give anglers easy lake access.

The park lies on the lakeshore in gently rolling terrain wooded with loblolly and shortleaf pines, mixed with hardwoods such as post oak, red oak, blackjack oak, sweet gum, elm, and river birch. A small island connected to the mainland by a footbridge is one of the park's more interesting features; at its east end is a primitive campsite for backpackers and boaters.

VISITOR INFORMATION

287 acres. Open all year. Hot and humid in summer, sometimes cold in winter. Moderate number of developed campsites with partial hookups and showers. Primitive campsites for boaters and backpackers. Screened shelters. Lighted fishing piers, boat ramps, picnicking, swimming, boating, waterskiing, and hiking and mountain-bike trails. Limited visitor services available in Tatum; full services in Henderson and Longview. For information: Martin Creek Lake State Park, Route 2, P.O. Box 20, Tatum, TX 75691, (903) 836-4336.

OPPOSITE PAGE, TOP:
Boat docks
OPPOSITE PAGE, BOTTOM:
Fishing pier
RIGHT:
Shoreline campsite

Martin Dies, Jr. State Park

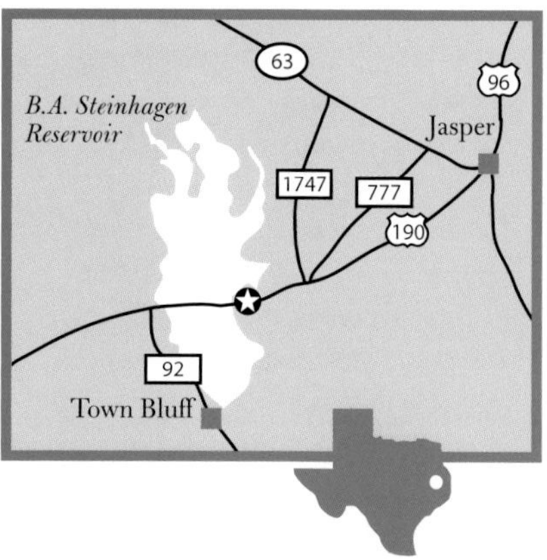

The popular Martin Dies, Jr. State Park lies on the shore of B. A. Steinhagen Reservoir deep in East Texas. Named for a Texas state senator, it is located on the northern edge of the Big Thicket, a vast, heavily wooded area with a unique mix of habitats. The Big Thicket forms a biological crossroads between eastern and western species of plants and animals. Visitors to the state park and surrounding areas in the thicket might see both roadrunners and alligators, and prickly pears as well as palmettos. Beech trees, common here, are actually at the southeastern limit of their range. The sugar maple and northern red oak are also found here, but are more common farther north. At one time, even the tropical jaguar and ocelot roamed as far northeast as the Big Thicket.

Slight changes in elevation and moisture create very different habitats within the Big Thicket. Swampy, primeval-looking cypress sloughs wind through lush floodplains, yet dry, sandy bluffs a hundred yards away may contain a mix of longleaf pines, post oaks, and yuccas.

At one time, the Big Thicket covered more than 3 million acres, but logging, agriculture, and urbanization have destroyed most of it. Today, remnants of the thicket are protected in parks such as Martin Dies, Jr. State Park and Big Thicket National Preserve.

The three units of the state park lie on an old terrace of the Neches River, which was dammed just below its confluence with the Angelina River to create the reservoir. Much of the lake is very shallow and, as in Caddo Lake in northeastern Texas, bald cypresses dot the water. Narrow sloughs lined with cypresses and willows wind through the two largest units of the park on the eastern shore of the reservoir. The park has not been logged for many years, so massive loblolly pines, beeches, magnolias, and oaks tower over the campgrounds and picnic areas. In spring, azaleas and dogwoods dot the forest understory and attract many park visitors. In fall, black gums and oaks add splotches of color to the woods.

Many people come to Martin Dies, Jr. to try their luck with a rod and reel in the lake. Various species of bass, crappie, and catfish all make popular catches. Other visitors enjoy canoeing through the backwaters of the 15,000-acre lake or simply relaxing under the tall pines and hardwoods that shade the state park.

VISITOR INFORMATION

705 acres. Open all year. Hot and humid in summer; mosquitoes can be pesky in warm weather. Most popular in spring, especially on weekends. Large number of campsites with partial hookups and showers, split into several areas. Screened shelters. Hiking and nature trails, picnicking, fishing, swimming, boat ramps, waterskiing. Bike, boat, and canoe rental. Full visitor services available in Jasper and Woodville. For information: Martin Dies, Jr. State Park, Route 4, Box 274, Jasper, TX 75951, (409) 384-5231.

Bald cypresses

Mission Tejas State Historical Park

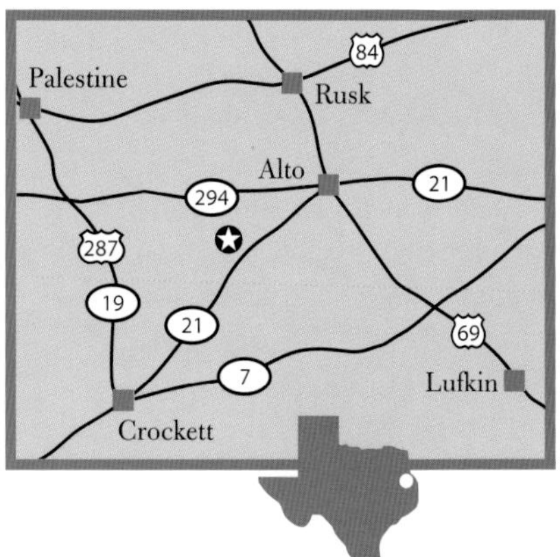

Today picnickers and campers relax under the tall pines of Mission Tejas State Historical Park on land where, 300 years ago, priests and Indians toiled. In the seventeenth century, the Spaniards laid claim to vast areas of land northeast of Mexico, including most of the area that now comprises Texas, but made little effort to colonize it. In 1685, a Frenchman, Robert Cavalier, Sieur de La Salle, established a small settlement on what is today Matagorda Bay. The Spaniards, worried about losing territory, began an effort to secure their claimed area. By the time an expedition led by Alonso de Leon found the French settlement in 1689, La Salle had died and only two members of his command remained.

The following year, de Leon set out from Monclova, Mexico with a large expedition to establish a mission in East Texas. In May, the expedition met a group of Caddoan-speaking Indians, the Nabadache. The Spaniards used *tejas*, the Caddoan word for friends, as the name for the Caddos and their land. Later, tejas became Texas. The Nabadache invited the Spaniards to their homeland on the Neches River. In their villages of conical, thatched huts, the Nabadache raised crops of corn, beans, melons, and squash, and they hunted in the surrounding country. The Franciscan priests accompanying the expedition built a cluster of rough wooden buildings for a mission and dedicated it on June 1, 1690, as San Francisco de los Tejas.

The missionaries settled in to learn the Caddo language, improve the Indians' agricultural methods, and foster Christianity. Initially, all went well and a second mission was established a few miles away. Unfortunately, the following winter brought a smallpox epidemic that killed several thousand people in the missions and surrounding villages. The Nabadache believed that the Spaniards' Holy Water of Baptism was causing the disease. One of the priests, Fray Casanas, worsened the situation by ridiculing the Indians' religious practices and their leaders. The summer of 1691 brought drought and increasing enmity. Spanish reinforcements and supplies arrived in August, but a second drought in 1692 worsened the missionaries' plight. In the spring of 1693, floods washed away the second mission. That fall, another priest, Fray Massanet, received word of an impending attack, so the missionaries loaded supplies, burned the mission, and fled to Mexico under the cover of night.

Domingo Ramón returned with an expedition to reestablish the mission in 1716, but lack of success, together with conflict between the French and Spanish, led to its abandonment only three years later. The Spaniards tried to reestablish the mission once again in 1721, but food and supplies continued to be in short supply, and few Indians joined the mission and converted to Christianity. Finally, in 1730, the mission was moved temporarily to the west, to a site on the Colorado River. The next year, it was moved to the San Antonio River and named San Francisco de la Espada; it thrived there for many years.

By modern times, nothing remained of the original mission buildings. During the Depression, the Civilian Conservation Corps built a wooden chapel to commemorate the original Spanish mission, and also constructed roads, trails, a pond, and a picnic area. In 1974, the home of the Rice family, early settlers in the region, was moved to the park from its original site 16 miles to the southwest. It was built between 1828 and 1838, and is one of the oldest structures in the area.

Today the park showcases the two historic buildings—the chapel and the Rice family home—and offers, too, a quiet retreat in the tall pines of the uplands above the Neches River. Campers, picnickers, hikers, and anglers enjoy the shady woods that once sheltered the Spaniards as they tried to colonize East Texas.

TOP:
Misty pond
ABOVE:
Commemorative chapel

VISITOR INFORMATION

363 acres. Open all year. Hot and humid in summer. Small campground with partial and full hookups, and showers. Historic buildings, hiking, picnicking, and limited fishing. Limited visitor services available in Alto; full services in Crockett and Rusk. For information: Mission Tejas State Historical Park, Route 2, Box 108, Grapeland, TX 75844, (936) 687-2394.

Starr Family State Historical Park

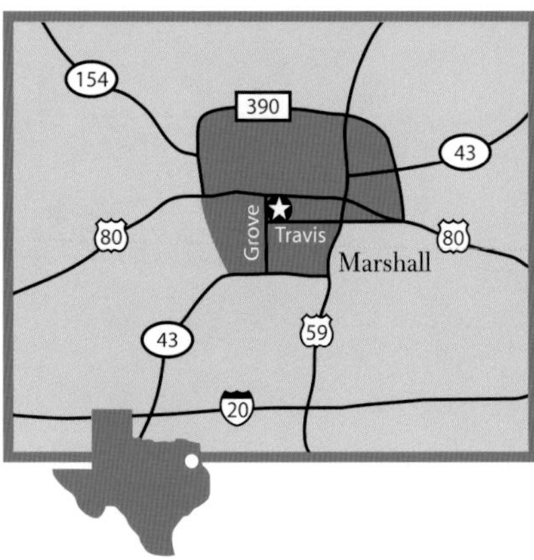

The Starr family had its start in Texas when Franklin J. Starr arrived in the state in 1834. He joined the volunteers fighting for Texas independence but saw little action, and settled in Nacogdoches with his wife after the fighting ended. His brother, Dr. James Harper Starr, and his brother's wife soon joined him in Nacogdoches. Sadly, Franklin Starr died of a fever in July 1837, saddling his brother with the responsibility of looking after his family and property.

Dr. Starr became active in the affairs of the new republic and was appointed President Mirabeau B. Lamar's secretary of the treasury in 1839. In 1844 he resigned and formed a very successful land agency with a partner in Nacogdoches. During the Civil War, Starr opposed secession, but supported the Confederacy by sending supplies to Southern troops. His eldest son, James Franklin (Frank) Starr, joined the Confederate Army in 1861 and served until the South was defeated.

After the war, Frank Starr attended the University of Virginia and in 1868 married Clara Fry Clapp in New Orleans. He then returned to Nacogdoches with his new wife to join his family's land business. In 1870, the family moved its home and business to Marshall, a thriving town served by the railroad and telegraph. Dr. Starr purchased a house called Rosemont on a large lot on the southwest side of town and retired from active business affairs. By the end of 1873, his son Frank was managing the family land and money, while his youngest son, Amory, handled the land agency. The Starr family acquired and sold lands that the State of Texas had granted as incentives for railroad construction, helping to open up the western part of the state for settlement.

The Rosemont house was the beginning of a large family compound, which eventually included several homes. Frank Starr purchased the southwest corner of the compound from his parents and built his home with the financial assistance of his father-in-law. His house, Maplecroft, is the centerpiece of the park today—and, fittingly, red maples still shade the grounds of the historic home. It was originally built in a transitional Italianate style, a precursor to the Victorian style. It contained four rooms on each of its two floors and had a detached kitchen and servants' room connected by a covered passageway. Most structural materials were acquired locally, but the trim and furnishings were, for the most part, shipped from New Orleans.

Over the years, the house was modified, modernized, and enlarged. A schoolhouse, a barn, and other outbuildings were added to the grounds. In 1925, Ruth Starr Blake inherited the house from her mother, Mrs. Frank Starr, and in the 1930s modified Maplecroft and the schoolhouse to reflect the Colonial Revival style of architecture. Other modifications were made to the internal layout of the home. When Ruth Blake died in 1969, the property passed to Clara Starr Pope Willoughby, the only surviving great-granddaughter of James Harper Starr. The home was acquired by the Texas Parks and Wildlife Department in 1976 and opened to the public in 1986.

VISITOR INFORMATION

3.1 acres. Open all year, Friday, Saturday, and Sunday. Call for tour times. Historic structure with interpretive exhibits. Wear flat-soled shoes to avoid carpet and floor damage. Full visitor services available in Marshall. For information: Starr Family State Historical Park, 407 W. Travis, Marshall, TX 75670, (903) 935-3044.

Starr family home

Texas State Railroad State Historical Park and Rusk/Palestine State Park

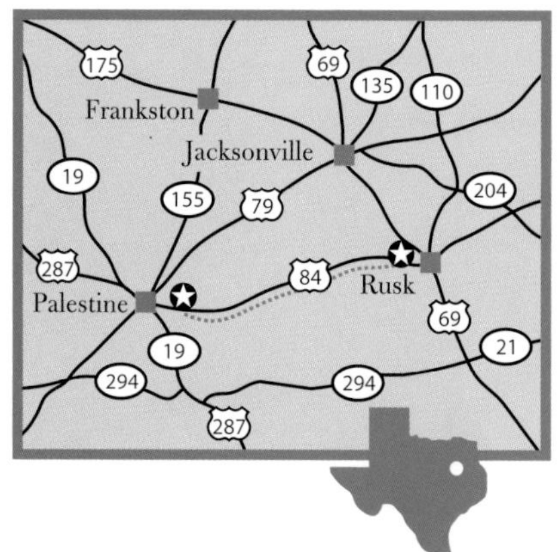

Deep in the Pineywoods of East Texas, the past still lives on where the steam trains of the Texas State Railroad carry passengers along 25 miles of track between the two units of Rusk/Palestine State Park. Construction of the railroad was begun by the state prison system in 1893, in an effort to make the prisons self-supporting. Penitentiary money, bonds, and legislative appropriations were used, and the railroad was built between Palestine and Rusk. The prison at Rusk had a foundry where pig iron and pipe were made for the state, and the railroad was needed to haul hardwood from Palestine to make coke for the iron plant.

In 1913, the iron plant in Rusk was closed and four years later the penitentiary was converted into a mental hospital. After that the railroad was only used intermittently. In 1921, it was taken from the Prison Commission's jurisdiction and placed under a separate board of managers. The state ceased regular railroad service and leased the line to the Texas and New Orleans, part of the Southern Pacific Railroad.

In the early 1960s the railroad lease was transferred to the Texas Southeastern Railroad. At the end of 1969, the railroad terminated freight operations and removed its rolling stock. In 1972, most of the railroad was transferred to the Texas Parks and Wildlife Department to preserve a part of the age of steam locomotives and railroading in Texas. A short, 3.7-mile stretch of track is still used commercially by the Missouri Pacific Railroad to serve a meat-packing plant near Palestine.

Today, passengers can board steam trains at both the Rusk and the Palestine depots, at either end of the line that connects the two units of Rusk/Palestine State Park. The stations are not original, but were built to resemble railroad architecture at the turn of the century. Food, drinks, and gifts are available at both depots; the one at Rusk also has a small theater with film presentations of the railroad's history.

Engineer

Steam train at Rusk Depot

For each run, steam locomotives dating from 1901 to 1927 chug out of both stations, pulling a string of open-air passenger cars. The route passes through 25 miles of thick East Texas woods, crossing 30 bridges. The longest bridge, over the Neches River, is 1,100 feet long. Near the halfway point, the east- and west-bound trains pass each other on a siding. At the stations, each train pauses for an hour so that passengers may eat lunch and stretch their legs before starting the return trip to the originating station.

Rusk/Palestine State Park's two units, located at either end of the Texas State Railroad, were designed to serve the passengers of the railroad, as well as to provide additional recreational activities. Both park units lie in the thick mixed pine-and-hardwood forests of East Texas. Loblolly pines, oaks, sweet gums, elms, and other trees dominate the forest canopy. Smaller trees and shrubs, such as dogwood, sumac, and sassafras, create an understory.

The area was settled in the early part of the nineteenth century; Palestine was founded in 1835 to succeed Fort Houston as the Anderson County seat, and Rusk followed soon after. Rusk was named after Thomas Jefferson Rusk, a signer of the Texas Declaration of Independence and inspector general of the Texas revolutionary army. The town is probably best known as the birthplace of Texas's first two native-born governors, James Stephen Hogg and Thomas Mitchell Campbell. Palestine, the larger of the two towns, was created when the county seat, Fort Houston, was found not to be in the center of Anderson County, and hence failed to meet one of the criteria for a county seat, as directed by the legislature. Thus the new town was created; it was named after Palestine, Illinois.

Although the terrain in the two park units and along the railroad line consists of gentle, unassuming hills with few visible rocks or minerals, the area is important geologically. Underlying it are thick beds of sedimentary rock containing enormous reserves of oil and gas. Some of the oil fields are found near salt domes, a number of which lie near Palestine. Near Rusk, shallow layers of iron-bearing rock were once mined and smelted for iron.

Small lake at Rusk unit

The Rusk unit is the larger of the two park units. It has a small 15-acre lake with rental paddleboats, fishing, a campground, and a picnic area. The Palestine unit has picnicking facilities and a small, less developed camping area. Both units center around the depots of the Texas State Railroad, a living remnant of the past.

VISITOR INFORMATION

Texas State Railroad: 499 acres. Open all year on weekends, and on additional days during busy times of the year. Reservations recommended. Trains depart from both stations at 11 A.M. and return at 3 P.M. Ice chests and food may be taken on the trains; food service is available at each depot. Call ahead for reservations and current dates, times, and ticket prices. For information: Texas State Railroad State Historical Park, P.O. Box 39, Rusk, TX 75785, (903) 683-2561 or (800) 442-8951.

Rusk/Palestine State Park: 136 acres. Open all year. Hot and humid in summer. Campgrounds and picnic areas adjoin railroad depots. Campsites with partial and full hookups and showers at Rusk unit, and with water hookups at Palestine unit. Fishing, paddleboat rental at Rusk unit. Full visitor services available in Rusk and Palestine. For information: Rusk/Palestine State Park, P.O. Box 39, Rusk, TX 75785, (903) 683-2561.

TYLER STATE PARK

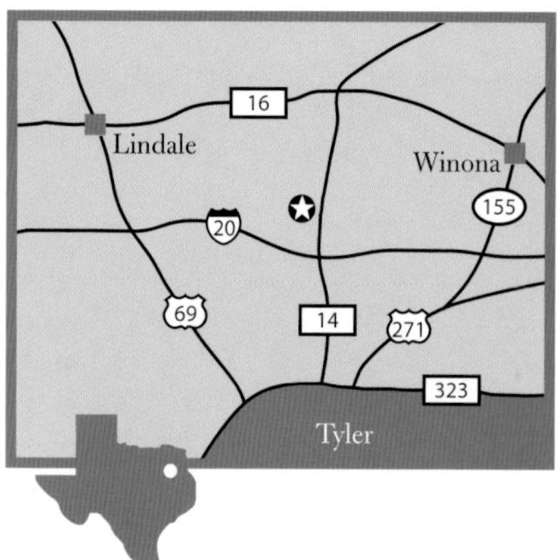

Tyler State Park is a popular, long-time retreat deep in the Pineywoods of East Texas. Heavily wooded hills surround a small 64-acre lake, the centerpiece of the park. The park site was purchased in the mid-1930s and, like many of Texas's older parks, was developed initially by the Civilian Conservation Corps during the Depression.

The park lies in dense forest in gentle hills north of the city of Tyler. A mix of loblolly and shortleaf pines, sweet gums, oaks, elms, eastern red cedars, and hickories creates a tall

Canoeist at Tyler State Park

forest canopy, while smaller trees, such as sassafras, dogwoods, and redbuds, create a lower understory. In spring, the dogwoods and redbuds sprinkle the forest with white and red blooms, and in fall, trees such as the sweet gum and the sassafras splash red and gold across the forest.

The lake hosts most of the activities at the park. A 5-mile-per-hour speed limit on the small body of water makes it ideal for small boats, such as canoes. The park concession rents paddleboats and canoes and sells snacks and fishing bait. The nearby swimming beach is usually crowded on hot days.

Fishing piers and a boat ramp cater to anglers, who, because the park is very popular, usually prefer to test their skill on weekdays and early in the morning or late in the evening. Several varieties of fish can be caught in the lake, including largemouth bass and catfish.

For those wishing to learn more about the park's natural history, a three-quarter-mile-long nature trail winds through the woods near the headquarters. For hikers desiring a longer walk, foot trails circle around much of the lake. There is even a small mountain-bike trail in the northwest corner of the park.

VISITOR INFORMATION

986 acres. Open all year. Hot and humid in summer. Campground with partial and full hookups, and showers. Screened shelters. No-wake boating, fishing piers, hiking, nature, and mountain-bike trails, picnicking, swimming. Seasonal concession with canoe and paddleboat rental and snacks. Full visitor services available in Tyler. For information: Tyler State Park, 789 Park Road 16, Tyler, TX 75706-9141, (903) 597-5338.

Stormy sunset over lake

Village Creek State Park

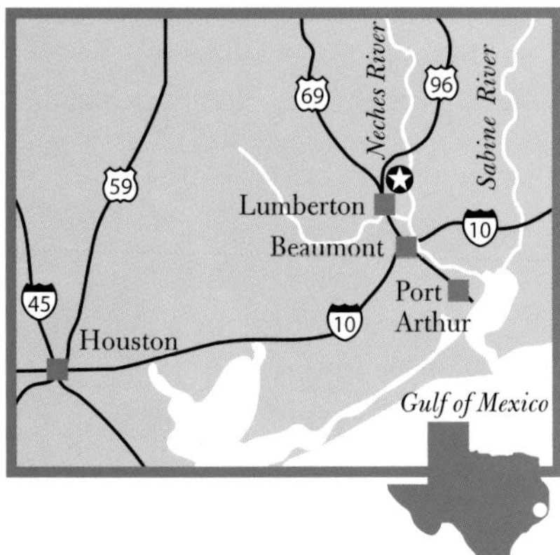

Village Creek winds through the heart of the Big Thicket of East Texas, its clear, tea-colored waters flowing through dense forest to its confluence with the Neches River. The boundaries of the Big Thicket through which the creek flows are not easily defined. A 1970 ecological survey defined an irregular band stretching from Conroe to part of the Sabine River near Newton, and extending from Woodville and Jasper in the north to Beaumont. The researchers used a type of mixed pine-and-hardwood forest, particularly the beech-magnolia-pine association, as the defining parameter for the boundaries of the ecological Big Thicket.

The Big Thicket is a melange of many different habitats reflecting slight variations in elevation, soil type, and available water. Amid the lush woods of the thicket there are places where the soil is so poor that plants have developed carnivorous traits to survive. Yet a few dozen yards away, the soil can be rich enough to support dense forests of beech, magnolia, and loblolly pine. Although the thicket has been greatly reduced in size and heavily impacted by human activities, it still contains a tremendous number of different plant and animal species. Village Creek State Park protects some of the thicket's unique biology.

The Big Thicket's location within North America adds to its biological importance, since it lies at an ecotone, or meeting place of different biological provinces. Its different soil types and moisture levels allow dry western desert plants such as yucca, mesquite, and prickly pear to thrive alongside the southeastern water tupelo and bald cypress. Southern orchids and ferns flourish alongside sphagnum moss more typical of Arctic bogs. Alligators bask on the banks of cypress sloughs, while roadrunners pursue lizards through the yuccas and oak scrub of dry sandhills.

The forest floor is shaded by 85 species of trees, while 1,000 species of flowering plants grow within the thicket. The beech tree reaches its southeastern limit of distribution here, as do trilliums and several orchid species, and the northern red oak and sugar maple found in the Big Thicket are more common much farther north. All four types of poisonous snakes found in the United States live here—the copperhead, the coral snake, the rattlesnake, and the water moccasin. More than 50 bird species call the Big Thicket home and

Cypress slough

flat-water creek winds for miles past lush forest, eerie cypress sloughs, and white sandbars. With multiple access points in the state park and national preserve, as well as on highway bridges, trips of varying lengths can be arranged. Local outfitters can help with canoe rentals and car shuttles.

Fishing for catfish, largemouth bass, perch, and crappie is also possible at the park, and hiking trails are another way to explore the dense Big Thicket forests. Whether it is visited by canoe or on foot, Village Creek State Park provides an excellent introduction to the unique and mysterious Big Thicket of East Texas.

at least another 125 either reside there part of the year or pass through during annual migrations. Evidence indicates that even the tropical jaguar and ocelot once roamed as far northeast as the thicket. Large temperate predators, such as the mountain lion, the black bear, and the red wolf, also thrived in the thicket before being exterminated by man.

Several Big Thicket habitats occur in the state park, including floodplain forests, swampy baygalls, acid-bogs, and cypress sloughs. The baygall's wet, junglelike habitat evokes the classic, mysterious image that the Big Thicket conjures up for most people. Black gum and bald cypress trees grow in the swampy terrain, anchored in the water and soft soil by wide buttresses. Smaller trees and shrubs, such as the black titi and the red bay, create dense thickets at the edges of the bogs and baygalls. The carnivorous bladderwort plant thrives in this environment. Here and there, alligators lurk deep in the swampy habitat, while water moccasins slither through the dark water in search of prey.

Close to the creeks and rivers, below the ancient waterway terraces that harbor baygalls and sandy uplands, are the low-lying floodplain forests which, as the term implies, flood regularly. The periodic flooding produces a fertile sandy or silty loam soil, and provides additional water for the plants of the creek and river bottomlands. A dense forest canopy grows in the floodplain, dominated by massive oaks and sweet gums.

Low ridges, backwater sloughs, oxbow lakes, and terraces break up the overall flatness of the floodplain. A few beeches and magnolias are found on the higher, drier areas. Bald cypresses and water tupelos grow directly out of the water in shallow sloughs and watery depressions. With thick, buttressed tree trunks and cypress knees poking out of the water, the sloughs are eerie, primeval-looking swamps. Unlike the baygalls, however, the fact that the cypress sloughs experience regular flooding, together with some water flow, prevents water in them from becoming highly acidic. The sloughs retain water most or all of the year, making them favorite haunts of water-dwelling animals such as alligators and water moccasins.

Of the original 3.5-million-acre Big Thicket, less than 300,000 acres remain. Of that remaining part, Village Creek State Park and Big Thicket National Preserve protect a sizable portion. The state park does more than just preserve important habitats, however; it also offers unique recreational opportunities. Village Creek provides one of the best canoeing experiences in Texas. The

VISITOR INFORMATION

942 acres. Open all year. Hot and humid in summer. Insect repellent advised in warm months. Moderate number of campsites with partial hookups and showers. Hiking, picnicking, canoeing, fishing. Full visitor services available in Lumberton and Beaumont. For information: Village Creek State Park, P.O. Box 8565, Lumberton, TX 77657, (409) 755-7322.

Canoeists on Village Creek

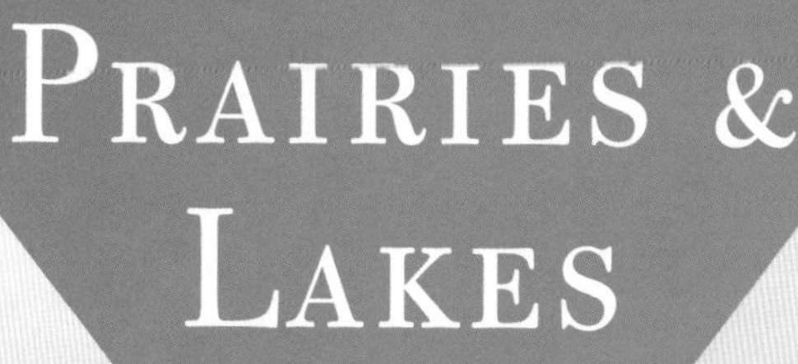

Prairies & Lakes

The Prairies and Lakes region covers a broad band of land stretching from the Red River to the north to as far south as east of San Antonio. Two major ecosystems, the Blackland Prairie and the Cross Timbers, run through the heart of the area, while its edges have ecological elements of adjoining regions, in particular those of the Hill Country and the East Texas Pineywoods.

Before European settlers arrived, more than 12 million acres of tallgrass prairie stretched through the Prairies and Lakes region. The gently rolling terrain was blanketed with a thick sod of grasses and wildflowers that often grew taller than a human. Lightning, as well as wild fires set by Indians, periodically burned the prairie and prevented trees and shrubs from encroaching. Huge herds of bison crossed the Red River from Oklahoma to graze the rich grasses and prairie wolves hunted the weak, sick, and young of the vast herds.

With the arrival of settlers, the prairie sod was cut by plows and built over with growing cities. Over the years, the fertile, dark, clay-rich soils were plowed under for farmland and pastures. As a result of this and the suppression of natural fires that allowed forest encroachment, maybe no more than 5,000 acres of original prairie remain today.

Within the Blackland Prairie region are north–south bands of Cross Timbers habitat. A thick, scrubby woodland of cedar elms, post oaks, hackberries, and hickories

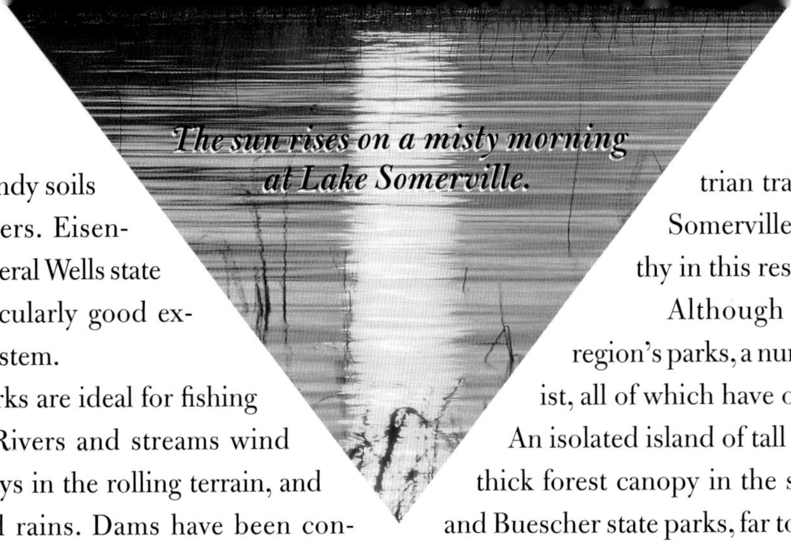

The sun rises on a misty morning at Lake Somerville.

grows in the thin, sandy soils of the Cross Timbers. Eisenhower and Lake Mineral Wells state parks contain particularly good examples of this ecosystem.

This region's parks are ideal for fishing and water sports. Rivers and streams wind through broad valleys in the rolling terrain, and are fed by plentiful rains. Dams have been constructed on many of these waterways to control water for city water supplies, agriculture, and recreation, as well as for flood-control purposes. Not surprisingly, many state parks lie on the shores of these reservoirs and offer a broad range of water-related activities, from fishing to waterskiing to swimming. Some of the lakes, such as those at Bonham, Cleburne, and Meridian state parks, are small no-wake lakes ideal for quiet activities such as canoeing and paddleboating, while others, such as Lake Whitney and Ray Roberts Lake, are large, sprawling impoundments of thousands of acres. Boaters with large sailboats, as well as waterskiers, favor such big lakes. Once they are open, Eagle Mountain Lake and Lake Bastrop promise to be equally popular water-oriented recreation sites.

Although the lake parks emphasize water recreation, many also offer other amenities, such as hiking trails. An extensive hiking, mountain-biking, and equestrian trail system makes Lake Somerville particularly noteworthy in this respect.

Although lakes dominate this region's parks, a number of exceptions exist, all of which have other notable features. An isolated island of tall loblolly pines forms a thick forest canopy in the sandy hills of Bastrop and Buescher state parks, far to the west of the pines' normal range. The wooden stockade of an early Texas fort has been reconstructed at Old Fort Parker. At Monument Hill/Kreische Brewery, visitors may enjoy one of the best views in this part of Texas, from a high bluff above the Colorado River; in addition, they can tour the ruins of one of the largest nineteenth-century breweries in the state.

Dinosaur Valley State Park is among other exceptions to the state parks dominated by water-related activities in this region. Dinosaurs once roamed the lands of this state park, leaving the largest concentration of preserved tracks in Texas in the Paluxy River bed near Glen Rose. Tiny Acton State Park contains the grave of Davy Crockett's second wife, while Fanthorp Inn preserves a prime example of an early Texas inn. Three of the parks in this region, Stephen F. Austin, Lockhart, and Bastrop, even offer golf courses in beautiful settings.

Prairies & Lakes

1 Acton State Historical Park
2 Bastrop State Park
3 Bonham State Park
4 Buescher State Park
5 Cedar Hill State Park
6 Cleburne State Park
7 Confederate Reunion Grounds State Historical Park
8 Cooper Lake State Park
9 Dinosaur Valley State Park
10 Eagle Mountain Lake State Park
11 Eisenhower Birthplace State Historical Park
12 Eisenhower State Park
13 Fairfield Lake State Park
14 Fanthorp Inn State Historical Park
15 Fort Parker State Park
16 Lake Bastrop State Park
17 Lake Mineral Wells State Park
18 Lake Somerville State Park
19 Lake Tawakoni State Park
20 Lake Whitney State Park
21 Lockhart State Park
22 Meridian State Park
23 Monument Hill • Kreische Brewery State Historical Parks
24 Mother Neff State Park
25 Old Fort Parker State Historical Park
26 Palmetto State Park
27 Purtis Creek State Park
28 Ray Roberts Lake State Park
29 Sam Bell Maxey House State Historical Park
30 Stephen F. Austin State Historical Park
31 Washington-on-the-Brazos State Historical Park

Acton State Historical Park

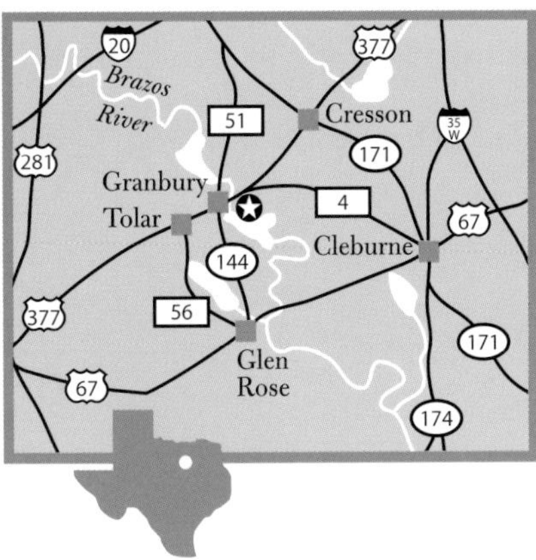

Tiny Acton State Park is the smallest state park in Texas and, with dimensions of only 12 feet × 21 feet, it might well be the smallest park in the nation. The little-known park contains the grave of Davy Crockett's second wife, Elizabeth Patton Crockett, together with the graves of her son, Robert, and his wife, Matilda.

Davy Crockett's first wife died of an unknown illness in 1813, leaving Crockett with three young children to raise by himself. Crockett met Elizabeth Patton while exploring the Shoal Creek area in Tennessee. She was a widow with two young children, which placed her in a similar situation to that of Crockett. In 1815 they married in Lawrence County, Tennessee. They raised their separate children together, and added three new children to the family. For many years, Crockett prospered as a businessman and Tennessee Congressman. In 1835, however, he lost a re-election effort and his businesses failed.

To make a new start, Crockett headed for Texas, arriving just in time for the Texas war of independence. Sadly, a few months later, he lay dead after the battle of the Alamo. Soon after, 20-year-old Robert Patton Crockett traveled to Texas to join the Texas troops, to avenge Davy Crockett's death. He later returned to Tennessee to live, and married in 1841. In 1854 he moved his wife and mother to Texas, ultimately settling on land in Hood County that was granted to Davy Crockett's wife by the Texas state government.

In 1860 Elizabeth Crockett died, and was followed soon after by her daughter-in-law, Matilda. Robert lived many more years, finally dying in 1889. All three were buried at the same site near the town now known as Acton. In 1911, the legislature authorized a memorial to Elizabeth. A stone shaft, capped by a marble statue of a pioneer woman searching the western horizon, marks the burial site. Tall oak trees and the other graves of Acton Cemetery surround the peaceful memorial to the widow of Davy Crockett.

VISITOR INFORMATION

0.006 acres. Open all year. Day use only. The state park lies within the Acton Cemetery—ask for directions in the town. Historic memorial site. Full visitor services available in Granbury. For information: Acton State Historical Park, c/o Cleburne State Park, 5800 Park Road 21, Cleburne, TX 76031, (817) 645-4215.

Memorial to Elizabeth Crockett

Bastrop State Park

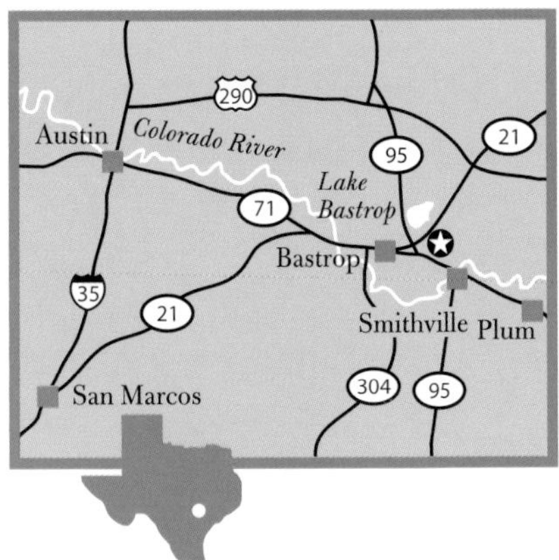

To the surprise of many, thick stands of loblolly pines thrive on sandy hills above the Colorado River only 30 miles southeast of Austin. Called the Lost Pines, they are isolated from the East Texas pine forests by more than 60 miles of post-oak woodland. During the wetter and cooler times of the last ice age, pine forests grew in an uninterrupted blanket from East Texas to the Bastrop area and westward. As the climate warmed and dried, the trees retreated eastward, leaving an isolated, 70-square-mile pocket of pines just east of the town of Bastrop, part of which is contained within Bastrop State Park. The Carrizo and Reklaw sandstone formations in this area created soil conditions that allowed the pines to survive in the drier climate.

The sandstones are rich in iron oxide, giving them a yellowish-to-reddish-brown color. The sandy land at Bastrop State Park has eroded into an area of small, steep hills and ravines. Pines dominate the forest canopy, but a mix of post oaks, blackjack oaks, junipers, and other trees adds variety.

Many mammals, such as raccoons, opossums, bobcats, and foxes, are common at Bastrop State Park. Lack of browse in the thick pine forest discourages the existence of large numbers of deer, however. A little-known creature, the endangered

Houston toad, lives in the park. Like the pines, a number of creatures reach the westernmost limit of their range at Bastrop; among these are the flying squirrel and the pine warbler.

Bastrop, together with its sister park, Buescher, attracts many birders every year. More than 200 species of birds, both migrants and residents, have been recorded at these parks. The parks' location on the migratory Central Flyway, combined with their unique pine-forest habitat, helps account for this high bird count.

ABOVE:
Bastrop State Park Lake
RIGHT:
Pine-forested golf course

Bastrop State Park was named for the town of Bastrop, which, in turn, was named for Felipe Enrique Neri, Baron de Bastrop. The baron was actually a commoner named Philip Hendrik Nering Bogel, who was wanted in Holland for embezzlement. Apparently he fled Holland, changed his name, and headed for the New World. He became friends with Moses Austin, Stephen F. Austin's father, and helped him gain an audience with the Mexican governor of Texas. Austin's petition to settle 300 families in Texas was granted, in part through Bastrop's negotiating efforts. In 1829, the first settlement of Stephen F. Austin's "Little Colony" was founded on the banks of the Colorado River at the western edge of the Lost Pines. Originally named Mina, the town's name was changed to Bastrop to honor the "baron."

The state park was established in 1938, when the city of Bastrop donated part of the land to the state. During the Depression, the Civilian Conservation Corps built many of the park facilities, using native stone and timber. The corps' enduring craftsmanship is first apparent at the park entrance, whose reddish-brown stone gates were built with the native, iron-rich sandstone. The workers used the same materials to build a large dining hall and 13 rustic cabins. One of their most popular developments is the 18-hole golf course, a rarity in the Texas state parks. The scenic course winding through the lush pine forest attracts golfers year-round.

In summer, a large swimming pool draws crowds of people to Bastrop State Park. Hikers come to walk the 8.5-mile loop hiking trail through the park's backcountry. Backpackers can hike to primitive forest campsites along the trail. The 14-mile scenic drive between Bastrop and Buescher state parks makes a picturesque but challenging ride for cyclists; the park road goes up and down many small hills, providing a good workout. Stephen F. Austin's first colonists settled at the edge of the Lost Pines; today, thousands of people come every year to relax under the tall pines of Bastrop State Park.

VISITOR INFORMATION

3,504 acres. Open all year. Hot and humid in summer. Moderate number of developed campsites with full hookups and showers, in two areas. Primitive camping for backpackers. Cabins—reserve well ahead. Groups may rent barracks buildings and dining hall. Swimming pool, picnicking, hiking trail, cycling, scenic drive. Golf course open all year. Park concession store. Full visitor services available in Bastrop. For information: Bastrop State Park, P.O. Box 518, Bastrop, TX 78602, (512) 321-2101.

CCC-constructed dining hall

Bonham State Park

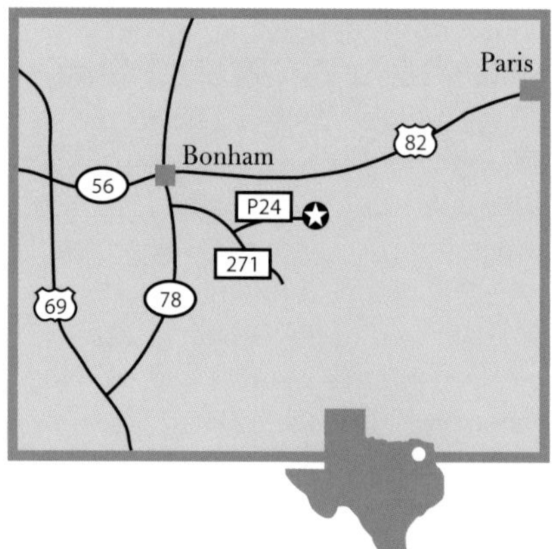

A small 65-acre lake is the centerpiece of heavily wooded Bonham State Park. Canoes slide quietly through its waters, while kids splash noisily in the shallows by the grassy shore of the swimming beach. The park lies in a gently rolling area of farms and grazing land south of the town of Bonham. Because the park has been protected since its acquisition in the 1930s, tall, mature stands of trees cover much of its area. Stately Shumard oaks, green ashes, cottonwoods, hackberries, pecans, and American elms line the lakeshore. Eastern red cedars are common also, especially in drier upland areas. Although much of the park is heavily wooded, wildflowers display their colors every spring in open grassy areas around the small earthen dam that impounds the lake.

The park was initially acquired from the town of Bonham in the 1930s and developed by the Civilian Conservation Corps (CCC), established during the Depression to provide jobs for unemployed young men. CCC work crews built and improved state and national parks all across the United States, including many in Texas. At Bonham, the CCC built the dam, as well as roads, bridges, picnic areas, and the boathouse. The combined headquarters and bathhouse building is probably the most prominent park structure built by the CCC. The durable, attractive building was constructed of locally quarried limestone.

Because the lake is small, boats must observe a 5-mile-per-hour speed limit. Quiet activities—fishing, canoeing, and picnicking—predominate at Bonham State Park which, as it has done for years, continues to attract families seeking a cool escape in the woods of East Texas.

VISITOR INFORMATION

261 acres. Open all year. Hot and humid in summer. Small number of campsites with partial hookups and showers. Picnicking, swimming, fishing, boat ramp, boating. Seasonal park store with canoe and paddleboat rental. Full visitor services available in Bonham. For information: Bonham State Park, Route 1, Box 337, Bonham, TX 75418, (903) 583-5022.

TOP:
Tree-lined park lake
BOTTOM:
Swimmers at lake

Buescher State Park

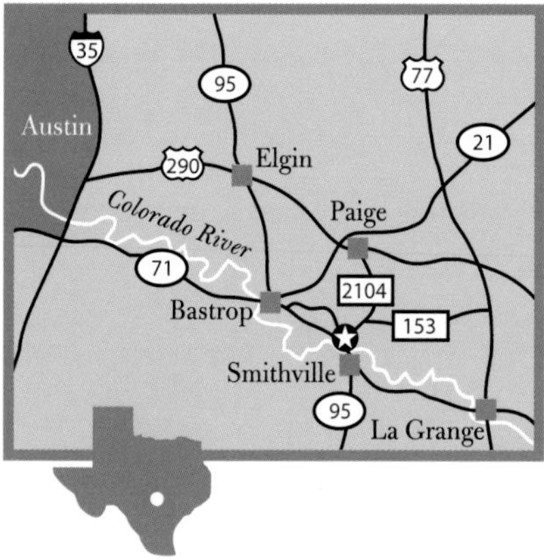

Buescher State Park lies in the Lost Pines of Texas, like its better-known sister park, Bastrop. Scenic, hilly Park Road 1 connects the two woodland parks. The fresh scent of loblolly pines wafts through the air, reminding visitors of the East Texas pine forests. Surprisingly, though, these pines are located on some hilly uplands only about 30 miles southeast of Austin.

During the wetter, cooler period of the Pleistocene, pine forests stretched westward, uninterrupted, from East Texas to and beyond the Bastrop area. As the ice-age glaciers melted and the climate warmed and dried, the pines slowly retreated east, leaving an isolated 70-square-mile stand in central Texas near Bastrop and Smithville. There, the Reklaw and Carrizo sandstone formations create a sandy soil conducive to the growth of loblolly pines, despite the drier climate.

RIGHT:
Lake Buescher
BELOW:
Fisherman

The north end of Buescher State Park lies, along with Bastrop State Park, in the Lost Pines. Toward its south end, the pines thin and post oaks, cedar elms, live oaks, hackberries, and other trees become more common. Buescher also has a large area of bottomland deciduous forest along drainages and around small Buescher Lake. This habitat helps attract more than 200 species of birds, including many types of waterfowl that may be seen on the 25-acre lake. Because Buescher has a more varied habitat than Bastrop State Park, it tends to attract more bird species and attendant birders. However, both parks, aided by their location on the Central Flyway, draw many migrant species at various times of year.

Buescher Lake lures anglers hoping to catch largemouth bass, crappie, and catfish. In winter, the lake gets cold enough that the Parks and Wildlife Department stocks the popular rainbow trout. Unfortunately, the water gets too warm in summer for a year-round population to survive and reproduce.

In the heat of summer, swimming in the lake is a popular activity, but because of its small size, boating activities are limited—the lake is only suitable for canoes and small boats powered with electric trolling motors. The 7.8-mile Buescher hiking trail winds through dense stands of loblolly pine and deciduous forests of oak and cedar elm. The scenic 14-mile road connecting Bastrop and Buescher state parks provides a good workout for cyclists willing to tackle its hilly terrain. If Bastrop State Park is too crowded on a given weekend, try its attractive but less well-known sister park, Buescher.

VISITOR INFORMATION

1,017 acres. Open all year. Hot and humid in summer. Moderate number of developed campsites with partial hookups and showers. Screened shelters. Picnicking, cycling, hiking, fishing, swimming, boating (small boats and canoes only) in Buescher Lake, trout fishing in winter and early spring—requires a trout stamp in addition to regular state license. Limited visitor services available in Smithville; full services in Bastrop. For information: Buescher State Park, P.O. Box 75, Smithville, TX 78957, (512) 237-2241.

Cedar Hill State Park

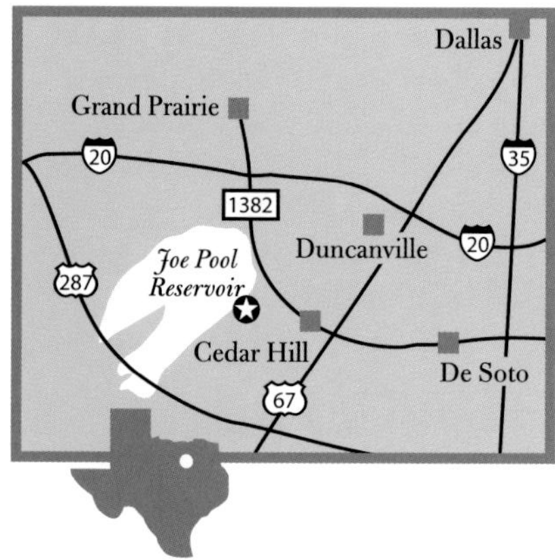

Cedar Hill State Park, one of the newer state parks in Texas, is quickly becoming one of the most popular. Its location in southwest Dallas County makes it a convenient escape for residents of the Dallas–Fort Worth metropolitan area. The park, which opened in 1991, was designed with elaborate facilities on the shore of Joe Pool Reservoir, to cope with the expected large influx of visitors. Among other features, it boasts a marina, two four-lane boat ramps, and 355 campsites, more than any other state park besides Garner.

To the surprise of many first-time visitors, the park lies on the edge of a particularly hilly area of North Texas sometimes known as the Cedar Mountains. The waters of Joe Pool Reservoir lap at the western slopes of these hills. A thick blanket of Ashe junipers, cedar elms, mesquites, and other trees covers the slopes, reminiscent of the Hill Country many miles to the southwest. Skunks, raccoons, coyotes, bobcats, and armadillos all make their homes on the steep, wooded slopes above the lake.

TOP:
Sailboat on Joe Pool Reservoir
ABOVE, RIGHT:
Marina

John Wesley Penn was an early settler in the area, establishing a homestead in 1854. In 1859, he purchased property in what would later become the park and constructed the first buildings. At one time, his farm occupied more than 1,100 acres. Bottomlands along Mountain Creek, now under the waters of the lake, were farmed, while upland areas were used for grazing and haying. As the years went by, the Penn family added more structures. The farm was operated by the family until 1970. The Parks and Wildlife Department is restoring the farm buildings as important relics of the family farms that once occupied this area of Dallas County. The buildings, built over the course of more than a hundred years, provide an architectural record of changes in construction techniques and building materials.

Joe Pool Reservoir, opened to the public in 1989, attracts many park visitors. Its 7,500 acres beckon to waterskiers, weekend sailors, and swimmers, and anglers are drawn by healthy populations of bass, crappie, and catfish. Fishing jetties and boat ramps, together with a long shoreline, provide plenty of access. Both the park's proximity to the Dallas–Fort Worth Metroplex and its many recreational facilities are sure to draw large numbers of visitors for years to come.

VISITOR INFORMATION

1,811 acres. Open all year. Hot and humid in summer. Large number of campsites, some primitive, most with partial hookups and showers. Picnicking, hiking and biking trails, fishing jetties, boating, boat ramps, waterskiing, swimming, historic structures at Penn Farm. Marina with park store, snack bar, and grill. Full visitor services available in Cedar Hill, Duncanville, Grand Prairie, and other Metroplex cities. For information: Cedar Hill State Park, 1570 W. FM 1382, Cedar Hill, TX 75104, (972) 291-6641.

Cleburne State Park

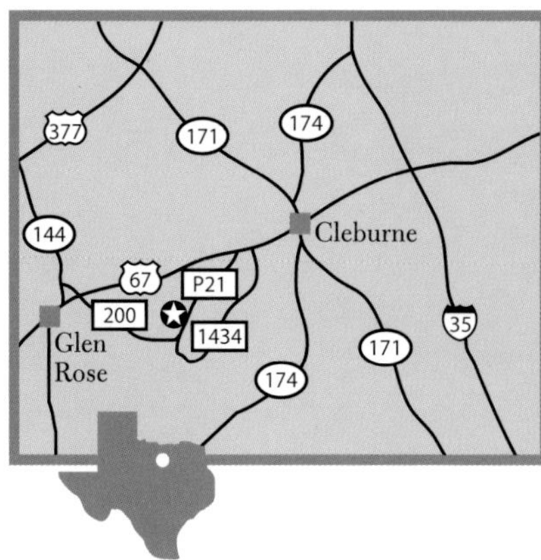

Springs feed the clear, cool waters of Cedar Lake, the centerpiece of Cleburne State Park. The 116-acre lake is tucked away in a small valley, in the breaks lining the broad Brazos River Valley. In 1934, local businessmen pushed the site as a suitable location for a state park and, like many of Texas's older state parks, Cleburne was built in the 1930s by the Civilian Conservation Corps (CCC), created to employ young men during the Depression. Both the nearby town of Cleburne and the park were named for Confederate general Pat Cleburne.

The CCC built the earthen dam that impounds Cedar Lake. Several springs, now under water, provide the primary water source for the lake. Because it is spring-fed, the lake's waters tend to be a little cooler than those of stream-fed lakes. In winter, when the water is coldest, rainbow trout are stocked. Other popular sport fish include largemouth bass, crappie, and catfish.

The narrow valley in which the lake lies is lined with bluffs of white limestone. Much of the uplands above the valley consist of open, grassy ranch land, but the valley slopes are densely wooded, particularly with Ashe juniper trees, also known as cedar. Along creeks in the valley bottom, hardwoods such as elms and oaks grow tall and thick. Wildflowers often blanket open, grassy areas near the park headquarters in spring. Deer, armadillos, raccoons, opossums, and squirrels are frequently seen.

Because the lake is small, a 5-mile-per-hour speed limit is enforced for boats. The low speeds not only keep the lake very quiet, they make it ideal for canoeing, paddleboating, and fishing. Facilities for swimming and hiking, together with the presence of shady campgrounds, provide several more reasons why Cleburne State Park makes an ideal retreat from the busy cities of Fort Worth and Dallas to the northeast.

Cedar Lake

VISITOR INFORMATION

529 acres. Open all year. Hot in summer. Moderate number of campsites with partial or full hookups and showers. Screened shelters. Boating (low-speed), fishing, swimming, picnicking, hiking, boat ramp. Seasonal store with rental of paddleboats, canoes, and fishing boats. Full visitor services available in Cleburne and Glen Rose. For information: Cleburne State Park, 5800 Park Road 21, Cleburne, TX 76031, (817) 645-4215.

Confederate Reunion Grounds State Historical Park

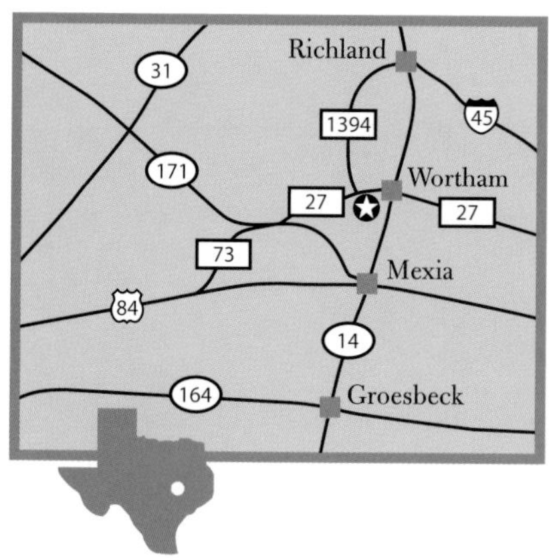

In spite of the hardships of Reconstruction after the Civil War, many Confederate veterans still retained a strong sense of brotherhood. In 1889, veterans in Limestone and Freestone counties formed Joe Johnston Camp No. 94 and established a constitution for their organization. Their stated purpose was to perpetuate the memories of fallen comrades, aid disabled survivors and indigent widows and orphans of deceased Confederate soldiers, and preserve the fraternity that grew out of the war.

Reunions were held almost every year in the late summer for 57 years. Over time, the organization purchased land at the confluence of the Navasota River and Jack's Creek. Some years, as many as 5,000 people congregated at the site to socialize, hold memorial programs, and listen to speeches. The reunion grounds were donated to the state in 1983.

Several historical items are displayed on the park grounds. In 1862, the Confederates captured six brass cannons from Union troops at the Battle of Val Verde in New Mexico. The cannons were assigned to a Texas artillery brigade led by Captain T. C. Nettles. Several other cannons captured in Louisiana were added to his brigade. After the war ended, Nettles hid the guns rather than surrender them to the Union, and later they were dug up. One of those cannons is at the park. Other historic items include the 1872 Heritage House, the 1893 dance pavilion, and Miss Mamie Kennedy's 1914 Confederate Flirtation Walk along the Navasota River.

In addition to visiting the historical sites, picnicking and a variety of other outdoor activities are possible at this park that lies in a peaceful woodland setting of gently rolling hills.

VISITOR INFORMATION

77 acres. Open all year. Hot and humid in summer. Day use only. Historic structures, picnicking, hiking, fishing, swimming. Canoes and other small boats on Navasota River. Full visitor services available in Mexia. For information: Confederate Reunion Grounds State Historical Park, c/o Fort Parker State Park, Route 3, Box 95, Mexia, TX 76667, (254) 562-5751.

Flirtation Walk footbridge

1893 pavilion

Cooper Lake State Park

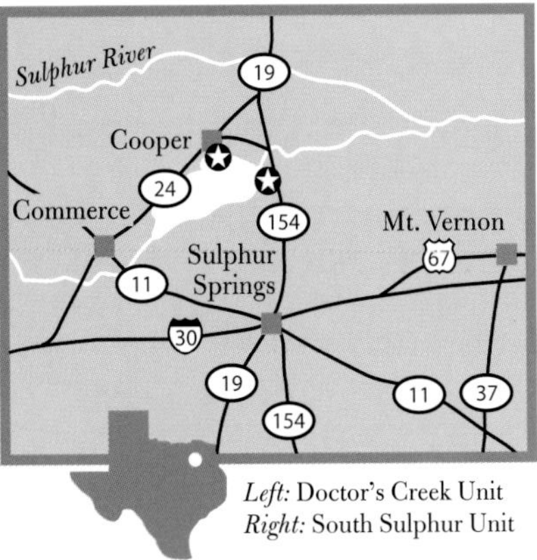

Left: Doctor's Creek Unit
Right: South Sulphur Unit

Cooper Lake State Park is a new park in northeast Texas with extensive facilities for everyone from anglers to campers to horse lovers. The two main units of the park lie on the shores of Cooper Lake, itself a relatively new reservoir. The U.S. Army Corps of Engineers began construction on the 5-mile-long earthfill dam in 1986 and began filling the 19,280-acre reservoir in September 1991. A little more than a year later, the lake was opened to boats. The main lake tributary is the South Sulphur River, although a number of other waterways add significant flows.

Cooper Lake was built primarily as a water-supply reservoir for Dallas, Sulphur Springs, and other communities, but has important secondary uses for recreation and flood control. Unlike other lakes, the entire shoreline and lake, except for dam and water-supply functions, is controlled by the Texas Parks and Wildlife Department. Most of the lakeshore lies within a wildlife management area; the rest is occupied by the two main units of the state park and the dam.

Cooper Lake lies in a mixed-habitat area a little west of the Pineywoods of East Texas. The gently rolling terrain is a mix of post-oak woodland—consisting of oaks, elms, hackberries, eastern red cedars, and other trees—and prairie. Among the most common wildlife species are white-tailed deer, opossums, armadillos, cottontails, and raccoons. Interesting, but less common, species include wild turkeys, falcons, and bald eagles. A lot of timber was left standing in the lake to provide a suitable habitat for fish, but it has proven to be valuable for waterfowl as well. Fishing on the lake has already showed good success, due in large part to heavy initial stockings of Florida largemouth bass.

The park has two main units, Doctors Creek and South Sulphur. Both units opened in 1996, and both have camping with partial hookups, picnic areas, fishing piers, and boat ramps. Doctors Creek has screened shelters, and South Sulphur has cabins and an equestrian camping area. Because the two units adjoin a wildlife management area, the combined large area allows long horseback-riding, hiking, and mountain-biking trails. Two boat ramps, separate from the main units, are also available.

VISITOR INFORMATION

Doctors Creek unit: 466 acres. *South Sulphur Springs unit:* 2560 acres. Open all year. Hot and humid in summer. Camping with partial hookups and showers. Equestrian campground (at South Sulphur) and backpacking campsites. Screened shelters and cabins. Fishing piers, boat ramps, picnicking, waterskiing, swimming, and hiking and equestrian trails. Limited visitor services available in Cooper; full services in Paris and Sulphur Springs. For information: Cooper Lake State Park, Doctors Creek Unit, RR 3, Box 231-A15, Cooper, TX 75432, (903) 395-3100; South Sulphur Unit, RR 3, Box 741, Sulphur Springs, TX 75482, (903) 945-5456.

Lake sunset

Dinosaur Valley State Park

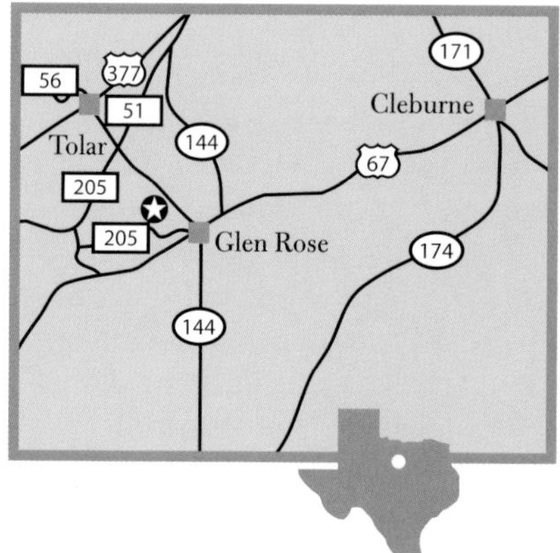

About 113 million years ago, during the early Cretaceous period, shallow seas washed over much of Texas. On mudflats near the shore of one of these seas, a giant sauropod called *Pleurocoelus* grazed on evergreen foliage. A hungry, carnivorous *Acrocanthosaurus* spied the larger herbivore and began pursuit, leaving a trail of footprints across the soft mud. The final outcome of the fight is unknown; only the tracks remain, preserved in a process beginning when the sun started to dry and harden the prints; tides from the sea then washed in muddy sediment that covered them. Over time, the mud hardened into rock, with the track-bearing layer becoming limestone. The Paluxy River eventually eroded away the softer overlying sediments, leaving the tracks exposed today in Dinosaur Valley State Park.

The tracks were first discovered in 1903, but were not widely known until Roland Bird of the American Museum of Natural History investigated the site in 1938. The tracks described above were excavated and are now displayed at the American Museum of Natural History in New York and the Texas Memorial Museum in Austin. Since their discovery, at least 1,000 tracks have been found in the riverbed of the Paluxy. The most common track is that of the three-toed *Acrocanthosaurus*. The footprints measure as much as 24 inches long and 17 inches wide. The 20- to 30-foot-long carnivore belonged to the same group as the later, and larger, *Tyrannosaurus rex*.

A second type of track that has been uncovered in the park belonged to one of the prey animals of *Acrocanthosaurus*, the 30- to 50-foot-long *Pleurocoelus*. This massive animal weighed as much as 40 tons and left tracks as large as 3 feet long and 2 feet wide. It was related to the even larger *Apatosaurus* (formerly called *Brontosaurus*), one of a group of the biggest land animals of all time. Two full-size models of *Apatosaurus* and *Tyrannosaurus rex* are displayed in the park.

The third type of track found in the park is much rarer than the other two and harder to identify. Researchers now believe that it belonged to a 30-foot-long, 3-ton dinosaur called *Iguanodon*. This was a plant-eating creature, as was *Pleurocoelus*; like the latter, it was probably pursued by the carnivorous *Acrocanthosaurus*.

Dinosaur Valley State Park contains one of the best displays of dinosaur tracks in the world. Other such sites are scattered throughout central Texas, from Glen Rose to Utopia, but they lie mostly on private land. The state park's visitor center has elaborate exhibits that explain much about the giant reptiles.

The dinosaur tracks are visible in several areas on the bottom of the Paluxy River. Hiking trails lead from the river to overlooks and primitive campsites in the hills to the north. The upland terrain, wooded with Ashe junipers, live oaks, Texas red oaks, and other trees, is similar to that of the Hill Country to the southwest. In the creek bottoms, cedar elms, American elms, green ashes, and other trees dominate. In the deep,

Fossil dinosaur footprint

Paluxy River

moist soils along the river, pecans, cottonwoods, sycamores, black willows, and walnuts thrive.

Many different animals inhabit the park, from wild turkeys to armadillos, and from raccoons to coyotes. They, too, leave tracks in the mud, but unless certain conditions exist to preserve them, their prints will quickly disappear, unlike those of the dinosaurs that roamed this area millions of years ago.

VISITOR INFORMATION

1,523 acres. Open all year. Hot and humid in summer, but possible to swim in the river to cool off. Relatively small developed campground with partial hookups and showers. Primitive campsites for backpackers. Picnicking, hiking, fishing in river, equestrian area for horseback riding, interpretive museum at visitor center. Park store. Full visitor services available in Glen Rose, Cleburne, and Granbury. For information: Dinosaur Valley State Park, P.O. Box 396, Glen Rose, TX 76043, (254) 897-4588.

Tyrannosaurus rex *model*

Eagle Mountain Lake State Park

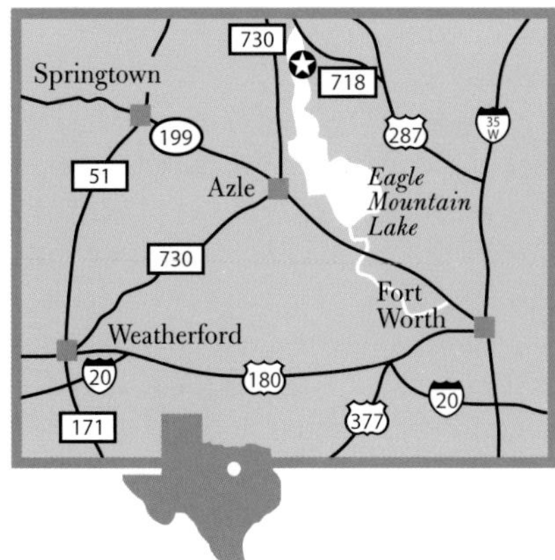

Eagle Mountain Lake State Park is an undeveloped tract of land on the shore of Eagle Mountain Lake, northwest of Fort Worth. The 9,000-acre lake was built in the 1930s by the U.S. Army Corps of Engineers by damming the west fork of the Trinity River. It provides water for the city of Fort Worth, as well as recreation opportunities and a means of flood control. The lake lies in a gently rolling area of native pasture partly wooded with oak, redbud, mesquite, juniper, and hackberry trees.

The only activities possible at present are bank fishing, hiking, and wildlife observation. Future development, however, will probably include boat ramps, fishing piers, campgrounds, and picnic areas. The area around Eagle Mountain Lake is experiencing rapid population growth and development, and once the park is developed, it should be a popular recreation site in the Fort Worth metropolitan area. Other public-access sites around the lake already offer campgrounds, boat ramps, and fishing opportunities.

VISITOR INFORMATION

401 acres. Undeveloped park site; access currently by special request only. Hiking, bank fishing, wildlife observation. Full visitor services available in Fort Worth. For information: Eagle Mountain Lake State Park, c/o Texas State Parks Region 2, 1601 E. Crest Drive, Waco, TX 76705, (817) 867-7959.

Eisenhower Birthplace State Historical Park

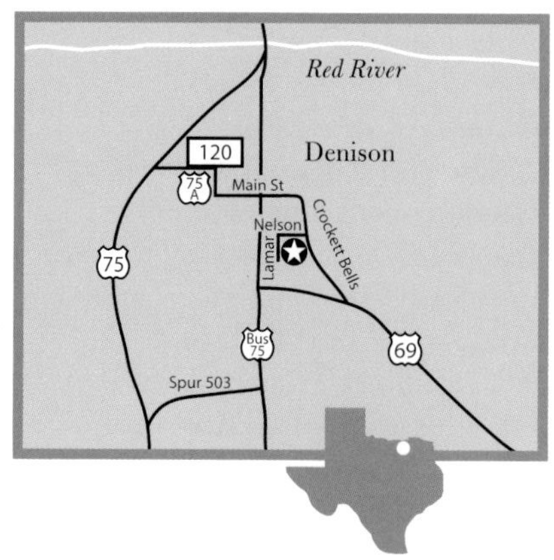

On October 14, 1890, Dwight David Eisenhower was born in a white, two-story frame house at 208 E. Day Street in Denison, Texas. His father worked in the yards of the Missouri, Kansas and Texas Railroad, known as the Katy. His parents lived in Denison for only three years; they moved to Abilene, Kansas, in the spring after the birth of Dwight, who was their only child born in Texas.

Eisenhower later became a five-star general of the U.S. Army and led the Allies to victory in Europe in World War II. Publicity surrounding his success in Europe awoke the memories of Jennie Jackson, the principal of Peabody Elementary School in Denison. She remembered an Eisenhower family that had lived in Denison and a baby named David (the future president's mother only later changed the order of the baby's given names to avoid confusion with his father, also David). Jackson wrote to General Eisenhower in an attempt to verify her memories. The general was at that time unaware of the house in Denison, and believed that he had been born in Tyler. He gave Jackson his mother's address, however, and she confirmed that he had indeed been born in Denison.

Jennie Jackson formed a group to preserve the home of one of America's most prominent generals. The group raised funds to purchase the house and donated it to the city of Denison. Jackson's interest was well-placed: in 1952, Eisenhower was elected President of the United States. On October 14, 1953, the president's birthday, the Eisenhower Birthplace Foundation was established, with the purpose of restoring the house and converting the surrounding property into a park. In 1958, the property was conveyed to the Texas State Parks Board.

VISITOR INFORMATION

6 acres. Open all year (call for hours), with guided tours of restored home. Interpretive exhibits on the life of President Eisenhower, plus some of his personal effects. Bookstore with titles related to Eisenhower and Texas history. Full visitor services available in Denison. For information: Eisenhower Birthplace State Historical Park, 208 E. Day Street, Denison, TX 75021, (903) 465-8989.

ABOVE:
Eisenhower birthplace
LEFT:
Dwight D. Eisenhower statue

Eisenhower State Park

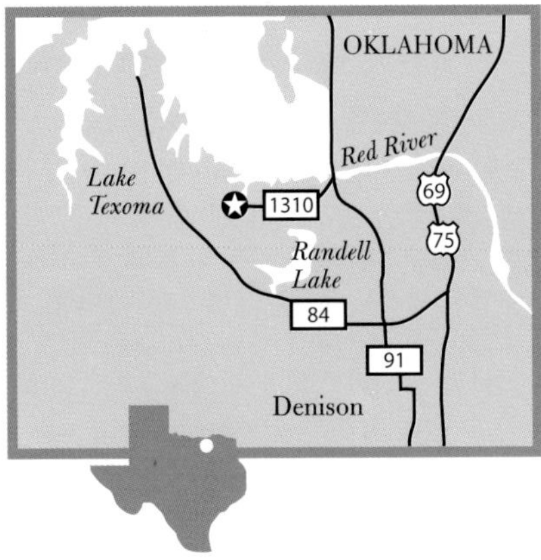

Although a nineteenth-century government report once described the area around Eisenhower State Park as "uninhabitable to man or beast," modern-day visitors and residents would hardly agree. The park, named for President Dwight D. Eisenhower, who was born in nearby Denison, lies on the shores of Lake Texoma in the heart of the Cross Timbers region. The Cross Timbers is a north-south belt of gently rolling land forested with a thick growth of shrubs and stunted trees, such as cedar elms, blackjack oaks, post oaks, hackberries, and hickories. Unlike the fertile Blackland Prairie soil to the east, Cross Timbers soil is thin and sandy and easily washes away, exposing rock and clay outcroppings.

The thick woods of the Cross Timbers were a major barrier to travel and culture for both Indians and settlers, despite the determined efforts of both to eradicate them. They were such a formidable obstacle that in 1832 Washington Irving likened travel through the region to "struggling through a forest of cast iron." Although modern civilization has made many inroads, much of the tenacious forest still exists.

In 1944, the U.S. Army Corps of Engineers created Lake Texoma by building Denison Dam, using earthfill, on the Red River just north of Denison. The 89,000-acre impoundment, the tenth-largest man-made reservoir in the United States, lies on the boundary of Texas and Oklahoma and has a sinuous 580-mile shoreline. The Red River, named for its heavy burden of red silt and clay, is the lake's principal water source, but the Washita River in Oklahoma also makes a significant contribution. The two rivers and numerous smaller tributaries give the lake a watershed of almost 40,000 square miles.

Eisenhower State Park perches on rocky bluffs above the lake, on the south shore. The rocks, called marl, were created 90 million years ago during the Cretaceous period, when seas covered what is now North Texas. They are made of interbedded layers of limestone and shale. Ammonoids and other fossils are common in these bluffs.

The area had a colorful history stretching back long before the creation of the lake. In the 1850s, the Butterfield Overland Stage had several water stops in the area, and the Chisolm and Shawnee cattle-drive trails crossed the Red River nearby. Indians, Fort Washita soldiers, outlaws, settlers, and cattle crossed the river at Colbert's Crossing, a busy

Lake Texoma

ford just below the dam. Later, a ferry replaced the ford, and eventually a bridge replaced the ferry.

Fishing attracts many people to Eisenhower State Park today. Fishing piers, a boat ramp, and a marina all make lake access easy. Introduced striped bass are probably the most popular and successful fish at the lake. The striper, a saltwater fish, reproduces and does well in the slightly saline water of the Red and Washita rivers. One bass caught in 1984 weighed 35 pounds, 2 ounces. Although they are not heavily fished, catfish lurk deep in the waters of Lake Texoma; in 1985, an angler pulled a record 116-pound blue catfish from the reservoir.

Another introduced fish, the smallmouth bass, favors rocky habitat such as that found under the bluffs of the state park. Although Texas's record largest smallmouth was caught at Lake Whitney, Oklahoma's record smallmouth, weighing 6 pounds, 8 ounces, was caught in Lake Texoma. Other popular fish caught there include black and white crappie, largemouth bass, spotted bass, white bass, and alligator gar. Even the rare paddlefish is found in the lake.

The massive lake attracts more than just anglers. Sailboats glide across the lake, pushed by North Texas breezes. Powerboats, often towing waterskiers, zip over the waters. The state park's marina, along with several others in the area, provides slips for permanent mooring, and some boats in the lake approach 60 feet in length.

Swimmers can paddle around a protected cove in the state park, while hikers are able to traverse a 6-mile trail that winds along the bluffs and through the campgrounds, providing excellent lake views. Campers can relax in shady campsites and escape fast-paced modern life here, at least for a while.

VISITOR INFORMATION

457 acres. Open all year. Very busy on weekends, spring through fall. Hot and humid in summer, but the lake is available for cooling off. Several large campgrounds, with partial and full hookups, and showers. Screened shelters. A recreation hall and pavilion are group facilities that can be reserved. Swimming area, hiking trail, picnic area, marina. Fossil collecting is not allowed. A special license is available that allows fishing anywhere on the lake; anglers with only a standard state fishing license must stay on their state's side of the lake. Full visitor services available in nearby Denison. For information: Eisenhower State Park, 50 Park Road 20, Denison, TX 75020, (903) 463-4696.

ABOVE:
Waterskiing on Lake Texoma
BELOW, LEFT:
Personal watercraft
BELOW, RIGHT:
Sailing on Lake Texoma

Fairfield Lake State Park

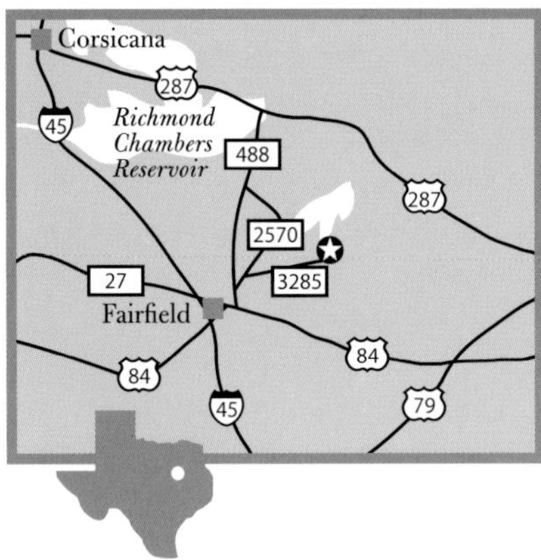

Fairfield Lake State Park lies in a transition zone known as post-oak savannah, between the pine forests of East Texas and the Blackland Prairies to the west. The area surrounding Fairfield Lake consists of gently rolling woodland with scattered farms. Trees such as post oaks, eastern red cedars, elms, white ashes, and hickories dominate the forest. In spring, wildflowers dot scattered open fields within the park.

The park hugs the shoreline of 2,400-acre Fairfield Lake, a reservoir that was built to provide cooling water for a Texas Utilities electricity generating plant. The power plant keeps the lake water warmer than normal all year, allowing the season for swimming and waterskiing to begin earlier in spring and extending it later into fall than at other area lakes.

Because they are suitable for other fish than those usually found in the waters of this region, the warm waters of Fairfield Lake provide a unique fishing experience. Red drum, commonly called redfish, is a salt-water species from the Gulf of Mexico that has been stocked in this freshwater lake where, surprisingly, it has done quite well. Redfish as large as 15 pounds are caught at the lake; unlike on the coast, there is no maximum-length limit on redfish catches in Fairfield Lake.

Other unusual fish also thrive in the reservoir. Another non-native fish, the blue tilapia, or African perch, flourishes in the warm lake waters. Unlike the redfish, however, the tilapia was introduced by accident and is unwelcome because it tends to dominate and overpopulate reservoirs. Despite this drawback, it is a good sport and eating fish. Because it feeds on plankton, it is not normally caught with a hook and line; instead, the most effective method is usually to use bowfishing gear in shallow waters.

Despite the presence of the tilapia, largemouth bass do very well at Fairfield, in part because of the abundance of smaller prey fish, such as threadfin shad, in the warm water. Bass as large as 13 or 14 pounds have been caught there. Other popular fish include hybrid striped bass, crappie, and both channel and flathead catfish.

The state park attracts more than just anglers; swimmers enjoy the warmer water at a sandy, buoyed swimming area, and boat ramps provide easy access for waterskiers and sailboats. Away from the lake, two easy hiking trails lead to quiet areas of the park. The longer trail of the two leads to a primitive camping area for backpackers which, despite its designation, isn't too primitive: it has water, flush toilets, and charcoal grills.

VISITOR INFORMATION

1,460 acres. Open all year. Hot and humid in summer. Busiest on week-ends, spring through fall. Large developed campground with showers; most sites have hookups. Picnic area. Primitive camp area for backpackers. Limited visitor services available in nearby Fairfield; more extensive services in Palestine and Corsicana. For information: Fairfield Lake State Park, 123 State Park Road 64, Fairfield, TX 75840, (903) 389-4514.

ABOVE:
Lake fishing
RIGHT:
Sunrise over Fairfield Lake

Fanthorp Inn State Historical Park

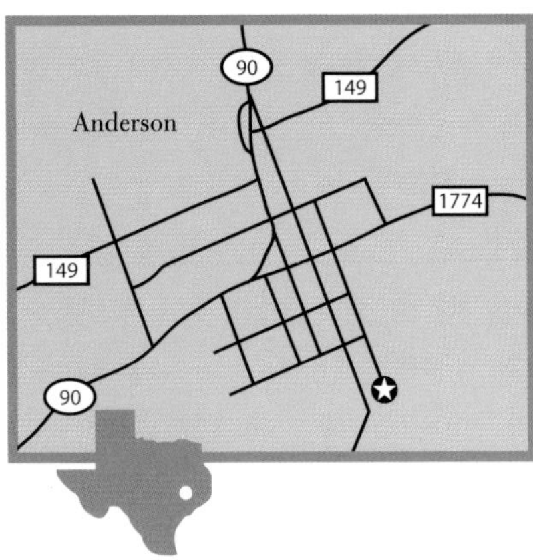

Travelers in the early days of the Texas Republic generally found accommodations to be either rough or nonexistent. Usually they ended up staying in the tiny, primitive houses of settlers. As time passed, however, roadside inns developed to serve the needs of travelers. Initially, the Fanthorp Inn was little more than a small log house shared with travelers, but it later became a sizable, prosperous inn, until its closure shortly after the Civil War.

Henry Fanthorp, an Englishman, purchased land on which to build the inn in 1832 from one of Stephen F. Austin's first colonists. Initially he built a corncrib and dealt in corn, buying when prices were low and selling when they were high. He soon built a two-room dogtrot log home, and in 1834, having been twice widowed, he married Rachel Kennard. They had three children over the next few years.

The Fanthorp home was well located on busy roads and became a popular stopping place for travelers. Several stage lines passed through, providing a steady flow of customers. Fanthorp charged between one and two dollars per night for food and accommodations for one person and a horse. The food served was basic: beef, pork, corn bread, and sweet potatoes, enlivened at times with chicken, turkey, and apple pie. One boarder described the coffee as "strong enough to bear up an iron wedge." Although the food received mixed reviews, it must have been better than the alternatives, because the inn grew in popularity.

To accommodate the increasing trade, Fanthorp steadily enlarged the inn. He built additions and a second story with an upstairs gallery, so that the building ultimately ended up with eighteen rooms. To lessen the risk of fire and to keep the main building cooler, the kitchen was built as a separate structure in back. Travelers' horses were boarded in a barn. Quite a few famous people, including Sam Houston, Anson Jones, and Henderson Yoakum, stayed at the establishment over the years. Others rumored to have visited include Jefferson Davis, Robert E. Lee, Ulysses S. Grant, and Zachary Taylor. Kenneth Anderson, the last vice-president of the Republic of Texas, died at the inn on July 3, 1845, and was buried in the Fanthorp family cemetery. The town developing around the inn was named Anderson in his honor.

The inn prospered during the Civil War, but Henry and Rachel Fanthorp died of yellow fever shortly after in 1867, and their one surviving heir, daughter Mary Fanthorp Stone, soon closed the inn. She and her descendants used the hotel as a private residence and kept it in the family until 1977, when it was conveyed to the Texas Parks and Wildlife Department. The department has done a meticulous job of restoring the inn to its appearance during its heyday from 1850 to 1867. For six generations, the historic inn remained in the Fanthorp family; today it provides a glimpse of Texas in bygone days.

VISITOR INFORMATION

1.4 acres. Open all year for tours Wednesday through Sunday, 9 A.M.–4 P.M. Historic structure with exhibits, picnicking. Limited food and gas available in Anderson; full visitor services in Navasota and Bryan. For information: Fanthorp Inn State Historical Park, P.O. Box 296, Anderson, TX 77830, (936) 873-2633.

Fanthorp Inn

Fort Parker State Park

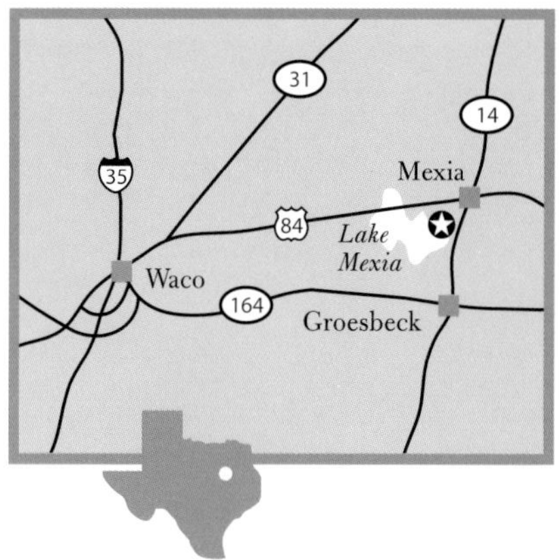

Fort Parker State Park lies in lush, gently rolling terrain in east-central Texas, south of Mexia. Its wooded facilities line the shore of 750-acre Lake Fort Parker. The small reservoir was created by the Civilian Conservation Corps (CCC) in the 1930s by building an earth-fill dam on the Navasota River. The CCC was established during the Depression of the 1930s to provide jobs for unemployed young men. Its workers were responsible for much of the construction at many state parks and other public facilities in Texas, as well as in the rest of the country. At Fort Parker State Park, in addition to constructing the dam, the CCC also built roads and buildings.

The park rests in an area where there are characteristics of both the post-oak woodland and the Blackland Prairie. Because the park was established many years ago, a tall canopy of oaks, cedar elms, pecans, hickories, and other trees has grown up. The thick woods shelter such wildlife as white-tailed deer, armadillos, opossums, raccoons, and many bird species. A short hiking trail provides good opportunities to view some of these creatures, especially early and late in the day.

The waters of Lake Fort Parker hide some of the park's most popular wildlife. Fishing piers, a boat ramp, and an extensive shoreline provide excellent lake access for anglers, and popular catches include largemouth and white bass, crappie, and channel, blue, and flathead catfish. Small boats can travel upstream on the Navasota River, adding more fishing opportunities.

In winter, the Texas Parks and Wildlife Department stocks rainbow trout in tiny Lake Springfield, located just east of the Lake Fort Parker dam. Cool spring water feeding Lake Springfield, together with colder winter weather, allows these cold-water fish to survive there. The lake is reached via a short hiking trail that starts near the group camp area.

Because Lake Fort Parker is small and shallow, it is better suited to canoes and small fishing boats than to large, fast boats and waterskiers. Although the lake's small size restricts some activities, it makes it a quiet retreat from everyday life, and one that continues to attract visitors, as it has been doing for more than 50 years.

VISITOR INFORMATION

1,459 acres. Open all year. Hot and humid in summer. Small campground with partial hookups and showers. Screened shelters. Fishing piers, boat ramp, short hiking trails, swimming, picnicking. Park store with seasonal canoe and paddleboat rentals. Full visitor services available in Mexia and Groesbeck. For information: Fort Parker State Park, Route 3, Box 95, Mexia, TX 76667, (254) 562-5751.

Lake Fort Parker fishing pier

Lake Bastrop State Park

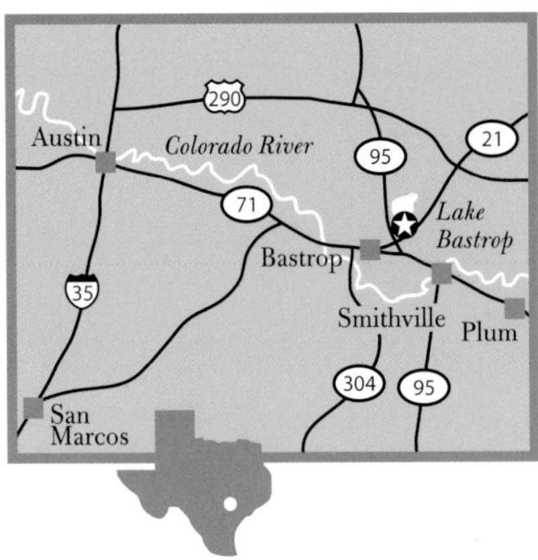

Lake Bastrop State Park lies on the shore of Lake Bastrop, about 3 miles northeast of the town of Bastrop. The 906-acre lake was created in 1965 when the Lower Colorado River Authority (LCRA) dammed Spicer Creek, a tributary of the Colorado River. The lake functions primarily as a cooling pond for the natural-gas-fired Sim Gideon Power Plant. The lake has since become popular for recreation, with camping, fishing, swimming, and boating facilities having been developed.

To the surprise of many, thick stands of loblolly pines thrive on sandy hills on the east side of the lake. Called the Lost Pines, they are isolated from the East Texas pine forests by more than 60 miles of post-oak woodland. During the wetter and cooler times of the last ice age, pine forests grew in an uninterrupted blanket from East Texas to the Bastrop area and westward. As the climate warmed and dried, the trees retreated eastward, leaving an isolated 70-square-mile pocket of pines—part of which lines the shore of Lake Bastrop—just east of the town of Bastrop. The Carrizo and Reklaw sandstone formations there created soil conditions that allowed the pines to survive in the drier climate. The sandstones are rich in iron oxide, giving them a yellowish-to-reddish-brown color. Pines dominate the forest canopy, especially on the east side of the lake, but a mix of post oaks, blackjack oaks, eastern red cedars, mesquites, and other trees also grows at the park.

The park has two sections, one on the north shore and the other on the south. The north-shore site offers day-use activities only, such as picnicking and fishing, while the south shore, recently developed by the Texas Parks and Wildlife Department, has a campground. Both facilities are operated by the LCRA.

VISITOR INFORMATION

785 acres. The park is scheduled to open in late 1996 or early 1997. Hot and humid in summer. Moderate number of campsites with partial hookups and showers. Lighted fishing pier, boat ramp, swimming, waterskiing, hiking trail, picnicking. Full services available in Bastrop. For information: Lake Bastrop State Park, c/o Bastrop State Park, P.O. Box 518, Bastrop, TX 78602, (512) 321-2101.

TOP:
Swimmers
ABOVE:
Boat docks and fishing pier

Lake Mineral Wells State Park

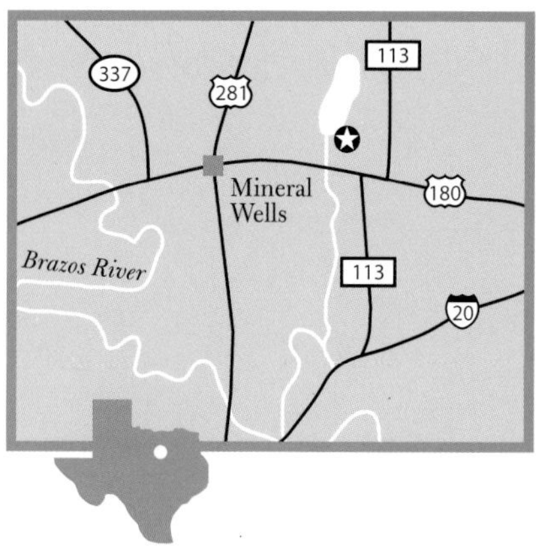

Lake Mineral Wells State Park has some of the most diverse recreational opportunities of any state park in Texas. The 646-acre lake offers swimming and boating, although waterskiing and jet skis are not allowed because of its small size. Several fishing piers and boats allow easy access for anglers. Extensive hiking trails lead to primitive campsites deep in the park's backcountry. There is also a 12-mile roundtrip trail for horseback riders and mountain bikes. At the trailhead there is even a developed equestrian campground, with adequate parking for 20 horse trailers. A 20-mile rail-trail for hikers, cyclists, and equestrians was created from an abandoned railroad grade.

Most surprising to first-time park visitors are the rock-climbing opportunities on bluffs on the east side of the lake. In only three other state parks in Texas—Enchanted Rock, Hueco Tanks, and Caprock Canyons—is rock climbing possible. The park is particularly popular with climbers from the Dallas–Fort Worth area. As would be expected in the rolling North Texas terrain, the cliffs are generally no more than 35–40 feet high. However, the sheer rock faces

Sunrise over Lake Mineral Wells

and overhangs offer plenty of challenges to climbers.

Much of the rock-climbing activity takes place in Penitentiary Hollow, a small but scenic maze of cliffs, narrow canyons, and massive boulders. Tall cedar elms and other trees dot the area, reaching toward the sun from deep, shaded canyon bottoms. The rock is a firm, durable conglomerate, which provides an excellent climbing surface. Climbs are rated on a scale of increasing difficulty, from 5.1 to 5.14. Climbs at Penitentiary Hollow rate as difficult as 5.10–5.11.

During World War II, the hollow was a boot-camp training center for Fort Wolters. The difficult, punishing military training they underwent there left veterans with less fond memories of the place than most modern-day rock climbers have.

The state park lies within the Cross Timbers region, where rolling hills of sandstone and shale are covered with thick, stunted woods of cedar elm, post oak, blackjack oak, Ashe juniper, and mesquite, interspersed with occasional grassy prairies. These dense woods made travel difficult in the early days. Pecans and cottonwoods thrive in the moister bottomlands along creeks and rivers. Wildlife commonly found in the park includes white-tailed deer, wild turkeys, and many bird species.

Much of the park's soil has a reddish color, due to the presence of iron. Coal was mined in the area, as close as 6 miles north of the park. The ghost town of Thurber, 30 miles to the southwest, depended for years on mining that began in the 1880s. The nearby town of Mineral Wells got its start in 1885, when the first mineral-water well in the county was discovered there. Crazy Well's highly mineralized water was said to cure mental illness, among other maladies. The town had become an important health spa by the early twentieth century, with 400 wells producing water with the same reputedly curative properties. Today, the state park is probably the largest draw in the Mineral Wells area.

VISITOR INFORMATION

3,010 acres. Open all year. Hot in summer. Large campground with partial hookups and showers. Screened shelters. Developed equestrian campground. Primitive campsites for backpackers. Hiking, mountain-bike, and equestrian trails, boat ramp, fishing piers, picnicking, and swimming. Rock climbers must register at park headquarters; there are restrictions on bolts, pitons, and other rock-damaging equipment. Seasonal park concession store. Full visitor services available in Mineral Wells. For information: Lake Mineral Wells State Park, 100 Park Road 71, Mineral Wells, TX 76067, (940) 328-1171.

LEFT:
Rock climbing in Penitentiary Hollow
RIGHT:
Lake Somerville Trailway

LAKE SOMERVILLE STATE PARK

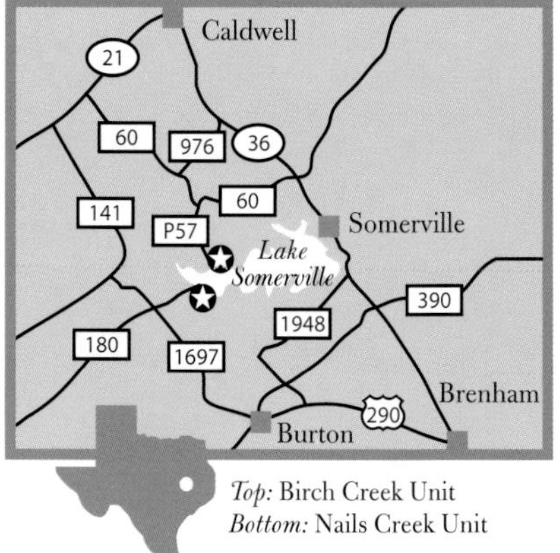

Top: Birch Creek Unit
Bottom: Nails Creek Unit

Lake Somerville State Park contains a surprisingly large undeveloped tract of land in the middle of the state, on the shores of Lake Somerville. In 1962, the U.S. Army Corps of Engineers began building Somerville Dam to control flooding and to provide municipal water. The dam was constructed on Yegua Creek, about 20 miles upstream from its confluence with the Brazos River. The two main units of the state park, Nails Creek and Birch Creek, lie across the lake from each other, and are connected by the extensive Lake Somerville Trailway that loops

around the undeveloped west end of the lake.

Both units contain campgrounds, boat ramps, picnic and swimming areas, and nature trails. Boaters and waterskiers can set out on the 11,460-acre lake from both units. Anglers try their luck from the shore or the fishing pier at Birch Creek, or else launch boats and search for a favorite fishing hole. Popular catches include white bass, crappie, large-mouth bass, and catfish. Children splash around in the lake, keeping cool on hot days.

Most people stay at one or the other of the two units, but the park's real jewel is the trail system, which contains almost 22 miles of trail. The main trail is 13 miles long and connects the two park units; spurs and side loops make up the rest of the trailway. The broad trail is open to hikers, equestrians, and mountain-bikers. Because some of the side trails have small bridges that cannot handle the weight of a horse, a few of them are not open to equestrians. Special developed equestrian campgrounds have been built at each unit at the start of the trail, and along the way there are several primitive campgrounds, with pit toilets, for equestrians and backpackers.

The trail passes through a mix of two habitats—the Blackland Prairie and the post-oak savannah. Lush meadows, carpeted with wildflowers in the spring, line parts of the trail and offer broad views of the lake and surrounding country. The hillsides often contain a mix of yaupons, post oaks, blackjack oaks, and other plants. In creek bottoms, a dense canopy of water oaks, elms, hickories, and other trees shades the trail. Waterfowl and wading birds favor Flag Pond, near the Nails Creek end of the trail. This large undeveloped area encourages abundant wildlife; raccoons, white-tailed deer, coyotes, rabbits, and many other creatures are commonly sighted.

VISITOR INFORMATION

5,970 acres. Open all year. Hot and humid in summer. Large number of developed campsites with partial hookups and showers, at both units. Equestrian campgrounds at both units. Primitive campsites for backpackers and equestrians between the two units. Hiking and nature trails, picnicking, waterskiing, swimming, boat ramps at both units. Fishing pier at Birch Creek. Extensive hiking, mountain-biking, and equestrian trail system connects units. Full visitor services available in Brenham, Giddings, and Caldwell. For information: Lake Somerville State Park, Birch Creek Unit, Route 1, Box 499, Somerville, TX 77879, (979) 535-7763; Nails Creek Unit, Route 1, Box 61C, Ledbetter, TX 78946, (979) 289-2392.

Lake Somerville

Lake Tawakoni State Park

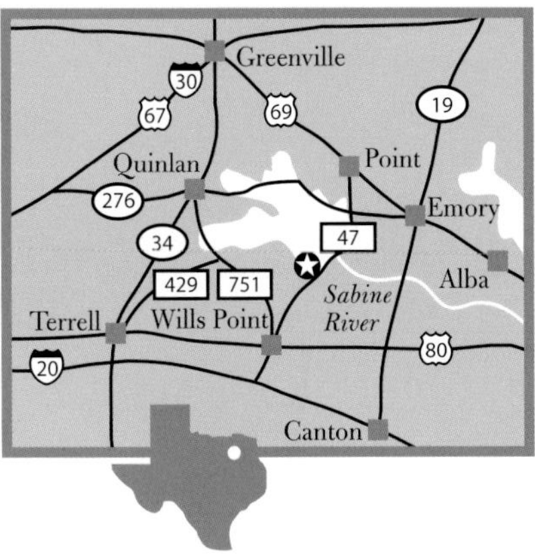

Lake Tawakoni is a new state park that is still under development. At present, facilities are under construction and it is accessible only by special request. The chief activities currently are birding, wildlife observation, and shoreline fishing.

Lake Tawakoni is a large 36,700-acre reservoir built on the upper reaches of the Sabine River east of Dallas. The lake was created primarily as a water supply for Dallas and other local communities. It was named for an early Indian tribe. The park lies on a small section of the approximately 200-mile-long lakeshore. Large areas of submerged timber encourage good fish populations, and anglers visit the lake in large numbers, hoping to catch striped bass, largemouth bass, crappie, and catfish.

The park and surrounding terrain is relatively flat, typical for the area. Post-oak savannah is the dominant habitat, with a mix of woodland and open prairie areas. Post oaks, along with cedar elms, red oaks, hackberries, eastern red cedars, and hickories, make up the forested sections.

Planned facilities include a day-use area, 78 multiuse campsites, 18 walk-in primitive sites, a swim beach, and a boat ramp. The Parks and Wildlife Department hope to have construction completed by Fall 2000.

VISITOR INFORMATION

376 acres. For information: Lake Tawakoni State Park, c/o Purtis Creek State Park, 14225 FM 316, Eustace, TX 75124, (903) 425-2332.

Lake Whitney State Park

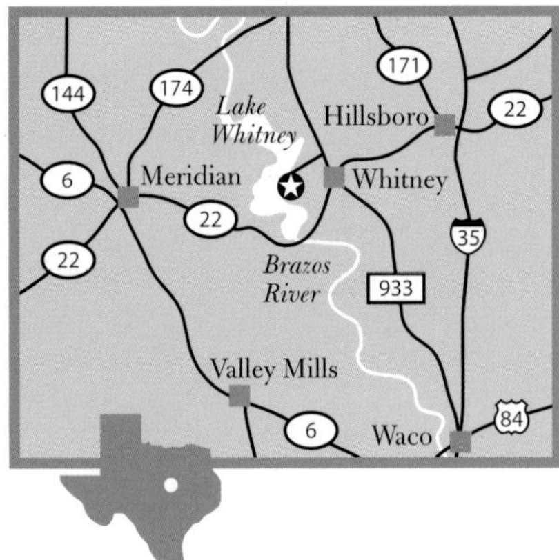

Lake Whitney State Park lies on a peninsula on the eastern shore of 23,560-acre Lake Whitney, created in 1951 when the U.S. Army Corps of Engineers completed a 2-mile-long dam on the Brazos River. The dam was built for flood control and power generation. The large lake winds upstream from the dam for 45 miles, providing plenty of room for large numbers of boaters, anglers, and waterskiers.

Without a doubt, the lake is the main draw of the popular state park, especially in summer and on warm weekends in spring and fall. Most camping and picnic sites lie near the lakeshore, within sight of water. There are no restrictions on the size of boats or motors used in the large, deep lake, and boat ramps in the park

Sailboat on Lake Whitney

make boat-launching easy. Water-skiers, too, love the broad, open lake and zip back and forth across the water. The wide expanse of water also provides a spacious setting for sailboats to glide across.

Lake Whitney is noted for its variety of fishing opportunities. Excellent smallmouth-bass fishing can be found along rocky sections of shore; the bass favor rocky areas under cliffs because they need such a habitat to spawn. That the lake is conducive to the smallmouth bass is clear from the fact that the largest smallmouth bass ever caught in Texas was caught here.

Largemouth bass, another popular Lake Whitney catch, favor a different type of habitat—shallow areas with aquatic vegetation and submerged trees and brush. The striped bass, a saltwater fish that lives mostly in the ocean and that breeds in freshwater rivers and streams, was introduced into Lake Whitney in 1973. It has done well there, and has even spawned, although stocking still continues. Catches of 20 pounds or more have not been uncommon. Other popular fish include white bass, crappie, and catfish.

The park lies above the lake, on gently rolling slopes covered with a mix of oak woodland and grasslands. The habitat consists of a mix of Blackland Prairie and Hill Country species. In spring, blankets of wildflowers, particularly such favorites as bluebonnets and Indian paintbrushes, attract large numbers of visitors. Frequently seen animals include white-tailed deer, squirrels, armadillos, rabbits, raccoons, and opossums.

When the dam was built, the lake flooded the early Texas settlement of Towash. The village was named for a chief of the Hasinai Indian tribe that moved into the area in 1835. A marker commemorating the village has been built in the park.

While most state parks in Texas can only be reached by car, Lake Whitney State Park caters also to visitors wishing to fly there—it has a paved airstrip that can accommodate small planes.

VISITOR INFORMATION

955 acres. Open all year. Hot and humid in summer. Large number of campsites with partial or full hookups, and showers. Screened shelters. Hiking and mini-bike trails, picnicking, swimming, boating, boat ramps, waterskiing, fishing, paved airstrip. Limited visitor services available in Whitney; full services in Hillsboro and Waco. For information: Lake Whitney State Park, P.O. Box 1175, Whitney, TX 76692, (254) 694-3793.

Lake Whitney campsite

Lockhart State Park

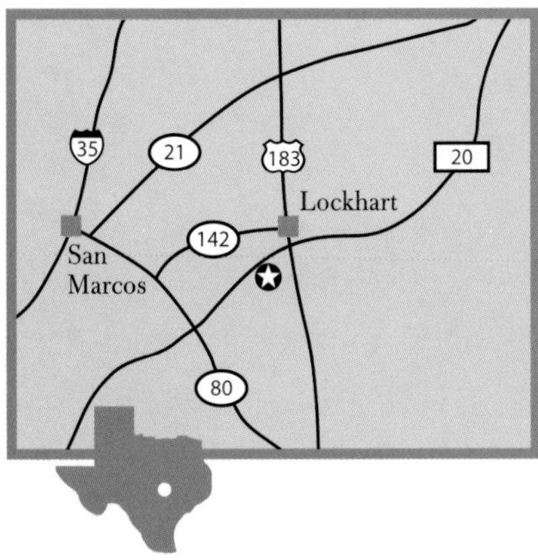

Lockhart State Park is a small, quiet retreat in the Blackland Prairie region of central Texas. An attractive golf course, of which there are few in the state-park system, draws local golfers, as well as many from further away. Its 9 holes follow the slopes along and above Clear Fork Creek, crossing it more than once. Hole distance ranges from about 150 yards to more than 500, with a total of 3,000 yards, and a par of 35.

Tucked deep in the trees on a bluff above the golf course is a recreation hall built by the Civilian Conservation Corps (CCC) in the 1930s. The CCC was started during the Depression to create jobs for unemployed young men. Its workers carried out all the construction work at this and many other new state parks during the dark economic days of the Depression. Until the late 1940s, the park was leased to a local country club, but since then it has been managed by the state. An adjoining rodeo arena is part of the park, but is leased to and managed by the Lockhart Kiwanis Club.

A swimming pool provides an opportunity to cool off, and other popular recreational pursuits include picnicking, camping, and fishing for bass, catfish, or sunfish in the creek.

VISITOR INFORMATION

264 acres. Open all year. Hot and humid in summer. Small number of campsites have partial or full hookups. Picnicking, fishing; swimming pool open during the summer months—call for hours and fees. Golf carts can be rented at park headquarters. Full visitor services available in Lockhart. For information: Lockhart State Park, 4179 State Park Road, Lockhart, TX 78644, (512) 398-3479.

ABOVE:
Lockhart State Park golf course
RIGHT:
CCC-built stone refectory

Meridian State Park

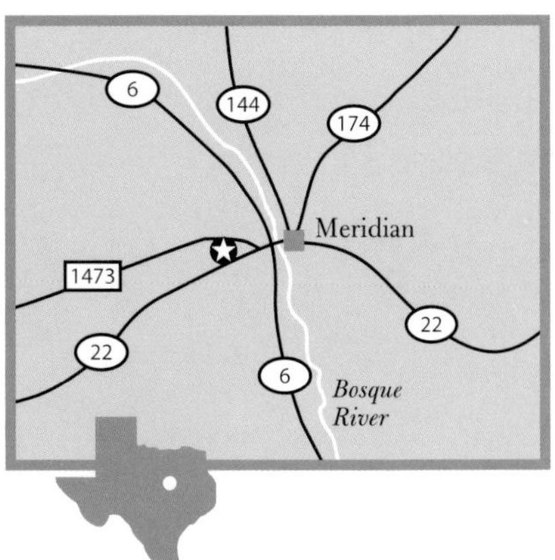

Meridian State Park lies in an area of gently rolling hills northwest of Waco. A mix of several Texas habitats covers the terrain, including elements of the Edwards Plateau, Blackland Prairie, and Cross Timbers regions. Ashe juniper, commonly called cedar, is the dominant tree, particularly on drier hillsides. Other trees include live oaks, post oaks, and blackjack oaks. In moist areas, such trees as cottonwoods, pecans, and cedar elms thrive.

A small 72-acre lake, created when a dam was constructed across Bee Creek, forms the centerpiece of the park. The dam and other park facilities, including an attractive, solidly built refectory, were built by the Civilian Conservation Corps during the Depression in the 1930s. Bee Creek originates in the hills a short distance north of the park and, downstream from the dam, flows into Meridian Creek. A short distance

further, the combined creek joins the North Bosque River, a larger watercourse that flows through the town of Meridian just east of the park.

The thick woods of Ashe juniper within the park attract a rare bird, the golden-cheeked warbler. The endangered warbler arrives early in the spring to build its nests using bark from the Ashe juniper. Probably because of its need for the juniper bark, it nests nowhere in the world but the Edwards Plateau area of Texas.

Offering a variety of recreational opportunities, as well as a quiet retreat, the park attracts a wide range of people. In spring, birders come, hoping to catch a glimpse of the golden-cheeked warbler or another rare bird, the black-capped vireo. Several miles of hiking trails wind through the woods and around the lake, providing excellent access for birders. In good years, wildflowers blanket the roadsides and open areas of the park, providing another attraction. During the hot days of summer, the lake is the park's main draw. Swimmers paddle through the cool waters and anglers cast their lines, hoping to hook bass, crappie, or catfish. Boating is allowed, but only at speeds of less than 5 miles per hour.

VISITOR INFORMATION

502 acres. Open all year. Hot and humid in summer. Small campground with partial hookups and showers. Screened shelters. Hiking and nature trails, picnicking, swimming, no-wake boating, fishing, birding. Limited visitor services available in Meridian; full services in Waco. For information: Meridian State Park, Route 2, Box 2465, Meridian, TX 76665, (254) 435-2536.

TOP:
Meridian State Park lake
BOTTOM:
Sunset over lake

Monument Hill • Kreische Brewery State Historical Parks

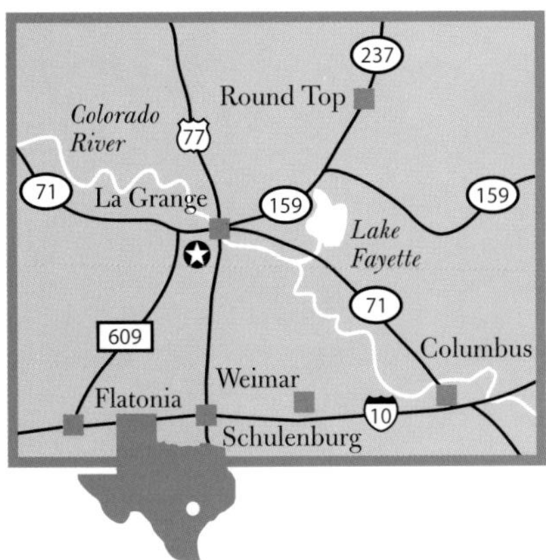

On top of a high bluff on the south side of the Colorado River, across from La Grange, are two sites of significance in the history of Texas. One is an early Texas brewery and the other is a tall granite and limestone monument that marks the tomb of Texans who died at the Battle of Salado Creek and on the ill-fated Mier Expedition.

After Texas won its independence from Mexico in 1836, ownership of the land between the Rio Grande and the Nueces River was a matter of dispute between the two countries. In February 1842, General Rafael Vasquez led Mexican troops on a raid of San Antonio and then retreated back to Mexico. Some months later, on September 11, a large body of Mexican troops under General Adrian Woll captured San Antonio. The next day, news of the attack reached the town of Gonzales, and Mathew Caldwell assembled Texas troops to go to San Antonio.

Three days after the attack, news reached La Grange, and a small group there assembled and marched on San Antonio as well. Others joined along the way, so that by the time it reached San Antonio, the group comprised 54 men. During the march, Nicholas Dawson was elected captain. On September 18, Dawson's men reached the San Antonio area, but were intercepted by 400 Mexican troops about two miles from Caldwell's position on Salado Creek. The outnumbered Texans were defeated: 36 were killed, 15 were captured, and 3 escaped. The next day, Caldwell's men buried Dawson's men at the battlefield. Caldwell and his men pursued Woll's troops back toward Mexico, but the Mexicans were able to retreat largely unscathed.

After learning of the Mexican raid, President Sam Houston assembled troops under Brigadier General Alexander Somervell and sent them to San Antonio. On November 25, Somervell and his men marched to the Rio Grande, but failed to find the enemy troops. Some of the Texans returned to San Antonio, but more than 300 remained on the border under Captain William Fisher. On December 25, they attacked the Mexican town of Mier after learning that it was defended by General Pedro de Ampudia and 350 men. The battle raged on into the next day, with the Texans having the advantage. Ampudia, who was about to retreat, bluffed, claiming that he had 1,700 troops in the city and 800 nearby. Even though they were, unknowingly, on the verge of victory, the Texans fell for the ruse and surrendered.

The captured Texans were marched toward Mexico City. At Rancho Salado, 188 Texans escaped, but 176 were caught again within two weeks. General Santa Anna ordered that one-tenth of the recaptured escapees be shot. To determine which of them would be executed, 17 black beans were put in a pot with 159 white beans. Those who drew the black beans were summarily executed and the others were jailed until September 12, 1844.

In 1847, during the Mexican-American War, American troops exhumed the remains of the Texans buried at Rancho Salado and shipped them to La Grange. Shortly after, the remains of Captain Dawson's party were retrieved from near Salado Creek and also brought to La Grange.

Colorado River from Monument Hill

On September 18, 1848, the remains of the men were given a full military burial in a tomb on the bluff overlooking the Colorado River above La Grange. Sam Houston and other dignitaries attended the ceremony.

In 1849, Heinrich Kreische purchased the property upon which the tomb lay. In the 1870s, Kreische built a brewery near the tomb, and by the late 1870s, his brewery was the third largest in Texas. At the time he purchased the property, a Fayette County committee agreed to buy 10 acres of land from him that included the tomb, and to build a monument there. It failed to follow through with the agreement, however, and over time, the tomb deteriorated. Finally, in the 1930s, a new granite vault was built around the tomb and a 48-foot-high marker was erected. The land was purchased in 1956 and the site became a park.

In 1977, the state also acquired adjoining land that included the old Kreische holdings. Among these was the old brewery, a large three-story structure constructed of locally quarried sandstone and with wood framing. Kreische had built his home in several sections above the brewery between 1855 and 1882, the year he died. Although the brewery seems to have been prosperous at the time of his death, it declined and went out of business soon after. Family descendants continued to live in Kreische's home until 1952, but the brewery fell into ruin. Today, visitors can tour the brewery, as well as the old tomb and its marker, and enjoy the sweeping view from the top of the bluff.

VISITOR INFORMATION

40 acres. Monument, tomb, and interpretive trails open all year; brewery tours are usually conducted on weekends. Call ahead for dates and times. Day use only. Historic structures and exhibits, nature trail, picnicking. Full visitor services available in La Grange. For information: Monument Hill/Kreische Brewery State Historical Park, 414 State Loop 92, La Grange, TX 78945, (409) 968-5658.

Historic Kreische home

Mother Neff State Park

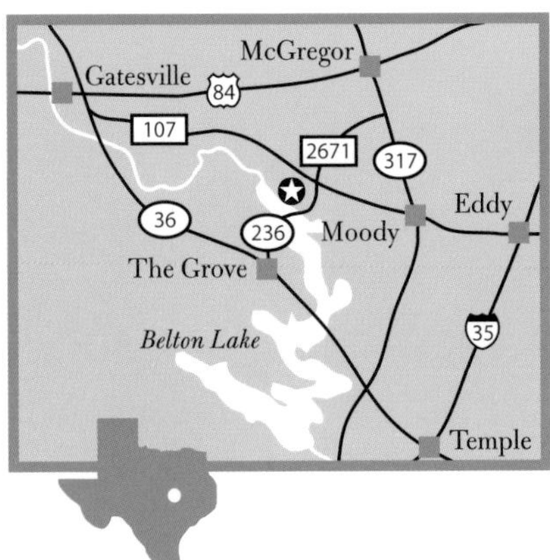

Mother Neff State Park, a quiet retreat on the shady banks of the Leon River, is the first state park in Texas. In the early part of this century, Isabella Eleanor ("Mother") Neff donated 6 acres of land along the Leon River floodplain to the state for community meetings. She and her husband Noah were early settlers of the region, arriving there from Roanoke, Virginia in 1855. One of her sons, Pat Neff, was governor of Texas from 1921 to 1925. During his tenure, he created the Texas State Parks Board and arranged for his mother's donated property to become the first state park in Texas.

Governor Neff was a tireless supporter of the parks system, traveling often and making many speeches in support of the program. In the 1930s, when Neff was chairman of the State Parks Board, he donated the remainder of the land that makes up the 259-acre park.

Mother Neff's legacy remains a popular retreat today. Most recreational opportunities are concentrated in the rich bottomland lining the Leon River. During the Depression, the

Civilian Conservation Corps developed the park, building attractive, durable stone structures—including a pavilion called the tabernacle, as well as the headquarters building—in the bottomland area. Tall pecans, sycamores, elms, oaks, and other trees thrive in the rich soil and shade the developed area along the river.

A short loop drive leads north away from the river along a narrow rocky ravine to the prairie uplands. Dense stands of Ashe juniper cloak the rocky slopes between the prairie and the river. A hiking trail winds through the ravine area and leads to a limestone rock shelter once used by Indians and to a pool called the Wash Pond, also thought to have been used by Indians and early pioneers. In spring, wildflowers blanket the upland prairie, a small remnant of the prairies that once covered much of central Texas.

The park lies at the extreme northeastern edge of the Edwards Plateau, the massive uplift from which the Hill Country was formed. It has mixed vegetation, with plants from the Edwards Plateau to the west, the Blackland Prairies to the east, and the Cross Timbers region to the north. Although Mother Neff State Park is small, it contains a variety of natural features and offers a range of recreational opportunities to visitors.

VISITOR INFORMATION

259 acres. Open all year. Hot in summer. Small number of campsites with partial hookups and showers. Hiking, picnicking, fishing. Limited visitor services available in Moody; full services in Temple and Waco. For information: Mother Neff State Park, 1680 Texas Highway 236, Moody, TX 76557, (254) 853-2389.

OPPOSITE PAGE, TOP:
CCC-built tabernacle
OPPOSITE PAGE, BOTTOM:
Limestone rock shelter
RIGHT:
Reconstructed fort

Old Fort Parker State Historical Park

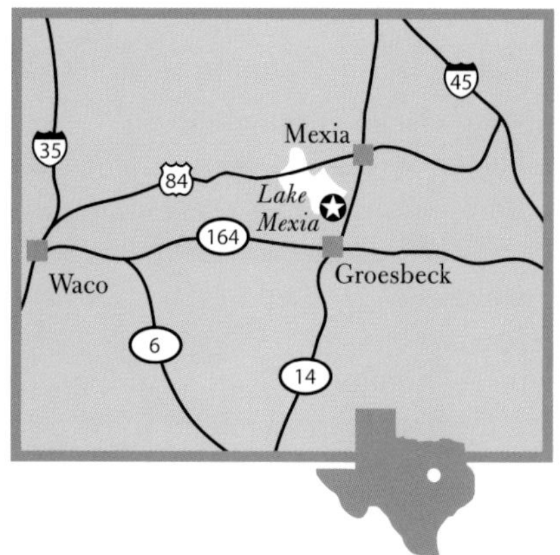

In 1833, the Parker family came with a group of pioneers to Texas from Illinois. Upon reaching Texas, one part of the group settled near the present town of Elkhart and the others settled near the Navasota River. Led by John Parker, the Navasota River settlers built a wooden stockade for protection against Indian attacks. It was constructed of split cedars that were sharpened at one end and buried three feet in the ground at the other. Two-story blockhouses built at opposite corners of the stockade provided good fields of fire along the stockade walls to help defend the fort from attack. Two rows of log cabins were built along the inside walls of the fort for residences.

By March 1834, the stockade was finished and the settlers moved in and started clearing surrounding land for fields. Life was difficult for them, but it seemed secure, especially after Texas's war for independence ended in triumph, in the April of 1836. However, the following month, on May 19, 1836, a band of Indians attacked the fort while most of the men were working in the fields. The raiders gained entry to the stockade before the gate could be closed. Five settlers were killed and five were captured; the

remainder abandoned the fort and made their way to the safety of Fort Houston.

The most famous of the captives was nine-year-old Cynthia Ann Parker. She was adopted by a group of Comanches and in time adopted their ways and language and took the name Naduah. In her teens, she married Chief Peta Nacona and bore three children.

In 1860, Captain Sul Ross and some Texas Rangers attacked a Comanche camp on the banks of the Pease River. One of the rangers captured Cynthia Parker and her infant daughter as they tried to escape. Sul Ross noticed the woman's blue eyes and realized that Parker was not an Indian. After he discovered her identity, he returned her to relatives in East Texas. However, she was unable to readjust to Anglo-American life and died about four years later, shortly after the death of her daughter, Prairie Flower.

Cynthia Parker's two older sons remained with the Comanches after she was taken by the rangers. One of them, Quanah Parker, became a warrior and chief of the Comanches and defended their land after most others had given up and gone to the reservation. Finally, however, in 1875, Quanah realized that the Comanches' situation was hopeless and took the remainder of his people to the reservation at Fort Sill in what would become Oklahoma.

Ironically, considering his mother's inability to readapt to Anglo-American culture, Quanah Parker helped his fellow Indians live with the white people's ways. He taught them ranching and farming and established schools on the reservation. He later became a judge for several Oklahoma reservations. He died in 1911, greatly respected by both Indians and the white community.

The fort from which the long history of Cynthia and Quanah Parker began has been reconstructed twice on the grassy prairie between Groesbeck and Mexia. Within the stockade walls today are exhibits that document the fort's short and turbulent life. The fort is operated by the City of Groesbeck. The park can be rented for special events or seminars.

VISITOR INFORMATION

38 acres. Open daily. Hot in summer. Campground with partial hookups and primitive camping available. Historic structure and interpretive exhibits. Visitor services available in Groesbeck and Mexia. For information: Old Fort Parker State Historical Park, Route 3, Box 746, Groesbeck, TX 76642, (254) 729-5253.

Palmetto State Park

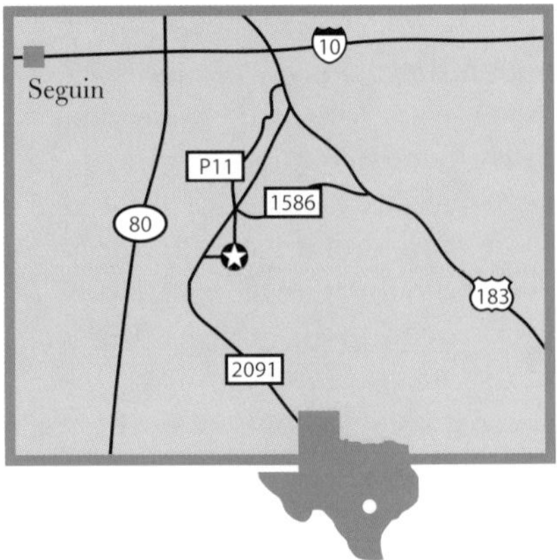

Palmetto State Park provides a surprising contrast to the gently rolling hills of post-oak woodland that surround it. It is located in the Ottine Swamp, which, with its lush, tropical appearance, lies on a terrace of the San Marcos River valley, nourished by underground water and intermittent flooding. The water feeds a boggy oasis most notable for the thick understory of dwarf palmettos, which usually grow further east, in wetter climates. A tall forest of green ash, Lacey and burr oak, sycamore, and other trees creates a thick canopy of foliage. Two species of iris, a purple native and a yellow import, add splashes of color to the margins of ponds.

Native iris in Ottine Swamp

Adolph Otto and his family settled in the area in 1879 and built a cotton gin and sawmill nearby. Because there was already a post office named Otto in the state and, in the days before zip codes, the postal service would not allow two post offices to have the same name, the village was named Ottine, a name created by combining Otto with Christine, the name of the wife of one of Otto's sons.

The lush vegetation that is now limited to the small swamp at Palmetto probably covered a much larger area during the cooler, wetter ice age 12,000 years ago. As the climate became warmer and drier, the greenery at Palmetto was able to survive only in its present isolated location, fed by springs and flooding.

The springs that feed the swamp issue out of Carrizo sands that are exposed at the base of the bluff that lines the river valley. At one time, thermal springs and mud volcanoes fed by underground water and natural gas existed in the park and, together with the unusual swamp, were a major draw for visitors at the turn of the century. Unfortunately, extensive groundwater pumping and other changes wrought by humans have caused them mostly to dry up. If the Civilian Conservation Corps (CCC) had not put in a well to provide supplementary water to the swamp, the remaining bog might have also disappeared by now. A faint sulfur smell rises from the water pumped from this well.

Before the park was established, the San Antonio and Aransas Pass Railroad offered weekend excursion trips to Palmetto. In 1933, the State Parks Board acquired part of the Ottine Swamp and established Palmetto State Park. During the Depression, the CCC helped build park facilities. The most notable structure is the large refectory, built from heavy blocks of reddish, iron-rich native sandstone and large wooden timbers.

Today, the unusual bog still attracts visitors. Birders, too, frequent the park, hoping to see some of the 240 species recorded there. In the spring, the area in and around the park is excellent for wildflower viewing. Three nature trails, one in the bog area and two in floodplain woodland, introduce the unique swamp of Palmetto State Park to visitors.

VISITOR INFORMATION

269 acres. Open all year. Hot and humid in summer. Small number of campsites with partial hookups and showers, in two areas. Fishing in river and small oxbow lake, picnicking, swimming, hiking and nature trails, canoeing on San Marcos River. Full visitor services available in Luling and Gonzales. For information: Palmetto State Park, 78 Park Road 11 S., Gonzales, TX 78629, (830) 672-3266.

CCC-built stone refectory

Purtis Creek State Park

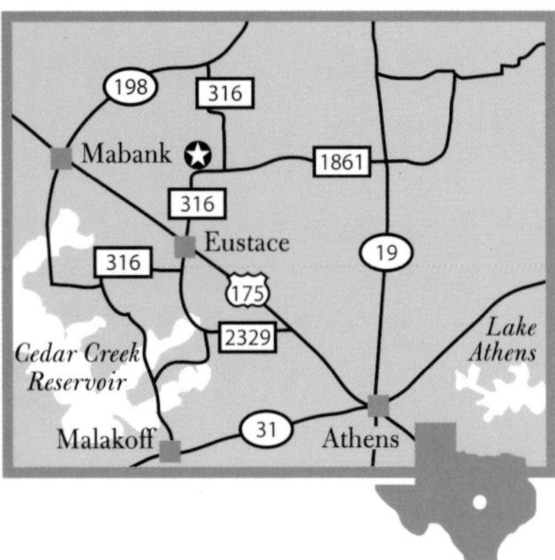

Purtis Creek State Park was literally built for anglers. The land was purchased in the late 1970s and dam construction began in 1981. As soon as the 355-acre reservoir had filled, the Texas Parks and Wildlife Department began stocking Florida largemouth bass, channel catfish, coppernose bluegills, shad, and redear sunfish. Before stocking began, all other fish were removed to ensure a pure strain of Florida bass. Timber was left standing in the lake to create good fish habitat.

To provide a pleasant fishing experience, no more than 50 boats are allowed on the small lake at one time and a no-wake rule is enforced. Bass fishing is restricted to catch and release to allow a healthy population of large fish to develop. Within size and bag limits, other fish, such as catfish, crappie, and bluegills, may be taken. As an added fishing bonus, two ponds near the dam are stocked in winter with rainbow trout.

Although the park lies in East Texas, it is not quite far enough east to have pines. Instead, it lies in post-oak habitat, with woods of post oaks, red oaks, white oaks, cedar elms, eastern red cedars, pecans, and other trees. Although fishing is the main draw of the park, other visitors come to camp and relax along the quiet lakeshore. A short hiking trail leads to a number of primitive backpacking campsites, allowing an easy escape from modern life.

VISITOR INFORMATION

1,566 acres. Open all year. Hot and humid in summer. Campground with partial hookups and showers. Primitive backpacking campsites. Fishing piers, boat ramp, picnicking, hiking, swimming. Full visitor services available in Athens. For information: Purtis Creek State Park, 14225 FM 316, Eustace, TX 75124, (903) 425-2332.

LEFT:
Anglers
OPPOSITE PAGE, TOP:
Ray Roberts Lake fishing pier
OPPOSITE PAGE, BOTTOM:
Ray Roberts Lake sunset

Ray Roberts Lake State Park

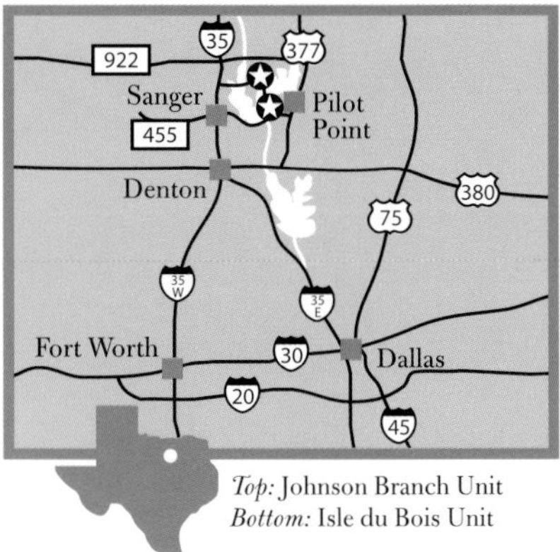

Top: Johnson Branch Unit
Bottom: Isle du Bois Unit

Ray Roberts Lake State Park is one of the newest additions to the state-park system in Texas. The park consists of several units. The large 29,350-acre lake was authorized in 1965 to provide water to Denton and Dallas, but obtaining funding for it and building it took many years. In 1980, the lake was named for Congressman Ray Roberts of Denton, and in the mid-1980s it began to fill, helped along by several major floods.

The lake was created when a dam was built to impound the Elm Fork of the Trinity River, below its confluence with Isle du Bois Creek. The Texas Parks and Wildlife Department began raising fish in brood ponds to stock the lake before it was filled, and today it is known for its largemouth bass, white bass, crappie, and catfish. Every year it draws many thousands of people, who come to fish its fertile waters, sail, swim, or waterski.

The Isle du Bois Unit near the dam on the east side of the lake was designed at the outset for large numbers of people and it has elaborate facilities, including large campgrounds, paved hike and bike trails, and a multi-lane boat ramp. The unit is set in the wooded hills of a large peninsula that juts into the eastern side of the lake. The hills lie in Cross Timbers woodland on the edge of the Blackland Prairie.

The Cross Timbers region is a narrow band of terrain heavily wooded by post and blackjack oaks, black hickories, winged elms, and other trees. Rust-colored Woodbine Sandstone underlies the dense Cross Timbers forest. Among commonly found wildlife species are white-tailed deer, armadillos, rabbits, opossums, raccoons, and skunks. A high point of this wooded terrain to the east of the lake became a landmark for early travelers in the area and hence became known as Pilot Point.

The large Isle du Bois Unit is only part of the park. Across the lake, the Johnson Branch Unit has also been developed. Several other sites around the lake have boat ramps and restrooms. A 12-mile hiking, biking, and equestrian trail connects the Isle du Bois Unit with the Jordan Park boat-ramp area and the Elm Fork area along the Trinity River below the dam. Downstream from Elm Fork, a 10-mile greenbelt offers hiking, biking, and equestrian trails, and canoe access to the river. Part of the land surrounding the lake is maintained by the Texas Parks and Wildlife Department as a wildlife management area. Planned developments along the shore of the lake will no doubt increase the popularity of Ray Roberts Lake State Park.

VISITOR INFORMATION

Isle du Bois Unit: **1,687 acres;**
Johnson Branch Unit: **1,514 acres.**
Open all year. Hot and humid in summer. Large number of campsites with partial hookups and showers. Primitive and equestrian campsites. Day-use group facilities. Hiking, biking, and equestrian trails, picnicking, swimming, fishing, boat ramps, waterskiing, fishing pier. Full visitor services available in Denton. For information: Ray Roberts Lake State Park, #100 PW 4137, Pilot Point, TX 76258, (940) 686-2148.

Sam Bell Maxey House State Historical Park

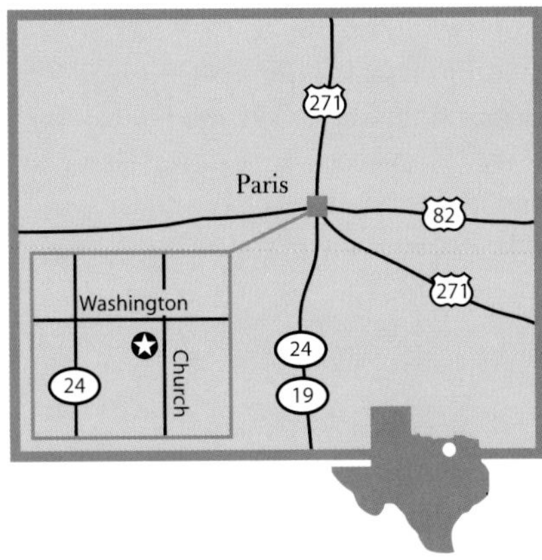

Samuel Bell Maxey was born in 1825 in Tompkinsville, Kentucky, to a socially prominent family. He attended West Point and although he ranked near the bottom of his class, he found that he liked the military life. After graduating in 1846, Maxey served with distinction in several battles of the Mexican War.

In 1849 he resigned his army commission and moved back to Kentucky, where he studied law under his father and became involved in state politics. In 1853 he married Marilda Denton. The family law firm became unprofitable, so in 1857 Maxey and his father moved their families to Paris, Texas. They settled on 5 acres just south of the town and opened a new law office. Soon after, Sam Bell Maxey became the county district attorney and in 1861 he was elected to the Texas Senate.

The outbreak of the Civil War prevented Maxey from taking office. He volunteered his services to the Confederacy and during 1861 organized the Ninth Texas Infantry Division, numbering 1,120 men. He was promoted to the rank of brigadier general in April 1862 and was detached from the Ninth Texas. He spent most of the first two years of the war in Tennessee and Mississippi. In December 1863, he assumed command of Indian Territory (later to become Oklahoma) to prevent any Union invasion into North Texas. After he helped capture a 170-wagon Union supply train in 1864, he was advanced to the rank of major general. During the war, the Maxeys adopted 7-year-old Dora Rowell after her father, one of Maxey's men, was killed at Shiloh. In February 1865, Maxey asked to be relieved as the war was obviously coming to a close, and he returned to Paris.

After two years of effort, Maxey obtained a presidential pardon for his services as a high-ranking Confederate officer, with the help of West Point classmate Ulysses S. Grant. In 1867, he resumed his law practice in Paris with his father and completed plans for a new home on his 5-acre tract. In late 1868, the Maxey family moved into their new house. The home was built as a two-story frame structure in High Victorian Italianate style. It was designed to be very symmetrical, with a central hall dividing each floor in half.

After failing to win a House seat in 1872, Maxey was elected to the U.S. Senate by the Texas legislature in 1874. During his Senate tenure, he worked hard to advance projects of benefit to Texas. In 1887, he lost his bid for a third term and returned to his law practice and family in Paris.

During the Senate years, the Maxey household expanded, with various relatives and in-laws living in the family home over the years. At an uncertain date, a large rear wing was added to the house. Maxey died in 1895 in Eureka Springs, Arkansas.

Indirect descendants of Maxey inherited the house in 1908, after Marilda died. They undertook a major remodeling of the home in 1911, the last major changes made to the house. Members of the Maxey family lived in the property until 1966; a year later, it was donated to the Lamar County Historical Society. In 1976, the Maxey home was conveyed to the Texas Parks and Wildlife Department. The historic house and its furnishings are now open to guided tours.

VISITOR INFORMATION

0.4 acres. Open all year, except Thanksgiving Day, Christmas Day, and New Year's Day; tours on Friday (1–5 P.M.), Saturday (6 A.M.–Noon and 1 P.M.–5 P.M.), and Sunday (1–5 P.M.); and by reservation on Wednesday and Thursday. Day use only. Historic structures and exhibits. Full visitor services available in Paris. For information: Sam Bell Maxey House State Historical Park, 812 S. Church Street, Paris, TX 75460, (903) 785-5716.

STEPHEN F. AUSTIN STATE HISTORICAL PARK

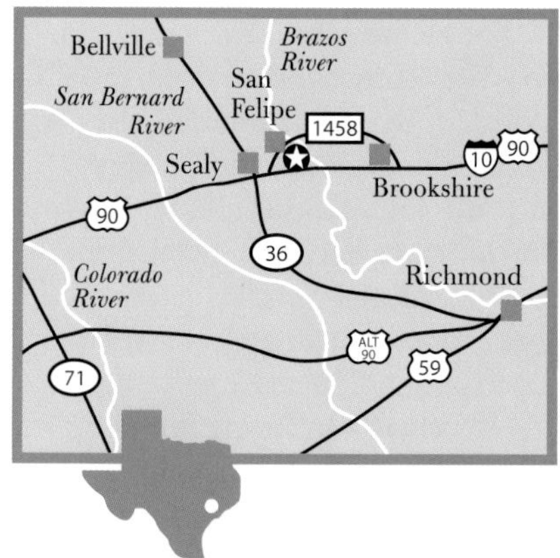

Early in the nineteenth century, Stephen F. Austin brought from the United States the first 300 families to colonize Texas under contract with the Mexican government. He obtained a land grant along the Brazos River from the Mexican government and founded San Felipe de Austin in 1828. Today, Stephen F. Austin State Historical Park marks the location of part of the original grant.

Austin lived in the settlement, along with such other early Texas heroes as Sam Houston and William Travis. Initially the settlement worked relatively well, with Austin working to smooth over cultural, political, and religious differences between the Americans and the Mexican government. However, tensions increased and finally came to a head when General Antonio Lopez de Santa Anna came to power as Mexico's president and dictator. Santa Anna's army was soon marching on the upstart immigrants to enforce his unquestioned authority. The Texans declared independence on March 2, 1836, during the Alamo siege. The fall of the Alamo was followed by the surrender and subsequent massacre of Colonel James Fannin's troops by Mexican forces.

Word reached San Felipe de Austin of the disasters and of the continuing advance of Santa Anna's army. On March 29, the settlers of San Felipe packed what they could carry and burned their settlement, to leave nothing for Santa Anna. With Santa Anna in pursuit, the Texans, under General Sam Houston, crossed the Brazos River and fled east, taking their provisional government with them. Houston realized that he and his troops were greatly outnumbered, so he continued to retreat eastward, hoping to find some way to gain the advantage on the battlefield. Finally, on April 21, when he found that Santa Anna had split up his troops and left himself with a much smaller numerical superiority, Houston attacked. The Battle of San Jacinto was a rout for the Texans. In 18 minutes, they overwhelmed the Mexican force, killing

ABOVE, LEFT:
Stephen F. Austin monument
ABOVE, RIGHT:
Cyclist
OPPOSITE PAGE:
Sam Bell Maxey House

630 Mexican soldiers while losing only 9 of their own. Santa Anna surrendered and independence was won.

The park is much more peaceful today, with little to break the quiet other than the sound of children playing or a golf club striking a ball. The park hugs the Brazos River, occupying both floodplain and upland areas of coastal plain. It is divided into two segments. The smaller historical section memorializes Stephen F. Austin and the early Texas settlers. Attractions include the old J. J. Josey General Store, which contains many items found in early general stores as well as other objects of historical interest. There is also a dogtrot cabin, a hand-dug water well, and a statue of Austin.

The 18-hole golf course is the most prominent feature of the recreational section of the state park. The beautiful fairways wind through lush woods draped with Spanish moss.

To get a feel for how the land appeared when the colonists first arrived, take the hiking trail along the back side of the park. Oaks, pecans, cottonwoods, elms, and other trees arch in lush profusion over the trail as it drops down through the floodplain to the banks of the muddy Brazos River. The river slides quietly by, much as it did for Austin's first Texans.

VISITOR INFORMATION

667 acres. Open all year. Hot and humid in summer. Moderate number of campsites with partial or full hookups, and showers. Screened shelters. Eighteen-hole golf course with pro shop, picnicking, hiking, historic structures and exhibits, fishing. Full visitor services available in Sealy and Houston. For information: Stephen F. Austin State Historical Park, P.O. Box 125, San Felipe, TX 77473, (979) 885-3613.

Washington-on-the-Brazos State Historical Park

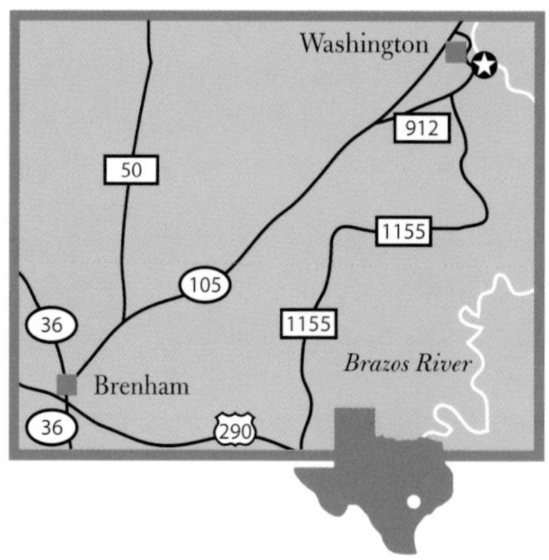

Although Washington was never a big town, it looms large in Texas history. In 1821, Andrew Robinson and his family first settled the site when they joined Stephen F. Austin's colony. They farmed and raised livestock on the west bank of the Brazos River and operated a ferry at the La Bahia river crossing of the old Spanish road between Goliad and East Texas.

In 1835, Robinson's son-in-law John Hall purchased the property and, with partners, laid out the townsite of Washington. The lots were sold at a public auction on January 8, 1836, on the eve of the Texas revolution. Even though the new town was rough and ragged, the provisional government of Texas designated it as the site of the convention that was to meet to determine Texas's fate. A Virginian visiting Washington in the February of that year was less than impressed:

Left Washington at 10 o'clock. Glad to get out of so disgusting a place. It is laid out in the woods; about a dozen wretched cabins or shanties constitute the city; not one decent house in it and only one well-defined street, which consists of an opening cut out of the woods. The stumps still standing. A rare place to hold a national convention. They will have to leave it promptly to avoid starvation.

Poor conditions or not, the delegates convened in Washington on March 1, 1836, in an unfinished frame building. As Santa Anna's Mexican forces besieged the Alamo, the delegates declared Texas's independence from Mexico, wrote a constitution for the Republic of Texas, and organized a government. On March 17, the newly formed government and the citizens of Washington fled east, ahead of the advancing Mexican army.

After the victorious Battle of San Jacinto on April 21, the residents of Washington returned home, finding the town little disturbed. Citizens of the town fought to retain its status as the Texas capital, but lost out, first to Houston and then to Austin. In 1842, however, Mexican troops captured San Antonio, giving President Sam Houston an excuse to move the capital back to Washington, owing to its greater distance from San Antonio. He did so in the fall of 1842, after a major political fight, bringing new life to the town. Although the accommodations there had improved since 1836, they were still, nonetheless, crowded and spartan.

The Republic of Texas was in poor financial condition and subject to invasions by Mexican troops. To help shore up the Republic, the new government worked to gain recognition and diplomatic relations with the United States and other countries. Many Texans thought that the way to solve their problems with Mexico was to be annexed by the United States. After extended negotiations, annexation was approved by the U.S. Congress and the people of Texas. On December 29, 1845, Texas officially joined the Union. The capital moved back to Austin, which remains the state capital today.

Washington prospered for some years after it lost its status as the capital, but it was dealt a mortal blow

in the mid-1850s when the railroad bypassed it, and it was finished by the Civil War. At some point, the town became known as Washington-on-the-Brazos.

Today, the state park contains the old townsite and several museums. The building where the Declaration of Independence was signed on March 2, 1836, has been reconstructed. Extensive exhibits chronicling the history of Washington and of Texas are displayed in the interpretive center and the Star of the Republic Museum. The home of Anson Jones, the last president of the Republic of Texas, was moved from a nearby location to the park and restored. Short walking trails and a pecan-shaded picnic area overlooking the Brazos River round out the park.

New construction at the park began in 1996. Among improvements are a new visitor services center with novel interactive exhibits and a full-service restaurant. The Barrington Living History Farm with costumed staff and period livestock demonstrates life in the 1850s.

Anson Jones home

VISITOR INFORMATION

240 acres. Open all year. Day use only. Historic buildings, Barrington Living History Farm, museums, interpretive exhibits, picnicking, short walking trails. Full visitor services available in Navasota. For information: Washington-on-the-Brazos State Historical Park, Box 305, Washington, TX 77880, (936) 878-2214.

South Texas Plains

From the edge of the Hill Country in San Antonio, the South Texas Plains sweep south in a broad swath to the Rio Grande. The land is relatively flat, especially in the lower Rio Grande Valley downstream from Roma. A mix of grassland and brush, particularly mesquite, characterizes the region's vegetation. Along its eastern edge, near the coast, the area receives moderate rainfall, but it becomes relatively dry farther west. Even in eastern sections with moderate rainfall, however, high evaporation rates tend to make the region fairly dry.

At one time the region had less brush, but heavy grazing has encouraged shrubby plants and cacti to encroach. Wildlife is plentiful in the brushy country; white-tailed deer and javelina are particularly prolific here. Numerous rare forms of wildlife found along the Rio Grande, especially in the lower valley downstream from Falcon Lake, attract many people to the region's parks and wildlife refuges.

The lower Rio Grande Valley, much of which is the delta of the Rio Grande, lies farther south than any other part of the United States except Hawaii and part of Florida. Its location and weather patterns give the area a warm, subtropical climate. Winter freezes are generally rare, mild, and short-lived, allowing even citrus trees to grow there.

Its subtropical climate and southerly location results in the Rio Grande Valley having many species of plants and animals found nowhere else in the United States. The

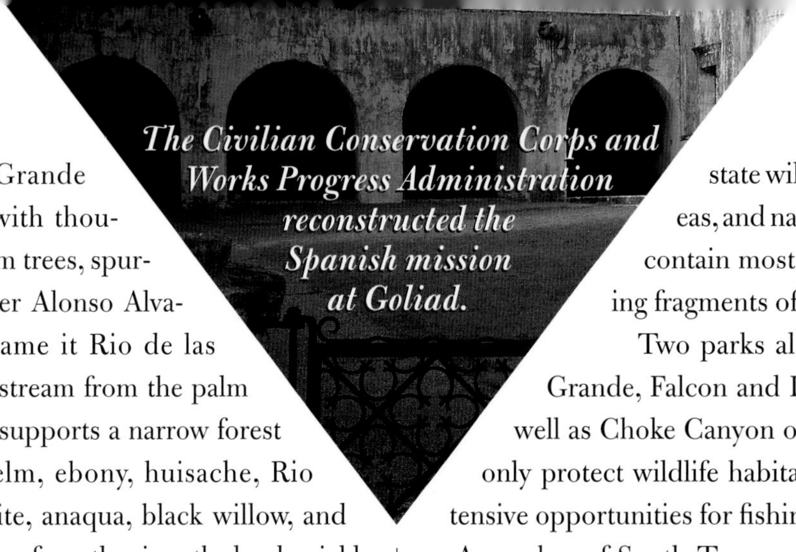

The Civilian Conservation Corps and Works Progress Administration reconstructed the Spanish mission at Goliad.

mouth of the Rio Grande once was wooded with thousands of acres of palm trees, spurring Spanish explorer Alonso Alvarez de Piñeda to name it Rio de las Palmas in 1519. Upstream from the palm woodland, the river supports a narrow forest corridor of cedar elm, ebony, huisache, Rio Grande ash, mesquite, anaqua, black willow, and many other trees. Away from the river, the land quickly dries and supports less lush brushlands of mesquite and other shrubs.

Small numbers of the rare ocelot and the even rarer jaguarundi live here in the thick, brushy woodlands. The elusive small wild cats slip quietly through the brush, making observation difficult. Long ago, even the jaguar, North America's largest cat, roamed the Rio Grande Valley.

Many species of birds range as far north as the Rio Grande Valley and no further. Birders come from all over the United States to see, among many other species, the chachalaca, the green jay, the Altamira oriole, the pauraque, the groove-billed ani, and the hook-billed kite. Almost 300 species of birds have been sighted in Bentsen-Rio Grande Valley State Park alone. More than 70 other species have been recorded elsewhere in the Rio Grande Valley.

Unfortunately for the native plants and wildlife, the soil of the Valley is fertile and the vast majority of the woodland has been cleared for farming. In addition, high birth rates and heavy immigration have increasingly urbanized the area along the river. The state parks, state wildlife management areas, and national wildlife refuges contain most of the small remaining fragments of the original habitat.

Two parks along or near the Rio Grande, Falcon and Lake Casa Blanca, as well as Choke Canyon on the Frio River, not only protect wildlife habitat, they also offer extensive opportunities for fishing and water sports.

A number of South Texas parks preserve important historic sites. In the 1930s, the Civilian Conservation Corps reconstructed Mission Espiritu Santo, an early Spanish mission, at Goliad State Park. Fannin Battlefield lies nearby, marking the Battle of Coleto Creek where Colonel James Fannin surrendered to superior Mexican forces during the battle for Texas's independence; a week later, Fannin and 342 of his men were executed after being promised honorable treatment.

In San Antonio, a large Spanish mission, San José, is managed under a joint arrangement with the National Park Service. Still another park, Casa Navarro State Historical Park, preserves the home of early Texas patriot José Antonio Navarro.

As well as preserving historic sites and protecting unique wildlife, the state parks of the South Texas Plains also offer many recreational opportunities. Many sites have camping and picnicking, as well as hiking trails, while others boast museums or water sports. But above all, the parks of the Rio Grande Valley offer something found in few other areas—the chance to see many rare and uncommon species of plants and animals.

South Texas Plains

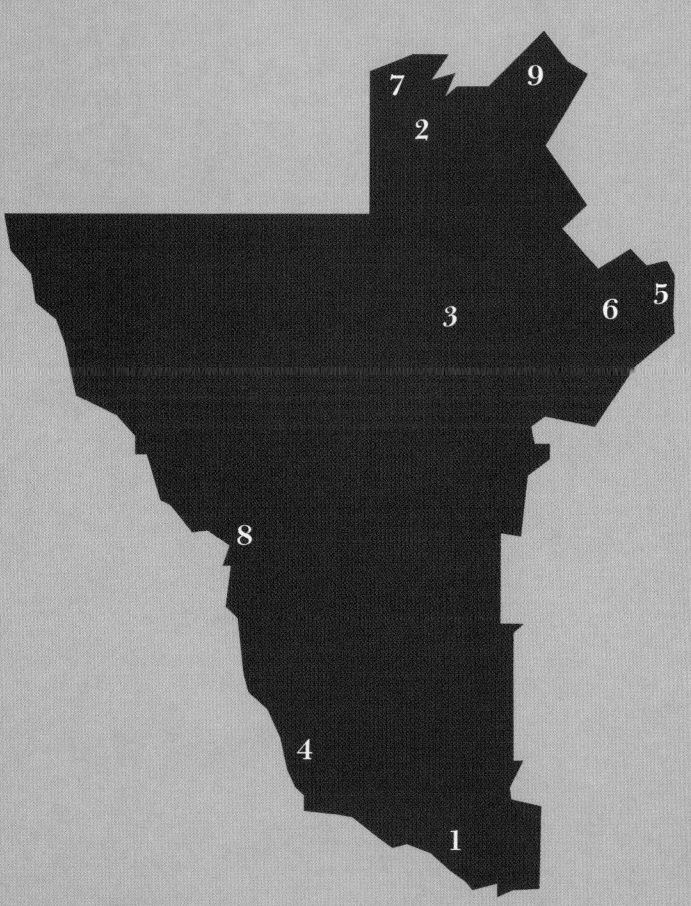

1 Bentsen-Rio Grande Valley State Park
2 Casa Navarro State Historical Park
3 Choke Canyon State Park
4 Falcon State Park
5 Fannin Battleground State Historical Park
6 Goliad State Historical Park
7 Government Canyon State Natural Area
8 Lake Casa Blanca International State Park
9 Sebastopol State Historical Park

Bentsen-Rio Grande Valley State Park

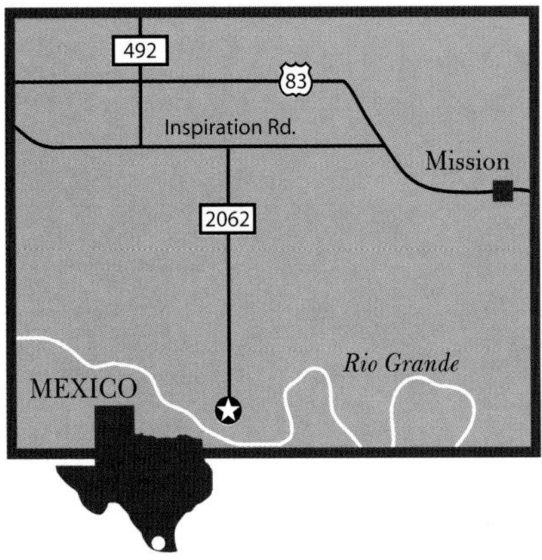

Deep in the Rio Grande Valley lies one of the southernmost state parks in the United States. Bentsen-Rio Grande Valley State Park adjoins the Rio Grande, near the city of Mission in South Texas. Unusual, rarely seen mammals such as the ocelot and possibly even the jaguarundi roam thick, brushy woodlands of cedar elm, Rio Grande ash, black willow, anaqua, ebony, huisache, and many other species. At one time even the jaguar, the largest cat in the western hemisphere, stalked prey on the banks of the Rio Grande.

The state park's unique avian life draws people even more than the mammals do: along with other areas of the Rio Grande Valley, the park provides a home for a tremendous variety of birds. Some 296 species have been recorded there, and another 74 have been sighted elsewhere in the Rio Grande Valley. Two major flyways, the Central and the Mississippi, converge here, funneling large numbers of migrants through the Valley. Many tropical species, limited by climate, reach the northern limit of their range here, and the nearby Gulf Coast draws many shorebirds. Birders come from all over the United States to see the green jay, the Altamira oriole, the chachalaca, the white-tipped dove, the pauraque, the groove-billed ani, the hook-billed kite, the ringed kingfisher, and many other species.

The lower Rio Grande Valley forms an ecosystem found nowhere else in the United States. Before the area was heavily developed, with farms and urban areas being built on both sides of the river, the Rio Grande shifted constantly, creating a broad, fertile floodplain. The Valley's southern location near the Tropic of Cancer, combined with its proximity to the warm Gulf of Mexico, creates a subtropical climate with a 320-day growing season. However, since rainfall is just moderate and evaporation is high, there is only a narrow corridor of lush woodlands lining the river; further away from the river, the woodland grades into brushland that is better adapted to dryness.

Unfortunately, urbanization and farming have destroyed virtually all of the original habitat of the Rio Grande Valley. Only a few islands remain of the once-extensive subtropical woodland. Many species, including the ocelot and the jaguarundi, have become endangered because of habitat loss and hunting. The state and federal government have an ongoing program to protect the remnants in a system of state parks, state wildlife management areas, and national wildlife refuges. The Rio Grande Valley is the highest-priority acquisition area in the country for the U.S. Fish and Wildlife Service.

Private entities, such as the Audubon Society, the Nature Conservancy, and the Valley Land Fund, have also protected pieces of the remaining habitat; the Audubon Society's Sabal Palm Sanctuary, for

ABOVE:
Prickly pear
RIGHT:
Resaca, or oxbow lake

Woodland hiking trail

example, preserves 37 acres of palm forest, a tiny remnant of the 40,000 acres that once covered part of the Rio Grande delta. As a mark of how extensive the palm forest once was, the early Spanish explorer Alonso Alvarez de Piñeda first named the river Rio de las Palmas when he sailed up it in 1519. Today, with so little natural habitat left, it's hard to imagine that such a name was once appropriate.

Unfortunately, even native woodland protected in the state park has suffered. Many trees have died, particularly cedar elms and ash trees. The creation of dams, with the siphoning off of water upstream for irrigation and other uses, together with the implementation of flood-control projects, has ended periodic flooding along the river and lowered the water table, drying out areas along the river. Recently, the state park management and the U.S. Fish and Wildlife Service undertook a large irrigation project to water much of the park and an adjoining Fish and Wildlife tract. Not only was the vegetation watered, one of the park's *resacas* (old cut-off river channels) was refilled. With such care, the Valley's unique ecology will be protected in Bentsen-Rio Grande State Park as well as in other refuges.

Two hiking and nature trails that wind through the state park's woodland provide an excellent introduction to the habitat of the Rio Grande Valley. Spanish moss drapes the trees along these trails, creating a tropical, primeval atmosphere. Observant hikers will see many plants, birds, and animals found nowhere else in the United States. If they are very lucky, they may even see the beautiful spotted ocelot, just one of this park's many unique sights, as it slips silently through the brush.

VISITOR INFORMATION

588 acres. Open all year. Hot and humid in summer. Campgrounds with both partial and full hookups, and showers. Very popular from December through April with "winter Texans" who stay there to escape the harsh northern climate during those months; reserve campsites well ahead during this time. Boat ramp and fishing on 60-acre *resaca*, hiking trails, picnic area. Full visitor services available in nearby Mission. For information: Bentsen-Rio Grande Valley State Park, P.O. Box 988, Mission, TX 78573-0988, (956) 585-1107.

Casa Navarro State Historical Park

Casa Navarro State Historical Park preserves the 1850s home of José Antonio Navarro (1795–1871), an important leader in early Texas history. Navarro's lifetime spanned the period when Texas underwent major changes in sovereignty, starting out as a Spanish colonial province and ending up as a state in the United States. In 1810, when Mexico's struggle for independence from Spain began, Navarro's family supported the movement, even though doing so forced them into exile for several years. After Mexico achieved independence in 1821, Navarro served as a representative of the Mexican state of Coahuila y Texas.

In 1828, Navarro's legislative term ended and he worked as a merchant and acquired large land holdings. In 1835, the Mexican president, Santa Anna, abolished the Mexican constitution and became dictator, helping to foment the Texas revolution. It was not only the Anglo settlers who resisted the totalitarian moves made by Santa Anna—many of the Mexican settlers did as well. A group of citizens of San Antonio elected Navarro to represent them in Washington-on-the-Brazos, at that time the state capital. There, Navarro signed the Texas Declaration of Independence on March 3, 1836. He was one of only two signers actually born in Texas. He also helped write the constitution of the new Republic of Texas and later helped revise it after Texas joined the United States. Navarro County was named in his honor.

In 1841, Navarro took part in the ill-fated Santa Fe Expedition, whose purpose was to open trade with New Mexico and take possession of lands in eastern New Mexico. He was captured by the Mexican Army and imprisoned in Mexico for three years, narrowly escaping execution.

During his life, Navarro worked to preserve the rights of the Mexican settlers of Texas, the Tejanos. He helped protect Spanish and Mexican land grants and defended Tejano rights in the Texas Constitution.

Navarro's home in downtown San Antonio has been preserved to honor his contributions to Texas history. Navarro and his wife moved to the house in about 1856 after selling their ranch near Seguin in 1853. To prevent its demolition, the San Antonio Conservation Society purchased the site in 1960 and restored the buildings—three stone and adobe structures, tentatively identified as the residence, the kitchen, and the store. The site was later donated to the State of Texas.

The store, a two-story building, was evidently used as a rental property. The residence does not contain any of Navarro's actual furnishings, but it does hold representative antiques from that period of Texas history. For the most part, the home and furnishings are plain and simple.

VISITOR INFORMATION

0.6 acres. Days of operation vary depending on the season; call ahead to check days and times. Historic structures, museum, guided tours, living history demonstrations. Full visitor services available in San Antonio. For information: Casa Navarro State Historical Park, 228 S. Laredo St., San Antonio, TX 78207, (210) 226-4801.

ABOVE, LEFT:
José Antonio Navarro home
ABOVE, RIGHT:
Restored bedroom

Choke Canyon State Park

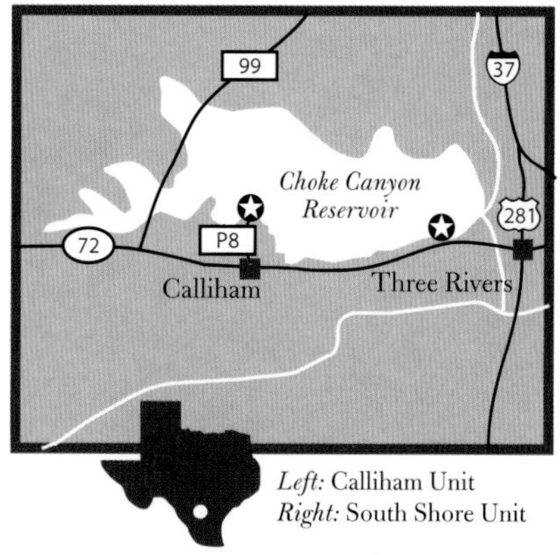

Left: Calliham Unit
Right: South Shore Unit

Although Choke Canyon State Park is relatively new—the first unit, South Shore, opened in 1986—it has quickly become a very popular park year-round. The two units, Calliham and South Shore, lie on the shores of Choke Canyon Lake, a large 26,000-acre South Texas reservoir. The dam project was initiated in the 1970s by the City of Corpus Christi and the Bureau of Reclamation to provide a water source for Corpus Christi and the surrounding area. To create the reservoir, the Frio River was dammed at a narrow "choke" point along its course. Most of the surrounding terrain consists of relatively flat grasslands invaded by brush such as mesquite and acacia.

The two park units were built within a 38,000-acre wildlife management area, and as a result there is plentiful wildlife within the park. Many of the animals have lost much of their natural shyness and can be viewed relatively closely, especially early and late in the day. White-tailed deer, javelina, and wild turkeys are some of the most popular and frequently seen creatures.

Birders are drawn to Choke Canyon, in the hopes of spotting

Sunset over Choke Canyon Lake

some of the almost 200 species of birds that have been recorded in the park. To the surprise of many visitors to the relatively dry brushlands surrounding the lake, even alligators are found in some marshy areas on the lakeshore. Choke Canyon is the westernmost site in which alligators are commonly found.

Wildlife viewing is only one of the attractions of Choke Canyon State Park. Boaters and waterskiers love the vast expanse of open water, and anglers actively pursue the many species of fish found in the reservoir's depths. Among the most popular fish are largemouth, striped, and white bass, catfish, crappie, and freshwater drum.

If wildlife viewing and lake attractions are not enough, the Calliham Unit has some of the state-park system's most elaborate facilities. A large swimming pool and bathhouse is probably the most popular attraction, especially in summer, but the park also offers basketball, tennis, and shuffleboard courts and a baseball diamond. There is even an auditorium, complete with dressing rooms and a raised stage.

Humans have been coming to the Frio River valley for thousands of years. Nomadic hunters are thought to have visited the area as long ago as 10,000 years. An archeological survey conducted before the lake was created found a number of Archaic sites that are several thousand years old. Evidence was also discovered of more recent Indian groups living there prior to the arrival of the Spaniards in the sixteenth century. Later, the area was settled under the jurisdictions of the Mexican, Texas, and U.S. governments. Then, as now, water was the primary draw for residents of and visitors to the area.

Mesquite tree

VISITOR INFORMATION

1,485 acres. Open all year. Hot and humid in summer. Large number of campsites, with partial hookups and showers, split between the two units. Screened shelters. Boating, boat ramps, waterskiing, fishing, canoeing (on Frio River below dam), lake swimming, picnicking. Calliham Unit's 90 Acre Lake not open to boats. Tennis, basketball, and shuffleboard courts at Calliham Unit. Baseball diamond, volleyball, nature trail, birding trails at both units. Swimming pool at Calliham Unit. Most visitor services available in Three Rivers. For information: Choke Canyon State Park, Calliham Unit, P.O. Box 2, Calliham, TX 78007, (361) 786-3868; South Shore Unit, P.O. Box 1548, Three Rivers, TX 78071, (361) 786-3538.

Falcon State Park

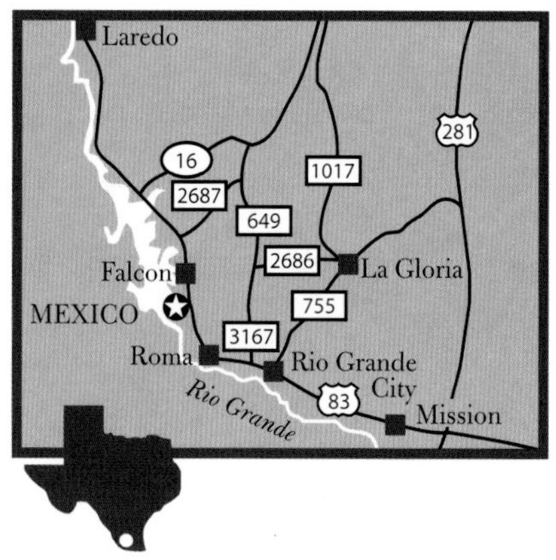

Deep in the dry brush country of South Texas lies sprawling Falcon Lake, a large reservoir fed by the Rio Grande and secondarily by the Rio Salado of Mexico. When the 5-mile-long dam was completed in 1953, the lake began to fill, eventually flooding 87,000 acres and extending 60 miles upstream. The reservoir was created jointly by the United States and Mexico for flood control, power generation, irrigation, and recreation purposes. Falcon State Park, on the east shore of the lake near the dam, provides excellent access to the enormous lake.

The brush country surrounding the lake contains many subtropical plant and animal species found only in Mexico and far South Texas. Brushy thickets of mesquite, huisache, palo verde, ebony, and other plants provide cover to birds such as the chachalaca, the groove-billed ani, the ringed kingfisher, and the green jay.

Tropical cats are of particular interest in the Rio Grande Valley, from Falcon Lake downstream. Although they were once more common, the spotted ocelot and especially the dark, thin jaguarundi are now very rare in South Texas. Most of their habitat, consisting of the woodland and brushland that once

lined the Rio Grande, has disappeared because of agricultural use and urbanization. The two cats have declined in tandem with many other plants and animals. At one time, even the jaguar, the largest cat in the New World, roamed the Rio Grande Valley. Today, the Texas Parks and Wildlife Department, the U.S. Fish and Wildlife Service, and other public and private entities are attempting to preserve undisturbed tracts of habitat in the Rio Grande Valley to protect the remaining cats and other rare animals and plants. Falcon State Park is one such site.

The state park lies in an area with an extensive human history. Nearby Roma was founded by the Spaniards in about 1767. It later became a trading center for steamboats that traveled up the Rio Grande from the Gulf of Mexico. Many historical buildings dating from the nineteenth century still stand around the town square.

Across the river and slightly upstream from Roma is the Mexican town of Mier. It was founded in the 1750s and is most famous as the site of the "black bean" incident. In 1842, during hostilities between Mexico and the newly formed Republic of Texas, a group of defeated Texans escaped from captivity; most were recaptured by Santa Anna and taken to Mier. As punishment, Santa Anna ordered that one-tenth of the recaptured escapees be shot. To determine which of them would be executed, 17 black beans were put in a pot with 159 white beans. Those who drew the black beans were summarily executed and the others were jailed until September 12, 1844.

Some history is visible to boaters on the lake. When the reservoir was built, it flooded the old Mexican town of Guerrero. Depending on water levels, boaters are sometimes able to view the ruins and foundations of a number of the town's buildings, including the old mission church, which was founded in 1750.

Falcon Lake provides the primary freshwater fishing opportunity in South Texas. Striped, white, and largemouth bass, crappie, and catfish all draw anglers to the lake. The vast expanse of open water also attracts waterskiers, boaters, and swimmers. In winter, the park is particularly popular with visitors from northern states seeking to escape cold, snowy weather by coming to the warm, temperate climate of Falcon Lake.

VISITOR INFORMATION

573 acres. Open all year. Hot from April through October. Very popular in winter. Large number of campsites with partial or full hookups and showers. Both screened and air-conditioned shelters. Boating, fishing, birding, boat ramp, picnicking, swimming, waterskiing, nature trail. Full visitor services available in Roma.

For information: Falcon State Park, P.O. Box 2, Falcon Heights, TX 78545, (956) 848-5327.

TOP:
Fishermen
BOTTOM:
Falcon Lake

Fannin Battleground State Historical Park

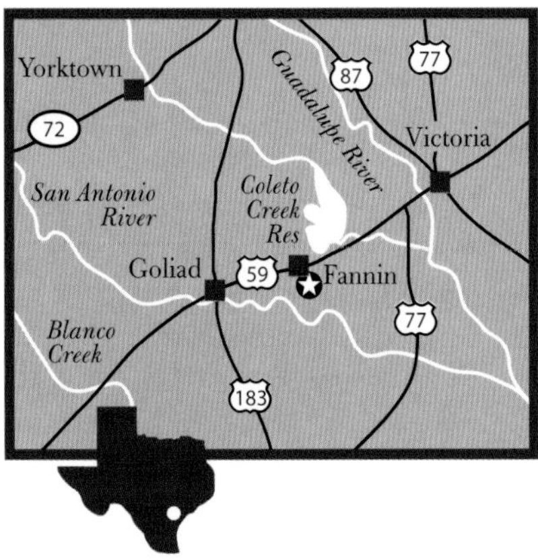

A handsome stone obelisk marks the site where Colonel James Walker Fannin, Jr., and his men surrendered to superior Mexican forces on March 20, 1836, after the Battle of Coleto Creek. The battle was one of a number fought during the course of Texas's struggle for independence from Mexico. After the surrender, which Fannin believed was done on honorable terms, the Texans were taken to the Presidio La Bahia in nearby Goliad. Against the wishes of local Mexican commanders, General Antonio Lopez de Santa Anna ordered Fannin and his men executed. On March 27, Palm Sunday morning, Fannin and 342 of his men were slain.

Word quickly spread of the massacre, giving the Texan troops a new rallying cry during the revolution—"Remember Goliad!" Fannin and his men were buried near the presidio in a site now enclosed in a small city park and marked by a large monument, the Fannin Memorial. The site of Fannin's surrender at the battleground is peaceful now. Landscaped grounds and a circular drive surround the stone obelisk on the flat coastal plain. A small museum tells of the battleground's history and a pavilion shades a cluster of picnic tables.

VISITOR INFORMATION

14 acres. Open all year. Day use only. Hot and humid in summer. Historic site and museum, picnicking. Full visitor services available in Goliad. For information: Fannin Battleground State Historical Park, P.O. Box 66, Fannin, TX 77960, (361) 645-2020.

Fannin Battleground memorial

Goliad State Historical Park

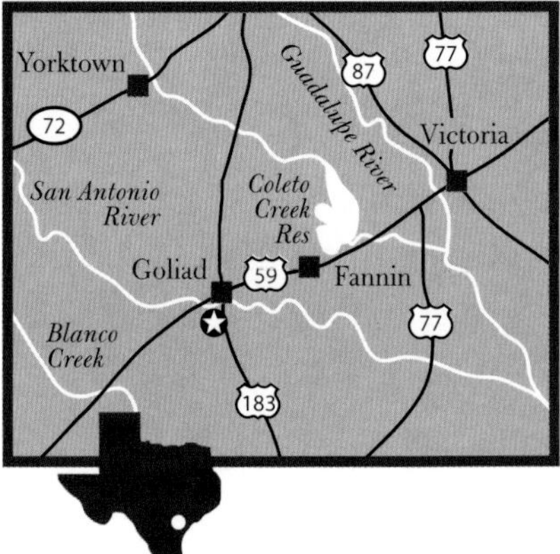

"Remember Goliad!" shouted Texans, in memory of the Goliad massacre, as they fought for independence from Mexico. After a day and a half of fierce fighting at Coleto Creek, Texas forces led by Colonel James Walker Fannin, Jr., had surrendered to superior Mexican forces on March 20, 1836. Expecting fair treatment, they were imprisoned at the Presidio La Bahia at Goliad. A week later, Fannin and 342 of his men were summarily executed under the orders of General Antonio Lopez de Santa Anna. Outrage over the massacre fueled the fires of the Texas war of independence.

Today, the San Antonio River slides silently by Goliad State Historical Park. The imposing white church of Mission Espiritu Santo de Zuniga dominates the quiet 178-acre park. In 1722, long before the Texas revolution, the mission was established by the Spaniards near Matagorda Bay to serve the Karankawa Indians and their allies. The Indians abandoned the mission in 1724 and it was moved to a site near Victoria, in the territory of the Aranama and Tamique Indians. Finally, in 1749, it was moved one last time to a hill lying in a large loop of the San Antonio River just south of the present-day town of Goliad.

The mission lasted 110 years, longer than any other Spanish colonial mission in Texas. Sporadic rains made farming difficult at the mission, but ranching thrived. With a 40,000-head herd, the mission operated the first large cattle ranch in Texas. Raids of the mission and its herds were common, and the mission was in poor shape when it was secularized in 1831. The mission lands were distributed to colonists and the buildings were used for schools for a number of years. An 1886 hurricane heavily damaged the buildings, which by then were already closed and in disrepair, and they collapsed into ruin. Area settlers salvaged stone and wooden beams for building materials, leaving little of the original mission by the time the site was designated a historical park by the state legislature in 1931.

Beginning in 1936, the Civilian Conservation Corps and the Works Progress Administration excavated and reconstructed the mission. Because of a lack of photographs or drawings of the original buildings, the reconstructed mission probably differs some from the original structure.

The ruins of another mission, Nuestra Senora del Rosario, lie a few miles west of Mission Espiritu Santo. The more short-lived Mission Rosario was founded by Franciscan missionaries in 1754 and was abandoned in 1807. The outlying park unit is not open to the public.

About a mile south of Espiritu Santo lies the birthplace of General Ignacio Zaragoza, in a small unit of the state park. After growing up in the area, Zaragoza was educated in Mexico and joined the Mexican Army. On May 5, 1862, he led his troops to victory over superior French forces in the Battle of Puebla, Mexico. His triumph is celebrated every year in Mexico as Cinco de Mayo.

Next to Zaragosa's birthplace is the privately administered Presidio La Bahia, the oldest fort in the western United States. It was built to house the Spanish troops who protected the mission complex. Like Mission Espiritu Santo, it has been reconstructed. Behind the presidio lies the Fannin Memorial, a large granite marker that commemorates Colonel Fannin and his men, who were executed there in 1836 under the orders of Santa Anna.

The tranquil facade of Goliad State Historical Park masks its rich history; events occurred there that were of vital importance to both Texas and Mexico. Listen carefully on a quiet moonlit night: maybe you can still hear the sound of church bells calling the faithful to prayer at the isolated Spanish outpost.

VISITOR INFORMATION

187 acres. Open all year. Both primitive and developed camping with partial hookups. Screened shelters. Restored mission church, adjoining granary housing excellent museum with artifacts and interpretive exhibits, short nature trail introducing South Texas brushland vegetation and the lush riparian corridor of the San Antonio River; fishing and canoeing in river, picnicking. Large swimming pool within park open during summer. Full visitor services in Goliad. For information: Goliad State Historical Park, 108 Park Road 6, Goliad, TX 77963, (361) 645-3405.

Reconstructed mission window

Government Canyon State Natural Area

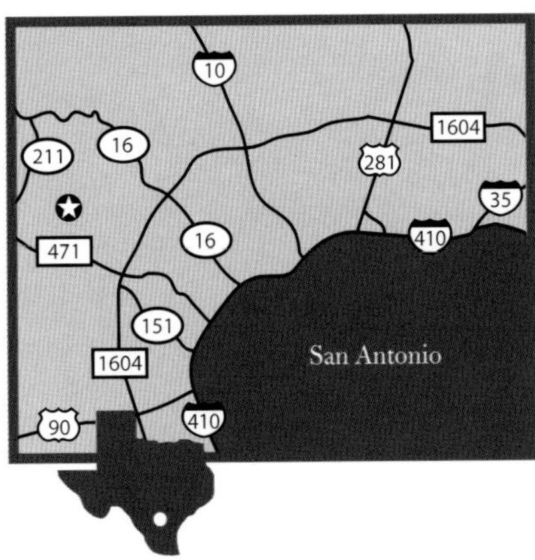

Government Canyon is a new state natural area that is still under development. The large park is located on the northwest side of San Antonio at the transition point between the Hill Country of the Edwards Plateau and the plains of South Texas. The rectangular park is oriented north-south, with dimensions of roughly 1.5 x 4 miles.

The Edwards Plateau was uplifted by the long Balcones Fault that stretches southwest from Austin through the northern part of San Antonio and then curves west toward Uvalde and Del Rio. Government Canyon State Natural Area straddles the fault, with the northern three-quarters of the property on the Edwards Plateau and the southern quarter in the plains. The fault line is quite distinctive in the park. To the north, the terrain becomes hilly and is wooded with typical Hill Country vegetation, such as live oaks, Ashe junipers, and cedar elms. To the south, the terrain flattens out and mesquite becomes much more common.

Not only did the fault create the Hill Country by lifting up a large piece of the Earth's crust, it also allowed the important Edwards Aquifer to develop. Some of the rain that falls on this part

TOP:
State natural area back road
BOTTOM:
Historic stage station

of the plateau seeps downward through cracks and fissures into buried layers of limestone in what is called a recharge zone. This water later resurfaces in springs or is tapped by wells. The water is extremely important to local farmers and ranchers, as well as to a number of cities. San Antonio is entirely dependent on Edwards Aquifer water. The three-quarters of the state park that lies north of the fault is part of the recharge zone. To protect this area's ability to direct water into the aquifer, most future park development will be concentrated in the southern quarter of the park.

The new park was named for Government Canyon, a large, normally dry drainage ditch that runs through the park. A rough, unimproved dirt road follows the canyon upstream, approximately following the old western travel route from San Antonio to Fredericksburg and El Paso. Within the park is an old stone house believed to have been built by troops from Fort Sam Houston, formerly Fort Government Hill, as a way station on the road west. The building is also believed to have been used as a stage station.

The park management plans eventually to develop campsites, an interpretive center, and other facilities in the southern quarter of the park. In the northern section, in the aquifer recharge zone, the old roads will be used in a system of hiking and mountain-bike trails. Access now available via volunteer activities and research projects. Once these developments have been completed, access should increase.

VISITOR INFORMATION

6,643 acres. Open for special tours only; call ahead for dates and times. No developed facilities at present. Full visitor services available in San Antonio. For information: Government Canyon State Natural Area c/o Park Manager, 12861 Galm Road, San Antonio, TX 78254, (210) 688-9055.

Lake Casa Blanca International State Park

Little-known Lake Casa Blanca International State Park provides one of the few public recreational retreats in Laredo. When it was impounded in 1946, it was the only lake of significant size in the area until Falcon Lake was built to the south in the 1950s. Unlike Falcon Lake, however, Lake Casa Blanca was not created by damming the Rio Grande. Instead, water from Chacon and

Lake Casa Blanca

Waterskier

San Ygnacio creeks feed the small 1,100-acre reservoir.

The lake lies in relatively flat country on the west side of Laredo, adjoining the airport. The land surrounding the park is dry and dominated by South Texas brush-country plants such as mesquite, palo verde, and prickly pear. Because the terrain has little relief, the lake averages only about 12 feet in depth. The shallow water encourages dense growth of reeds and other water plants along the lakeshore. These plants provide an excellent habitat for fish, a little-known fact beyond the Laredo area. Largemouth bass exceeding 10 pounds in weight are frequently caught at the lake. Among other species caught are sunfish, white and black crappie, and channel, flathead, and blue catfish.

The park was formerly managed as a county park, but its operation was taken over by the Texas Parks and Wildlife Department in 1991. Early in the morning and late in the evening, anglers practice their skills along the banks and from boats. During the middle part of the day, boaters and waterskiers zip across the blue waters, taking their turn at enjoying the oasis of Lake Casa Blanca International State Park.

VISITOR INFORMATION

371 acres. Open all year. Hot from April through October. Moderate number of campsites, with partial hookups and showers. Group pavilions. Lake swimming, fishing, boat ramp, waterskiing, picnicking. Full visitor services available in Laredo. For information: Lake Casa Blanca International State Park, P.O. Box 1844, Laredo, TX 78044, (956) 725-3826.

Sebastopol State Historical Park

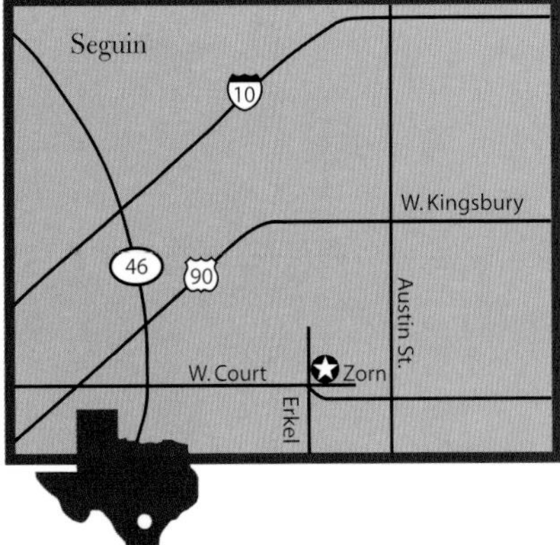

Seguin has been called the "mother of concrete cities," because of its many concrete-built structures dating back to the nineteenth century. The fact that a number of concrete buildings had already been built in Seguin by 1850 is surprising, given that the use of concrete in wall construction was by then still less than 20 years old. Frederick Olmsted, the famous architect of New York

Sebastopol home

City's Central Park, passed through Seguin in 1854. He found it worthy of note that a small, isolated town in Texas was using such a new building technique.

In the seventeenth century the Spanish used a type of aggregate wall-construction material utilizing shells from along the coast. One of the oldest known aggregate buildings in the United States is Castillo de San Marcos in St. Augustine, Florida, begun in 1672. However, it was not until 1819, with the building of the Erie Canal, that cements were used that hardened even when wet. Concrete soon became popular for such structures as canals and bridges that required strength and weather resistance, but it was not used in homes until the 1830s, when it was used in a New York residence. Historians are uncertain how the technique came to Seguin, but it may have been brought there by Dr. John Park, who came from Georgia in about 1847. Over the years, he acquired several patents on concrete use.

Seguin proved to be an ideal site for concrete—or limecrete, as it was then called—construction. The town lies on a thick bed of coarse gravel lying close to the surface, and ideal for use in concrete when mixed with lime and water.

In 1854, Colonel Joshua W. Young built a large home, that later became known as Sebastopol, using gravel dug at the site to make limecrete. Sadly, his wife died just before the home's completion; he sold it shortly afterward to his widowed sister, Catharine Young LeGette. Although Young's children opposed the sale, eventually LeGette obtained the house for herself and her children. Her family lived in the house until 1874, when the property was sold to Joseph Zorn, Jr., a local merchant.

Although Zorn's personal fortunes waned in the 1890s, he held prominent civic positions in Seguin, including the mayorship for 20 years. Zorn died in 1923 and his wife, Nettie, died in 1937. Family members continued to live at Sebastopol until 1952. Because the house's condition had deteriorated, it was threatened with demolition in 1960, but was saved by the Seguin Conservation Society. The home was later obtained by the state and was recently restored.

The origin of the home's name is unknown. It may have come from the Battle of Sevastopol in the Crimean War, made famous by Tennyson's poem "The Charge of the Light Brigade." The war took place from 1853–1856, the time of the house's construction.

As many as 90 limecrete buildings had been built in Seguin by 1900, although many are now gone. The restored Sebastopol house is an important site that both exhibits an early innovative construction technique and provides a window into the lives of the home's past residents.

VISITOR INFORMATION

2.2 acres. Day use only. Open Friday through Sunday, 9 A.M.–4 P.M. Guided tours. Call ahead for days and hours. Historic structure with interpretive exhibits and period furnishings, picnicking. Full visitor services available in Seguin. For information: Sebastopol State Historical Park, P.O. Box 900, Seguin, TX 78156-1500, (830) 379-4833.

Index

Page numbers in italics refer to information found in visitor information boxes.